SO-CEW-387

PRINCIPLES OF BANKING

Second Edition

ERIC N. COMPTON
Vice President
The Chase Manhattan Bank, N.A.

AMERICAN INSTITUTE OF BANKING

AMERICAN
BANKERS
ASSOCIATION
1120 Connecticut Avenue, N.W.
Washington, D.C. 20036

© 1979, 1980, 1983
By the American Bankers Association
Second Edition, 1983
All rights reserved
Printed in the United States of America

Contents

Figures

Tables

Preface

Commercial banking in the United States has often been looked on as an industry in which changes take place very slowly. Banks are frequently thought of as institutions that operate today as they did many years ago, and bankers themselves have been characterized as resistant—often actually hostile—to change.

No student of banking, and certainly no bank employee, should accept or promote this false notion. The fact is that the past 30 years have witnessed changes far more numerous, meaningful, and long-lasting than those that occurred in the previous 170 years of U.S. banking history.

In the single decade from 1961 through 1970, a number of dramatic changes took place. The basic deposit structure of commercial banking changed, largely because of the introduction of the large-denomination negotiable certificate of deposit. Bank cards became part of a new life-style for many millions of individuals. The bank holding company concept was introduced, enabling banks to broaden their range of services. The first applications of EFTS (electronic fund transfer systems) appeared. Global banking systems on a large scale became far more commonplace.

In 1979, the first edition of *Principles of Banking* attempted to present an overview of *what* commercial banks were doing and *why* they were doing it, and it mentioned some of the foregoing developments and events. In the few years since that original text appeared, however, so many additional changes, both evolutionary and revolutionary, have taken place that an updated and revised edition appears necessary. Some of these new developments may be classified as purely internal within the banking industry; others, although external, shook the industry to its very foundations. To be unaware of them, and of the adjustments banks have had to make to cope with them, is to align oneself with those who have the inaccurate perception of banking as a purely tradition-oriented institution. Consider that, since 1979, for example,

- New time-deposit instruments (e.g., the All-Savers Certificate) have been authorized and offered; the NOW account has become increasingly important; and the range of Keogh and IRA opportunities has been broadened;

- Money market funds have displayed incredible growth and, in many cases, have offered a package of financial services that eliminates or reduces their customers' needs for bank accounts;

- Savings and loan associations and mutual savings banks have encountered financial crises unknown since the era of the Great Depression, and reports of their losses have appeared with increased frequency;

- Mergers, of a nature and magnitude previously unknown, have occurred among different types of financial institutions and in some cases have crossed state lines for the first time;

- Nonbank enterprises, such as American Express, Merrill Lynch, and Sears Roebuck, have announced their intentions of being the financial supermarkets of the future and have already captured a significant share of what traditionally was the commercial banks' marketplace;

- Interest rates have fluctuated widely, including increases in the prime lending rate to previously unheard-of levels;

- Foreign banks have steadily expanded their U.S. operations, both by acquiring American banks and by becoming aggressive marketers of loan and nonloan business;

- The Monetary Control Act of 1980 has brought about major changes in pricing of services, reserve requirements, and the competitive environment.

- The Garn-St. Germain Depository Institutions Deregulation Act of 1982 increased the competitive spirit by providing for new types of interest-free accounts, and by extending the powers of federal regulatory authorities to assist banks and thrift institutions that encounter financial difficulties.

A knowledge of the basic principles of commercial banking has been, and remains, essential for those who wish to prepare for leadership roles in the future. The timeliness of that knowledge becomes even more important in a financial marketplace that is changing so rapidly and significantly. Every effort has been made to provide students with that timeliness through this second edition of *Principles of Banking.*

Acknowledgments

The success of any venture can usually be measured by the degree of assistance, support, and enthusiasm generated by the individuals involved in the endeavor. Grateful acknowledgment is tendered here to the many bankers whose efforts contributed to the completion of this book. Special thanks go to the members of the ABA Task Force assembled for the project who willingly gave of their time and expertise. The members include: T. Eugene Allred, Vice President, First and Merchants National Bank, Fairfax, Virginia; Bethany S. Brown, Branch Manager, First National Bank of Boston, Brighton, Massachusetts; David V. McCay, President and Chief Operating Officer, Boatman's Bank of Concord Village, St. Louis, Missouri; M. A. Muirhead, Vice President, RepublicBank-Dallas, Texas; James D. Reese, Director of Marketing, Affiliated Bank Shares of Colorado, Denver, Colorado; James H. Treanor, Assistant Vice President, Northwest Bancorporation, Minneapolis, Minnesota; and John S. Wilson, District Credit Supervisor, Seattle–First National Bank, Seattle, Washington.

For their cooperation and continued guidance with the manuscript, I acknowledge: Roy E. Bruner, Vice President, First National Bank of Dona Ana County, Las Cruces, New Mexico; James Devereaux, Assistant Vice President, Union Bank and Trust Company, Grand Rapids, Michigan; Carl Sakamoto, Assistant Vice President, First Hawaiian Bank, Honolulu, Hawaii; Richard C. Obst, Sr., Director of Personnel, Thunderbird Bank, Phoenix, Arizona; M. P. Romano, Vice President, First Interstate Bank of California, Los Angeles, California; Raymond E.

Sacher, Assistant Vice President, Barclay's Bank of New York, Ossining, New York; Roger A. White, Group Vice President, First National Bank of Atlanta, Georgia; and Alvin G. Wilner, Vice President, Harris Trust & Savings Bank, Chicago, Illinois.

Throughout this project, I have had the consistent support and encouragement of the staff of the Education Products and Services Division, Education Policy and Development Group of the American Bankers Association. Special appreciation is extended to George T. Martin. His continued guidance has been invaluable in the preparation of this text.

Francis A. McMullen, Executive Director of the American Institute of Banking in New York, has been a constant source of encouragement. His counsel and friendship are deeply valued, and his constructive criticisms are here acknowledged with sincere thanks.

Finally, to Maire Cathleen, Maureen, Eric, Margaret, Anne, and their spouses, my gratitude for their patience, their involvement, and their loving support of my efforts.

Eric N. Compton
May 1983

Chapter 1

Banking in Today's Economy

LEARNING OBJECTIVES

After completing this chapter, you will have an understanding of

- the concept of "full-service" banking;
- the importance of banks in the economy;
- the three basic functions of banks;
- what is meant by the nation's money supply;
- the reasons why deposits are made with banks;
- the distinction between demand and time deposits;
- the definition of a NOW account;
- the importance of the credit function; and
- the definitions of such terms as share drafts, commercial paper, and electronic fund transfer systems.

Gary Johnson operates a ski resort. The drought has severely affected his business, and his profits have fallen far below their normal level. As a result, he does not have the $25,000 that he needs to put the resort into proper condition for this season's customers. If he could borrow the funds now, he is confident he could repay them out of profits in 6 months.

Joe Terry's daughter will be a student at a Canadian university next semester. Joe has never tried to transfer money to another country. He would like to find a convenient way of sending money to his daughter when she needs it.

Ellen Smith lives in one of the problem areas of a large city and receives public assistance payments for herself and her children. She has lost three of her welfare checks in the past year because of mailbox thefts. In each case, she had to wait for replacement checks to be issued, and the government agency had to incur the effort and expense of issuing new checks. Both Ellen and the welfare authorities would like some form of payment that would eliminate this problem.

Lynn De Palma started her own business as an interior decorator and has been very successful. She has never worked for a firm that had a pension plan. Lynn has heard that federal laws allow her to set money aside each year for retirement security, but she does not know how or where she can do this. In addition, Lynn's sister works for a company that does have a pension plan; however, she has heard advertisements stating that she can also establish her own retirement fund and wonders how to do this.

Charlie McGowan is treasurer of a department store in his community and also serves on the local school board. Because of changes in its billing and collection system, the board now possesses a fairly large sum of money that will not be needed for several months. For the taxpayers' benefit, Charlie would like to place the funds in an investment vehicle at an attractive yield.

Matthew and Verna Robinson came to the United States from the Caribbean some time ago. They have both worked and have always wanted a home of their own. They have now found the house they want but will need a mortgage loan to buy it.

What do all these situations have in common? In each case, the individuals *could* have gone to some type of financial institution for the services they needed. A savings and loan association, credit union, finance company, savings bank, insurance company, or brokerage firm might have been able to offer them financial help. However, by going to a commercial bank, each person could have obtained the required services under one roof. Indeed, if all eight people lived in the same town, they might all have gone to the same commercial bank and found the answers to their needs and problems.

THE FULL-SERVICE BANK

Competition in today's financial marketplace is intense. Many types of financial institutions compete aggressively with the commercial banks. However, it is *only* the latter group that can provide *every* form of financial service to *every* type of customer. The commercial bank is truly a full-service bank.

There are over 14,000 such banks in the United States, ranging in size from institutions with many billions of dollars in deposits to small community banks handling only a small fraction of that amount. Yet the smallest is like the largest in one respect: Each is a business organized to generate profits by rendering services, and each is designed to offer its customers a complete range of financial services. Whether the bank's customers want to save money, deposit it for near-term or long-term use, borrow, invest, move funds from one place to another, or provide for future security, the commercial bank *alone* has the experience and capability to meet their needs.

For example, Gary Johnson could have discussed his borrowing needs with a loan officer, supplied all the necessary information, and, if he met the bank's credit standards, could have obtained the loan that would enable him to start the new skiing season. Joe Terry would have found that commercial banks can quickly, cheaply, and efficiently transfer funds to other countries. Ellen Smith could have asked the bank to open an account into which her public assistance payments could be directly deposited. She would then have the convenience and safety of an account, and the welfare agency would be spared the expense and effort of processing claims resulting from check thefts, tracing stolen checks, and issuing replacements. Lynn De Palma and her sister would both have found out that the commercial bank offers retirement accounts tailored to their needs. The bank's officers or customer service representatives would have been ready and willing to assist Charlie McGowan with information on investment opportunities so that the school board's idle funds could be put to work to provide income. The Robinsons could have applied for a mortgage loan that would help them buy the house of their choice; the monthly payments would be in keeping with their income, and the bank, by financing housing, would be helping the community.

There are over 4,000 savings and loan associations and over 400 mutual savings banks in the United States. They encourage thrift and use the deposits they attract primarily for home mortgage loans. Over 20,000 credit unions, often organized by employees of the same firm, also exist; they provide such financial services as loans and deposit accounts and give the customer ways to save, borrow, and earn interest at attractive rates. Financial conglomerates such as Merrill Lynch, American Express, and Sears Roebuck have expanded their range of services to become much more competitive with the banks. Nevertheless, the fact remains that commercial banks, by meeting the financial needs of every type of user, are dominant in the marketplace.

THE IMPORTANCE OF BANKING

If one wishes to measure the importance of commercial banking in today's economy, there are several approaches that can be taken. For example, consider size alone. The 14,000 banks employ over one million workers and operate some 40,000 banking offices with over $1 trillion ($1,000,000,000,000) in total assets. The figures are impressive, but they are not the real yardstick by which the importance of banking can be measured.

It is more meaningful to consider the ways in which banks directly affect every segment of the economy. America's status among world nations is often calculated in terms of gross national product (GNP)—the total value of all the goods and services we produce. The country's GNP is now in the $1 trillion dollar range—a figure that staggers the mind. What contributions to this do the commercial banks make?

The automobile industry is always considered one of the most important elements in the economy, not only because millions of cars, costing billions of dollars, are sold each year, or because the industry directly employs over one million workers, but also because so many other industries—steel, aluminum, glass, and textiles—are tied to it. By the same standards of measurement, commercial banking can be viewed as the one industry that is related to every other. It is the one on which all others depend for financial services in some manner and at some time. Without those services, the other industries would find it difficult or impossible to carry out their own daily operations.

How, for example, does banking affect the automobile industry? Assume that John Smith buys a car from his local dealer (possibly using the proceeds of a bank loan to do so) and gives the dealer a check on a local bank. The dealer, in turn, deposits that check with his bank and draws a check of his own to pay the manufacturer. The manufacturer uses a commercial bank, in which all its receipts are deposited, and issues checks on its bank to pay taxes, wages, and vendors. If necessary, the manufacturer can borrow money from its bank, move funds from one account to another anywhere in the world, obtain daily computerized information on the status of its accounts, establish profit-sharing and pension plans with the bank for the benefit of its employees, ask the bank to perform various duties in connection with stockholders, use the bank for investing excess funds, and so forth. If the commercial bank did not exist and did not offer the full range of financial services that it does, the automobile industry would be seriously affected, for there is no other single agency or institution to which it could turn for all its needs.

It is not just the largest industries and companies that are directly involved with commercial banks' services and operations. The smallest business, the consumer, and the agencies of federal, state, and local governments also rely on them to meet every type of financial need.

A giant commercial bank located in a major city may offer as many as 200 financial services and products. However, not all of these are absolutely essential to banking. If many of them were eliminated, a bank could still operate and serve most of its customers. The key question, then, is this: What are the real essentials of banking? What are the basic functions of commercial banks, without which they would not exist and without which the economy could not remain productive and healthy?

If all the functions of a bank are studied, three essentials stand out above the others as major contributions to the economy. They are

- The deposit function;

- The payments function; and

- The credit function.

These are the foundation blocks on which both banking and the economy rest. They also provide the means through which banks are able to grow and prosper. American commercial banks, unlike those in many other countries, are not owned and operated by the government. There is no central bank in the United States comparable to the Bank of England, Sweden, Italy, or Japan. U.S. banks are owned by their stockholders, and the basic objective, again, is to render services while generating profits. The deposit, payment, and credit functions make it possible for that objective to be achieved.

THE DEPOSIT FUNCTION

Why are hundreds of billions of dollars deposited with commercial banks each year? What is deposited? Who are the depositors who create this inflow? The answers to these questions require an understanding of what is known as the U.S. **money supply**. This term is used to describe the total amount of funds available to the public for spending, that is, funds in nongovernment hands. The most recent definition of the money supply includes the following components:

$M_1 =$ Coin and currency in circulation; demand deposits at commercial banks (with certain exceptions); travelers checks of nonbank issuers; and funds withdrawable on demand at other financial institutions.

$M_2 = M_1$ plus savings and small-denomination time deposits.

$M_3 = M_2$ plus large-denomination time deposits.

$L = M_3$ plus certain other liquid assets.

Of these, M_1 is the most widely quoted because it reflects funds available for spending. It has recently amounted to some $450 billion (see Table 1-1); however, only 25 percent of that total was in the form of currency (paper money) and coin. The remainder consisted of various types of **demand deposits**—funds that could be withdrawn at any time, without prior notice to the bank or other type of financial institution.

The most common type of demand deposit is the checking account. As the name implies, the total amount on deposit, or any part of it, is payable on demand and is convertible into coin and currency if it represents collected funds and is classified by the bank as available to the customer. If an individual has a checking account with an available balance of $100, he or she can issue a check for that amount, present it to a teller, and immediately receive $100 in cash.

But is a check money? Under the true definition of the word, it is not. It may be acceptable as a form of payment, and, in fact, over 90 percent of all payments in America today are made by check. However, a check can be refused, because there can be doubt as to whether it is "good." With actual money, this problem does not exist. The currency circulating in the United States today consists of Federal Reserve notes, each of which bears the printed legend, "This note is legal tender for all debts, public and private." Legal tender is issued and backed by a government; a check is accepted on faith.

Because the largest single element in the money supply is the demand deposit, against which checks are issued, it follows that the bulk of a bank's daily deposit activity involves checks rather than currency and coin. The dollar value of all the checks deposited with banks each day is far greater than the amount of coin and currency, simply because checks are far more widely used than money as a means of payment. Almost 40 billion checks now pass through the banking system each year—an average of over 100 million per day.

Converting Checks Into Money

When a check is used to make a payment, what can the recipient do to convert it into money? That person could physically take it to the bank on which it is drawn and ask for legal tender in exchange. However, with over 14,000 commercial banks, against any of which the item could be drawn, this is obviously impossible for every recipient to do. The check may be drawn on a bank across the street or on one

Table 1-1
Money Stock Measures and Components
Billions of dollars, averages of daily figures

Item	1978 Dec.	1979 Dec.	1980 Dec.	1981 Dec.	1982 Jan.	1982 Feb.	1982 Mar.	1982 Apr.	1982 May
Seasonally adjusted									
Measures									
1 M1	363.2	389.0	414.5	440.9	448.6	447.3	448.3	452.3	451.5
2 M2	1,403.9	1,518.9	1,656.2r	1,822.7r	1,841.3	1,848.0	1,865.2	1,880.7	1,897.5
3 M3	1,629.0	1,779.4r	1,963.1	2,188.1r	2,204.3	2,215.0	2,235.8	2,258.1	2,278.6
4 L²	1,938.9	2,153.9	2,370.4	2,642.8r	2,666.1	2,687.2	n.a.	n.a.	n.a.
Selected Components									
5 Currency	97.4	106.1	116.2	123.1	123.8	124.6	125.1	126.3	127.4
6 Traveler's checks[3]	3.5	3.7	4.2	4.3	4.3	4.3	4.4	4.4	4.5
7 Demand deposits	253.9	262.2	267.2	236.4	239.3	234.5	233.0	233.0	232.6
8 Other checkable deposits[7]	8.4	16.9	26.9	77.0	81.1	83.8	85.7	88.6	87.0
9 Savings deposits[4]	479.9	421.7	398.9	343.6	348.8	348.6	350.7	350.5	350.9
10 Small-denomination time deposits[5]	533.9	652.6	751.7	854.7	852.3	859.4	870.0	881.6	894.1
11 Large-denomination time deposits[6]	194.6	221.8	257.9	300.3r	302.6	308.0	312.5	317.1	321.3
Not seasonally adjusted									
Measures									
12 M1	372.5	398.8	424.6	451.2	453.4	437.2	440.0	455.5	445.1
13 M2	1,408.5	1,524.7r	1,662.5r	1,829.4r	1,849.2	1,842.9	1,861.9	1,887.9	1,888.8
14 M3	1,637.5	1,789.2	1,973.9r	2,199.9r	2,217.2	2,216.0	2,237.4	2,266.1	2,266.6
15 L²	1,946.6	2,162.8	2,380.2	2,653.8r	2,680.4	2,695.0	n.a.	n.a.	n.a.

8

Selected Components									
16 Currency	99.4	108.2	118.3	125.4	123.3	123.0	123.8	125.7	127.2
17 Traveler's checks[3]	3.3	3.5	3.9	4.1	4.1	4.1	4.2	4.2	4.3
18 Demand deposits	261.5	270.1	275.1	243.3	243.6	228.5	228.2	236.1	228.2
19 Other checkable deposits[7]	8.4	17.0	27.2	78.4	82.5	81.4	83.7	89.5	85.3
20 Overnight RPs and Eurodollars[8]	24.1	26.3	35.0	38.1	43.2	42.9	43.0	40.4	42.8
21 Savings deposits[4]	478.0	420.5	398.0	343.0	346.8	344.5	346.1	348.1	347.4
22 Small-denomination time deposits[5]	531.1	649.7	748.9	851.7	857.5	868.5	879.6	888.2	895.3
Money market mutual funds									
23 General purpose and broker/dealer	7.1	34.4r	61.9r	151.2r	154.9	156.0	159.2	161.9	164.3
24 Institution only	3.1	9.3	13.9	33.7	32.5	30.5	31.5	31.5	32.8
25 Large-denomination time deposits[6]	198.6	226.0	262.3	305.4r	307.6	314.2	317.4	317.9	320.0

1. Composition of the money stock measures is as follows:
M1: Averages of daily figures for (1) currency outside the Treasury, Federal Reserve Banks, and the vaults of commercial banks; (2) traveler's checks of non-bank issuers; (3) demand deposits at all commercial banks other than those due to domestic banks, the U.S. government, and foreign banks and official institutions less cash items in the process of collection and Federal Reserve float; and (4) negotiable order of withdrawal (NOW) and automatic transfer service (ATS) accounts at banks and thrift institutions, credit union share draft (CUSD) accounts, and demand deposits at mutual savings banks.
M2: M1 plus savings and small-denomination time deposits at all depository institutions, overnight repurchase agreements at commercial banks, overnight Eurodollars held by U.S. residents other than banks at Caribbean branches of member banks, and balances of money market mutual funds (general purpose and broker/dealer).
M3: M2 plus large-denomination time deposits at all depository institutions, terms RPs at commercial banks and savings and loan associations, and balances of institution-only money market mutual funds.
L: M3 plus other liquid assets such as term Eurodollars held by U.S. residents other than banks, bankers acceptances, commercial paper, Treasury bills and other liquid Treasury securities, and U.S. savings bonds.
2. Outstanding amount of U.S. dollar-denominated traveler's checks of nonbank issues.
3. Savings deposits exclude NOW and ATS accounts at commercial banks and thrift institutions and CUSDs at credit unions.
4. Small-denomination time deposits — including retail RPs — are those issued in amounts of less than $100,000.
5. Large-denomination time deposits are those issued in amounts of $100,000 or more and are net of the holdings of domestic banks, thrift institutions, the U.S. government, money market mutual funds, and foreign banks and official institutions.
6. Includes ATS and NOW balances at all institutions, credit union share draft balances, and demand deposits at mutual savings banks.
7. Overnight (and continuing contract) RPs are those issued by commercial banks to other than depository institutions and money market mutual funds (general purpose and broker/dealer), and overnight Eurodollars are those issued by Caribbean branches of member banks to U.S. residents other than depository institutions and money market mutual funds (general purpose and broker/dealer).
NOTE: Latest monthly and weekly figures are available from the Board's H.6 (508) release. Back data are available from the Banking Section, Division of Research and Statistics, Board of Governors of the Federal Reserve System, Washington, D.C. 20551.
Revisions in M2, M3, L, and money market mutual funds reflect the inclusion of three general purpose and broker/dealer money market funds that began reporting in May 1982 though their operations had begun earlier.
SOURCE: *Federal Reserve Bulletin*, July 1982, p. A 14.

3,000 miles away. To resolve this problem, the commercial banking system provides a mechanism for converting a check into money.

Consider a cross section of the depositors at a commercial bank. A state government receives checks from its citizens in payment of taxes. A farmer receives checks in payment for his produce. A manufacturer is paid for goods sold by means of checks. A worker receives salary checks. A retired person receives pension checks from a former employer and a social security check from the federal government. Stockholders receive dividend checks from corporations. By depositing their checks with banks, all these customers can convert the otherwise worthless pieces of paper into spendable, available funds quickly, cheaply, and efficiently.

Safety and Convenience

Two additional reasons for depositing with banks are safety and convenience. Every depositor—business, government unit, or individual—believes that every deposit turned over to a bank will be fully protected at all times and that the bank will be responsible for safeguarding it and making it available at some future date. If a bank robbery or embezzlement occurs, the depositor is protected against loss. Whenever a bank puts money to work and generates profits by making loans and investments, most of the funds it uses come from depositors. The bank must always be conscious of the need to protect the funds, using them prudently and *never* being unable to honor a request for payment against an account.

Many banks strive to make their offices and facilities available to customers at the most convenient times and locations. Extra banking hours, drive-in facilities, and automated teller machines (ATMs)—of which more than 20,000 have been installed—have become commonplace. Banking at home by telephone and automatic transfers of funds between accounts are offered by many institutions. Banks often go where their customers are and try to simplify transactions for them.

Checking account customers realize that they will have bills to pay and expenses to meet. The deposit function, then, also involves the payment function; deposits must precede payments. Checks are a convenient and safe way of disbursing funds. They are widely accepted because the public in general has come to believe in their validity. When we receive a check as payment, we assume that it is good and that funds are on deposit to cover it. Indeed, unless prior arrangements (e.g., overdraft privileges) have been made with the bank, the issuing of a check by someone who knows that there are insufficient funds to cover it is an act of fraud.

Demand Deposits Versus Time Deposits

At a commercial bank, the deposit may be made into either a checking or a savings account, or it may be used to establish a time deposit relationship. Is the intent of the depositor identical in each case? Obviously it is not. Checking account deposits are made because the customer intends to withdraw the funds in the very near future to meet current expenses. On the other hand, savings and time deposits are made because the funds will not be needed for a period of time and are being set aside for future goals or emergencies.

There is a legal distinction between **savings accounts** and **time deposits.** The customer who opens a savings account does not establish a specific maturity date when it will be closed; deposits and withdrawals through it may be made over a period of many years. On the other hand, time deposits have a stated maturity—7 days or more from the date of deposit. Whenever a time deposit is withdrawn before maturity, the bank must impose penalties for early withdrawal.

All savings and time deposits can earn interest. The typical standard checking account cannot. However, under recent federal legislation, all financial institutions can offer accounts known as NOW (negotiable order of withdrawal) accounts, which are interest-bearing but also give the depositor the privilege of issuing checks against the balance.

The most common examples of time deposits include certificates of deposit (CDs) and special club accounts (e.g., Christmas, Hanukkah, or Vacation).

It was traditional in the past that only commercial banks could offer checking accounts, and there was no type of account relationship that could combine the ability to earn interest with the ability to draw checks against it. More recently, these restrictions have been removed through federal laws. Thrift institutions (savings banks and savings and loan associations) now offer checking accounts. Credit unions provide their customers with instruments called **share drafts**, which serve exactly the same purpose as checks. Finally, as mentioned earlier, NOW accounts have become popular because they give the customer both interest-earning and check-issuing capability (Figure 1-1).

Figure 1-1
Growth of NOW Accounts

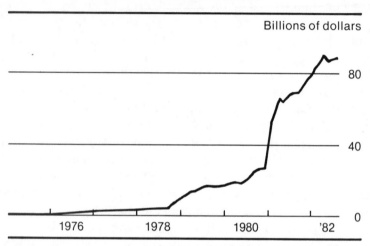

SOURCE: *Federal Reserve Bulletin*, July 1982, p. 395.

Federal laws also allow banks to offer **Automatic Transfer Service** (ATS). The depositor who uses this service can issue checks against insufficient or nonexistent funds in a checking account; the bank will then move funds from a savings account to cover them. If the bank offers banking-at-home plans, the customer can issue instructions for payments and conduct other banking business by telephone.

Because banking, in its simplest form, consists of obtaining money through deposits and then putting that money to profitable use, it is logical to expect banks to watch the types of deposits on hand very closely as well as to be aware at all times of the actual amounts on deposit. The ratio between demand and time deposits is extremely important to a bank for two reasons: there is a need to pay interest on all forms of savings and time deposits, thus increasing the bank's expenses, and there is an essential difference in the rate of turnover. Demand deposits do not stay with a bank for any appreciable length of time. Depositors, aware that interest cannot be paid on checking accounts, keep those balances to a minimum and find various ways of putting the funds to work. The turnover rate on demand deposits is extremely high. Time deposits, however, remain with the bank for longer periods of time and are used differently—for example, in long-term loans and investments.

At the time they are accepted from customers, all forms of deposits become *both* assets and liabilities for the bank. The coin, currency, and checks that make up the deposit can be considered assets, which is the term used in accounting for owned property of value, because they are legally in the bank's possession and can be put to profitable use. At the same time, they represent liabilities because the amount of each deposit is owed to the customer and will have to be repaid at some future date. Whenever a bank prepares its balance sheet showing its financial condition, all deposit balances are shown as liabilities, that is, debts of the bank.

THE PAYMENTS FUNCTION

With each succeeding year, the volume of checks used in the United States increases; the fact that 100 million checks change hands on an average day indicates the importance of the payments function. From the largest corporation to the average individual, every bank customer relies on the efficiency, safety, speed, and convenience of the commercial banking system through which most checks are processed. The universal use of checks also testifies to the faith and trust evidenced every time a check is issued and accepted.

Before checks gained this wide acceptance, the payments function involved other methods that often left a great deal to be desired. For one thing, money can obviously be lost or stolen. If a payment is made in cash, any receipt that is given can also be lost. If no receipt is issued, it may be impossible for the payer to prove that a payment was actually made.

By contrast, every customer who uses a bank as a payment vehicle benefits from the existence of certain guarantees that have become implicit in the system. From the time a deposit is made until checks are issued against it, the bank is responsible for safeguarding the funds. Thus, the risk of losing cash disappears. The customer also receives additional protection through the check processing system. Each check is a letter of instruction, directing that a specific payment be made. If those instructions are not complied with in every detail, the bank, not the customer, is liable. Each customer receives a periodic statement showing all activity on the account, and a cancelled check remains the best evidence of payment.

Electronic Fund Transfer Systems

By operating and continually improving the payments mechanism, and by supplying the personnel, equipment, and technology to handle almost 40 billion checks per year, commercial banks have contributed a great deal to the economy. However, they have also had to consider the costs and problems that this huge volume creates for them. Even with all the benefits of automation, the cost to banks for exchanging and processing checks continues to increase, so there is a constant search for a better way to serve the interests of both customers and banks. This search has led to the development of various forms of **EFTS**—electronic fund transfer systems.

Whenever paperless, automated bookkeeping entries can be used so that one account is debited and another credited, tremendous benefits can be realized because these electronic transfers are far less costly, more accurate, and faster than traditional systems.

Instead of issuing a large volume of payroll checks, a corporation can now supply magnetic tape data so that each employee's account, wherever it is held, can be credited with the net pay. Social Security Administration officials have successfully introduced direct deposit of payments to retirees, avoiding the use of checks and guaranteeing payment on the due date. In increasing numbers, customers use their plastic cards in automated teller machines to obtain cash without issuing checks. Depositors can authorize their banks to make automatic charges to their accounts for insurance premiums, mortgage and installment loan payments, and other fixed charges. Point-of-sale terminals have been installed in many stores and supermarkets; they use a customer's plastic card to initiate a transfer of funds in payment for merchandise purchased.

When electronic transfers of funds were first introduced, it was thought that a "checkless society" would develop and that the total use of checks would gradually diminish. This no longer appears to be realistic. Although each application of EFTS reduces the volume of checks, it now seems that there are still a great many situations in which checks will be used.

The increasing emphasis on EFTS applications is only one manifestation of the changing nature of banking. Commercial banks must now make customers aware of the EFTS services that are available, the improvements that have become possible, and the benefits that can be gained. Just as they gradually educated their customers to issue and accept checks as a payment medium, they must now make a major effort to demonstrate that even better payment vehicles can be used, with reduced costs and greater efficiency. Checks can never be entirely eliminated from the payment system, but the volume can be significantly reduced as a new generation of customers emerges in our society. That new generation appears more willing to accept change and to take advantage of new technology. That willingness can be seen in many ways, such as the fact that over 20,000 automated teller machines are now in active use throughout the country at all types of financial institutions, and that by the end of 1980 over 10 million social security recipients had agreed to accept direct deposit of payments.

In the meantime, the sheer volume of checks used each day, and the costs incurred in handling them, have also led to systems of check **truncation**. This term describes any of the ways in which a bank may try to reduce check-handling expenses. Truncation may involve the electronic transmittal of the information contained in a check so that the item itself does not have to be sent physically from one bank to another. In another form of truncation, cancelled checks are not returned to the depositor unless there is a specific request for them.

THE CREDIT FUNCTION

The borrowing and lending of money have been an accepted part of the conduct of financial affairs since the earliest days of civilization.

In the ruins of ancient Babylon, archaeologists found evidence of a farmer borrowing from a temple and agreeing to make repayment, with interest, after his crops were harvested and sold. In agricultural areas of the United States today, commercial banks perform the identical lending function, and the farmers who borrow from them execute a written promise of repayment just as their predecessor did in Babylon 5,000 years ago.

In the Middle Ages, goldsmiths often acted as lenders, in addition to providing safekeeping for their clients' precious metals and other assets. When a goldsmith made a loan, those assets served as the security, just as some form of marketable asset often serves as security for today's lending bank. Other early examples of the credit function abound. Shakespeare's money lender, Shylock, has become a legend. The American Revolution was financed in large part through the loan certificates issued by Congress, and all subsequent wars in which the United States has been involved were financed by heavy government borrowing.

Today, many sources of credit are available to every category of borrower, large or small. Individual consumers can approach personal finance companies for loans, borrow from insurance companies against the cash surrender value of their policies, obtain a mortgage loan from a thrift institution, finance automobiles and appliances through a host of credit agencies and stores, borrow from the credit union to which they belong, or, as savings depositors, use their passbooks as security for loans.

Businesses of every size and type likewise have many avenues of credit open to them. Commercial financing firms will lend to them against their accounts receivable; one business may extend short-term credit to another by supplying needed raw materials or other inventory and awaiting payment. Insurance companies frequently make the large, long-term loans that permit the construction of office buildings, factories, and shopping centers. Many corporations with outstanding credit ratings borrow money by issuing their own short-term, unsecured promissory notes; these notes are called **commercial paper** and are actively traded every day. Federal, state, and local governments use a variety of long- and short-term borrowing techniques to raise the funds they need. Banks often find it necessary to borrow from one another or from the Federal Reserve.

Despite the number of other lenders, the commercial banking industry remains the dominant force in the credit market. More money is borrowed each year from commercial banks than from any other source; total loans outstanding at these banks now exceed $1 trillion. In keeping with their full-service philosophy, commercial banks extend credit under virtually every conceivable set of conditions to every segment of the market. No other lender can match banking in either the size or the diversity of credit extended. There are bank loans to meet the needs of the business, the consumer, and the government. Commercial banks throughout the United States may simultaneously be granting a $250 loan to an individual for some personal need, a $25,000 loan to a business, and an even larger loan to an agency of government. Some bank loans are backed by a form of security, known as collateral; most are made on an unsecured basis, with the bank relying entirely on the borrower's written promise to repay. Some bank loans are made for 30 days, others for 30 years.

Commercial banks supply $70 out of every $100 borrowed by businesses throughout the United States. By purchasing bonds, bills, and notes issued by every level of government, they supply $50 out of every $100 raised by those agencies. Commercial bank loans to consumers are about $180 billion, and this figure does not include the amounts loaned through bank credit cards or for home mortgages.

Businesses, consumers, and governments represent the three main categories of borrowing customers. The commercial banks' ability to serve their credit needs keeps the American economy prosperous and growing. The extending of credit also provides by far the largest single source of bank income; typically, two-thirds of a bank's yearly earnings result from interest on loans. The commercial bank's credit function provides a basic and much-needed service to the community; at the same time, it is the most important element in bank profits.

There is another important aspect to the credit function at commercial banks. By approving loans and adding the proceeds to customers' accounts, they are responsible for the creation of money and thereby directly affect the nation's money supply.

Here is how. Assume that a new account is opened with a bank or that a customer increases the account balance through a deposit. Assume that in each case the amount involved is $1,000. The bank must set aside a portion of that $1,000 as a reserve, but the remainder

17

can be used by the bank to make loans and investments. In this case, assume that the reserve requirement against the $1,000 is 12 percent, or $120, and that the bank takes the remaining $880 and uses it to lend to another customer. The original depositor's funds remain as a balance in an account, but the loan proceeds have been deposited to the borrower's account; therefore, a new deposit has been created by the bank and $880 has been added to the total money supply.

Banks can build up their deposits by increasing loans as long as they keep enough on hand to redeem whatever amounts customers want to convert from balances to currency and coin. When a loan is approved and the proceeds are credited to the borrower's bank account, loans (an asset for the bank) and deposits (a liability) both increase. The customer has spendable funds that, in effect, did not exist before; new money has been introduced into the picture. If the customer demanded payment of the loan proceeds in currency, the effect would be the same.

SUMMARY

It is impossible to visualize a national economy that could operate efficiently, grow steadily, or survive for any length of time without the support of a strong banking system. Commercial banks in the United States form the cornerstone of that system because they offer every type of financial service to every category of customer. Not every bank may find it necessary or advisable to offer every service, but the fact remains that banks, as a group, are indeed full-service institutions.

In today's financial marketplace, credit unions, thrift institutions, brokerage firms, insurance and finance companies, and new "financial supermarkets" such as American Express, Merrill Lynch, Sears Roebuck, and Prudential compete with the commercial banks in many ways. However, none of them covers the entire spectrum of financial services as completely or as well.

Three of the services provided by commercial banks are so important that they are considered fundamental to our economy. They involve the deposit, payment, and credit functions. While international, trust, safe deposit, investment, and other specialized services help to meet the financial needs of customers and contribute to the bank's profits, they do not have the same overall significance to the monetary system.

Commercial banks are dynamic, rapidly changing institutions. They employ over one million individuals, handle over one trillion dollars in assets, and, through their daily operations, touch the lives of the entire population.

QUESTIONS FOR DISCUSSION

1. Is a check money?

2. What two elements make up the bulk of the nation's money supply? Which of the two is larger?

3. How are most payments made in the United States?

4. What is the legal difference between a savings deposit and a time deposit?

5. How does the customer's purpose determine whether a demand deposit or a time deposit is to be made?

6. How do deposits create both assets and liabilities for banks?

7. With what three categories of borrowers do banks primarily deal?

8. What advantages does an automated teller machine (ATM) provide to depositors? What is its benefit to the bank?

Suggested Readings

American Bankers Association. *Bank Fact Book.* Washington, D.C.: American Bankers Association, 1981.

Boreham, G. *Money and Banking.* 2nd ed. New York: Holt, Rinehart & Winston, 1979.

Candilis, Wray O. *The Future of Commercial Banking.* New York: Praeger, 1975.

Chandler, Lester V., and Stephen M. Goldfield. *The Economics of Money and Banking.* 7th ed. New York: Harper and Row, 1977.

Compton, Eric N. *Inside Commercial Banking.* New York: John Wiley & Sons, Inc., 1980.

Savage, Donald T. *Money and Banking.* New York: John Wiley & Sons, Inc., 1977.

Staats, William F. *Money and Banking.* Washington, D.C.: American Bankers Association, 1982.

Chapter 2

The Evolution of American Banking

LEARNING OBJECTIVES

After completing this chapter, you will have an understanding of

- the basic differences between American banking and the systems in other countries;

- banking conditions in colonial times;

- the importance of the First and Second Banks of the United States;

- major provisions of the National Bank Act;

- weaknesses in the banking system after 1864;

- the organization of the Federal Reserve;

- the importance of the Monetary Control Act;

- such terms as wildcat banking, national bank, Comptroller of the Currency, and transaction account.

Any attempt to compare the banking system that exists in the United States with systems found in other countries leads to one inescapable conclusion: the American system is unique. The differences between our system and others can be seen both in the variety of institutions in America that compete in offering services—savings and loan associations, mutual savings banks, and credit unions, for example—and in the commercial banking system itself. In many other countries, the banking system is dominated by a handful of giants; in the United States, over 14,000 commercial banks are in business. In France, England, and Sweden, among others, there are strong central banks owned and run by the government; no identical bank can be found in the United States. In Canada and Great Britain, the largest banks operate over 1,000 branches extending from border to border; in the United States, no bank is permitted to open full-scale branches across state lines.[1]

All of these differences combine to create a banking structure that has no parallel in other parts of the world. Our banking system has gradually evolved over 200 years, through a succession of money crises. It is profitable and strong today because bankers and legislators have learned the lessons of history. They have continually sought to eliminate the sources of past problems and have worked to serve customers more efficiently, providing more and/or better services at reduced costs. Today's system is not perfect. There will always be a need for further adjustments in response to new customer needs, the demands of a dynamic economy, and legislative developments. Yet the fact remains that our commercial banks serve more individuals, businesses, and units of government in more ways than do their counterparts in other areas of the world.

Newspapers, magazines, and television are all quick to capitalize on bank failures or problems; these make news. A ready market exists for anyone who wants to publicize the flaws in bank operations or the ways in which a customer received less-than-ideal service. It is unfortunate that equal publicity is not given to the ways in which banks render a positive and vital service to the economy. The strength and efficiency of a trillion-dollar system often seem to be taken for granted, and the millions of transactions of every type that are handled quickly, accurately, and at low cost seem to go unnoticed.

The journey from colonial times to the present has been long and difficult for commercial banks. It is a most interesting history, and one that is closely tied to the history of the nation itself. The evolution of banking reflects the philosophy and mood of the population at different times.

BANKING IN COLONIAL AND POST-REVOLUTION TIMES

The earliest settlers on our shores were a very diverse group. They came from a wide variety of national, ethnic, and religious backgrounds. Yet they all shared one basic desire—the fierce hunger for freedom. The willingness of these pioneers to risk everything in leaving their familiar homelands and coming to a primitive, largely unexplored New World was a reflection of their wish to escape from every form of persecution, tyranny, and government control over speech, religion, and other aspects of daily life. The colonists wanted as much independence as possible. Free enterprise, freedom of religious worship, freedom of thought, expression, and assembly, and minimal government control were the aspirations.

Many of the colonists came from countries where a central bank dominated the financial scene. Institutions such as the Bank of Sweden, the Banque de France, the Reichsbank, the Bank of Amsterdam, and the Bank of England predated the colonizing of America. It would have been logical for the colonists to establish some comparable institution, closely affiliated with their new federal government; however, the spirit of free enterprise prevailed.

Instead of following the pattern that existed in European countries, the early settlers moved toward the opposite extreme. They believed that anyone who wished to open a general store, a tavern, or a blacksmith's shop should be free to do so, and they applied this same principle to those who wanted to establish banks. Because the colonists strongly opposed any form of centralized control, there was no rigorous system of bank chartering by the federal government. Each of the original 13 colonies stoutly defended its right to regulate banking within its own borders. The requirements for opening and operating a bank, while they varied from one colony to another, were, in general, easy to meet. As a result, banks opened their doors—and, unfortunately, closed them—with great regularity.

Of course, not all the banks of the colonial era failed, defrauded customers, or otherwise contributed to a rather unhappy history. The Bank of New York and commercial banks organized in Massachusetts and Philadelphia during the 1780s have survived to the present day. These, however, were the exceptions.

One basic weakness that led to so many bank failures in our early history was the system of currency that existed. **Specie**, also known as hard currency, consisted of gold and silver. There was not enough of it to meet the needs of the economy. Specie also tended to flow out of the colonies in payment for goods purchased abroad. As a result, various types of paper money began to appear on the scene. In making loans to customers, individual banks had begun the practice of issuing their own notes, which presumably could be redeemed in specie. The concept of depositing loan proceeds to customers' accounts had not yet been introduced. In theory, bank notes would be used as money in payment of debts. In actual practice, this was not the case. Instead of having confidence in the system, the public came to distrust it. Counterfeiting of bank notes became rampant. Creditors often refused to accept bank notes, doubting whether the issuing bank was still in business. Even if the bank were still functioning, there was also a question of whether it would be willing or able to exchange the notes for specie.

Robert Morris, who had been named Superintendent of Finance by the Continental Congress, was largely responsible for establishing the Bank of North America. This bank opened in Philadelphia in 1781. Its stock subscription was open to both the government and private individuals, but Congress retained the right to supervise the bank's affairs. Notes issued by this bank were generally accepted, a fact that made it an exception to the general rule.

The Bank of the United States

People were becoming painfully aware of the fact that a sound monetary system was essential to the health of the nation's economy. In the absence of sufficient quantities of gold and silver money, a system had to be devised with some form of circulating medium, whether paper or wooden money, lightweight coins, or other accepted standard of value. Moreover, regardless of its form, people had to have confidence in the medium. Paper money was acceptable only if the public believed it was actually worth its equivalent in specie and could be redeemed on request. If everyone shared that confidence, paper money would not necessarily be redeemed but would pass freely from hand to hand at face value.

Alexander Hamilton had been responsible for the founding of the Bank of New York in 1784. Under the nation's new Constitution, he was appointed Secretary of the Treasury and turned his attention to the weaknesses of the banking system. He proposed the formation of a new bank to Congress and stipulated that the new bank would have the direct involvement and backing of the federal government. His plan was approved, and the First Bank of the United States opened in Philadelphia in December 1791. It was established under a strict set of provisions regarding capitalization; it could issue its own paper currency only up to the amount of its own capital. The federal government itself deposited funds with the bank and used it for payments. Its charter was granted for a 20-year period, subject to renewal if Congress so voted.

The memory of the central banks of other nations and of the control that a strong central government could exert was still fresh. The First Bank became the object of strong opposition from several sides. Its very existence was criticized by those who pointed out that the Constitution contained no provision for government involvement in banking. Independent, private bankers, whose institutions operated under the liberal terms of their individual states, saw the First Bank as the forerunner of centralized bank supervision and insisted on their right to conduct business as they saw fit. More important, the bank acted as a policeman by accepting the note issues of other banks from its customers and presenting those notes for redemption in specie. This police role benefited the public but was vehemently resented by banks that did not want to redeem their outstanding notes and thus surrender any of their precious supplies of gold and silver. The capitalization of the First Bank and its sound, prudent operations generated a good deal of public confidence; however, the opposition to it was too great to be ignored. In 1811, Congress vetoed renewal of its charter, and the bank went out of existence.

The period from 1811 to 1816 witnessed the same weaknesses that had existed prior to the formation of the First Bank but on a much larger scale. The population had grown considerably, and the economy had expanded. The federal government had arranged the necessary financing for the War of 1812. More than ever before, the growing nation needed a sound banking system, but the need was not met.

The number of undercapitalized and poorly run state-chartered banks continued to increase, as did the number of failures. Issues of individual bank notes continued to appear in large quantities, since the fear of policing had disappeared with the demise of the First Bank, and public confidence in the banking system deteriorated during this 5-year period. These factors led to congressional approval for chartering the Second Bank of the United States in 1816.

THE 1816–1863 PERIOD

Like its predecessor, the Second Bank operated under a 20-year charter and was soundly capitalized. It had the direct support of the federal government. In a landmark Supreme Court decision (*McCulloch vs. Maryland*, 1819), the Second Bank was declared a necessary and proper instrument of the U.S. government for carrying out its fiscal operations. The overall conservatism of the bank generated public confidence. Because it acted as a government depository and collection agent for notes issued by state banks, however, it was resented as the First Bank had been. It was also bitterly opposed by President Andrew Jackson. In addition, the question of constitutionality had never actually been resolved. For all these reasons, Congress failed to renew the charter, and the Second Bank went out of existence in 1836.

The subsequent period, from 1836 to 1863, has been described as the darkest in U.S. banking history, for at no point in the country's existence was there a greater need for a sound and trustworthy banking system, yet so little response to that need. The geographic expansion, population growth, and economic prosperity of the pre-Civil War period combined to create an ideal climate for the growth of commercial banking. However, many of the banks that opened lacked sufficient capital, prudent management, or both, and failed completely in their presumed task of serving their communities.

Many banking abuses also crept into the system. The term **wildcat banking** became part of the nation's vocabulary, describing the practices of those banks that discouraged customers from presenting notes and demanding specie in exchange by establishing offices in remote locations in the wilderness, where wildcats supposedly roamed.

By 1858, counterfeiting had become so widespread that thousands of fraudulent bank notes circulated. Merchants, often suspicious about the existence of the bank on which the notes were drawn or about the genuineness of the notes themselves, frequently refused to accept them in payment. In other cases, notes were accepted only at a discount from their face value. Banks sometimes issued their own notes to customers (Figure 2-1) but demanded repayment in specie. Public faith and trust in the banking system were at their lowest point, especially in the South and West, where new banks opened and operated indiscriminately. Communities that needed banking facilities and services were deprived of them.

Figure 2-1
Bank Note
Issued by The Bank of Morgan, Georgia, 1857

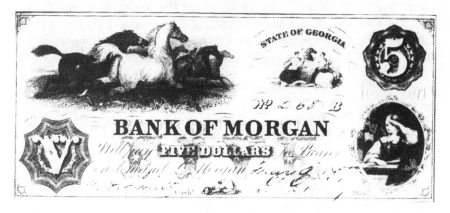

1863–1864: THE NATIONAL BANKING ACT

In 1863, for the third time in less than a century, America was engaged in a war, this time one that divided the nation against itself. Two years of conflict had created a severe fiscal crisis in the federal government, forcing President Lincoln to seek new methods of obtaining the funds he so desperately required. Salmon P. Chase, Lincoln's Secretary of the Treasury, was given the dual task of finding these new sources of revenue and, at the same time, overhauling and reforming the banking system. Chase introduced dramatic and drastic legislation, passed by Congress in 1863 as the National Currency Act and amended a year later as the National Banking Act. The legislation is commonly known by the latter, shorter title. It not only forms the basis for today's banking structure but also provided a solution to the government's financial woes by opening up a new market for Treasury bonds. The basic provisions were as follows:

1. A new type of financial institution, called a **national bank**, was created. Each such bank was to be privately owned but chartered directly by the federal government. Rigorous qualifying standards for charters were drawn up; individuals of questionable character were disqualified from participation. The stockholders whose contributions made up the required capital for forming a national bank were made personally liable in the event the bank failed, and Congress set limits on the bank's lending operations. Existing state-chartered banks were invited to convert to national bank charters if they wished and if they could meet the standards.

2. A new office in the Treasury Department was established, and the person placed in charge of it was given the title of **Comptroller of the Currency**. The title may be misleading; the Comptroller does *not* regulate the nation's supply of currency but is responsible for chartering, examining, and regulating all national banks. The Comptroller is authorized to call for periodic financial reports from each national bank and reports directly to Congress on the findings and operations of the office.

3. A new, uniform type of currency was created, called the **national bank note**. Except for the issuing bank's name, these notes were to be standard in design (see Figure 2-2). Before issuing them to its customers, a national bank was required to purchase a certain amount of government bonds and to pledge them with the Treasury Department. This technique not only gave the public a measure of confidence in the soundness of the notes but also raised money for the government and kept the amount of each bank's outstanding notes proportionate to its capital.

Figure 2-2
National Bank Note, 1900

4. A system of required **reserves** was established. As an additional confidence-building measure for the public, each national bank was required to keep reserves against both its deposits and its notes. A reserve might consist of cash in the bank's own vaults plus a balance maintained with another national bank in a money center. Because New York City was the nation's financial center, there was a concentration of reserves in New York's banks.

It was Salmon Chase's intention to have the state-chartered banks voluntarily join the national system, but few chose to do so. They preferred to stay with a system that did not call for the chartering procedures, regular examinations, and other restrictions that national banks had to contend with. Therefore, Congress passed additional legislation in 1865, imposing a 10 percent federal tax on all notes issued by state banks. This law, together with the increasing acceptance of checks throughout the country, led the state banks to discontinue issuing notes. Thereafter, loan proceeds were usually deposited directly to customers' accounts.

The Dual Banking System

The 1863–1864 legislation was responsible for much of what we see today in the U.S. banking system. The Office of the Comptroller of the

Currency functions today under basically the same guidelines, supervising the entire system of national banks—which number about 4,500. These banks can easily be recognized by the word "national," which must appear somewhere in their legal names. Examples include First National Bank (of Boston, Chicago, etc.); Bank of America, N.T.&S.A. (National Trust and Savings Association); and Citibank, N.A. (National Association). National banks exist competitively and side-by-side with the far more numerous state-chartered banks, generally offering the same services and operating in the same fundamental way. If it gains the necessary approvals, a bank may at any time convert from one type of charter to the other. The fact that every commercial bank must be chartered either by the federal government or by the banking authorities in its own state has created what is known as the **dual banking system.**

Weaknesses of the National Banking Act

The National Banking Act was a landmark in U.S. banking history. In terms of addressing the abuses and problems that had existed prior to its passage, in terms of providing a new fund-raising technique for the government in a time of fiscal crisis, and in terms of establishing the basis for a sound banking system in which the public could place its trust, it served its purposes very well. In retrospect, it is difficult to imagine how the banking system could possibly have survived much longer without the reforms that the act introduced. With the passage of time, however, it became apparent that the nation was faced with monetary problems not addressed by the act and that new legislation would be needed to correct the deficiencies that Congress could not have foreseen in 1863 and 1864.

Lack of a Check Collection System. One such deficiency resulted from the increased use of checks. By 1913, America was a nation of 48 states, and the daily flow of checks from coast to coast created a major problem. No system for the quick presenting and collecting of checks existed. It might take weeks for a merchant in Texas who accepted a check drawn on a bank in North Carolina to receive payment or learn that the check had not been honored. Banks began to establish direct ties with other banks, often for the purpose of having a depository for their reserves, but also for check-collection purposes. A bank that maintains an account for another bank is called a **correspondent bank.**

An Inflexible Currency. A second weakness identified after 1864 involved the nation's money supply. The amount of outstanding national bank notes at any one time was legally tied to the amount of government bonds in circulation. When business conditions were good, it would have been desirable to increase the supply of bank notes to finance transactions. However, the opposite took place. When the government found that its revenues, chiefly derived from taxes, had increased because of a prosperous economy, it naturally tried to reduce its outstanding debt and its interest payments by calling in some of the bonds for redemption. The outstanding amount of national bank notes then had to decrease in proportion. The requirements of the National Banking Act thus created a safer, uniform currency, but did so in a way that had an adverse effect on the needs of the rapidly growing national economy.

Pyramiding Reserves. The third defect resulted from the system of reserve requirements created by the act. Each national bank was compelled to keep reserves with another bank, and "city banks" were designated to serve as depositories for the smaller "country banks." The "city banks," in turn, used larger, stronger banks as their reserve depositories, and national banks in New York City—the apex of the pyramid representing this upward flow—received funds from the entire country. All reserves on deposit with other banks could earn interest. To meet that interest expense, each bank put the reserves of its correspondents to work. The reserves concentrated in New York banks were used for short-term loans, primarily to brokerage firms.

When banks outside New York City needed large amounts of currency, they were forced to draw down their reserves. This caused an eventual drain on the New York banks, which were then forced to call in loans in order to raise immediate funds. In some cases, actual money panics ensued, since the stockbrokers whose loans had been called in were forced to liquidate their own securities holdings to make the required repayments. As forced sales usually do, these liquidations drove market prices down, and the entire economy suffered.

THE FEDERAL RESERVE SYSTEM

The weaknesses in the banking system could not have been expected to disappear by themselves; indeed, their effects increased with each succeeding year. In 1912, President Woodrow Wilson publicly stated that further reforms were absolutely necessary. After much congressional discussion and analysis of proposals presented by national monetary commissions, economists, bankers, and government officials, the Federal Reserve Act was enacted in 1913. It is a fascinating example of compromise legislation, responding to the wishes of many different groups while correcting the defects in the banking system. To those who feared an excessive concentration of power in Washington, it provided a measure of local control. To those who opposed the idea of a strong central bank, it provided for private ownership. To those whose chief concern was the money supply, it offered a new type of currency, the Federal Reserve note, which did not have to be backed by bonds but would be accepted as official legal tender (see Figure 2-3). In every way, the act served to remedy the previous drawbacks to sound and efficient banking, and thus gave the economy a far more responsive system.

Figure 2-3
Federal Reserve Bank Note, 1914

The three basic weaknesses in the 1864–1913 period had been identified as the lack of a check collection system, the inflexibility of the money supply, and the pyramiding of reserves. To correct the first of these, the Federal Reserve Act divided the country into 12 geographic districts, established a Federal Reserve bank in each one, and provided that member banks could send out-of-town checks directly to those banks for collection; thereafter, the Fed itself would take care of presenting the checks to the individual banks on which they were drawn (see Figure 2-4). The new check collection system contained the necessary mechanisms to ensure that the presenting and collecting process would require far less time than previous methods.

To solve the problem of an inflexible money supply tied to the amount of outstanding government bonds, the Federal Reserve Act gave the Fed authority to issue notes and removed the requirement that these be backed by government obligations. Today, these Federal Reserve notes form our basic currency. National banks stopped issuing their own notes after passage of the act. The Federal Reserve Act also made it possible for banks to obtain ready supplies of the coin and currency they need, since the Fed can, on very short notice, deliver cash to its member banks.

The problem of pyramid reserves was also solved through the concept of the 12 geographic districts. Member banks in the Federal Reserve System were told to maintain their reserves with the Federal Reserve bank in their own districts, so that there was a pool of reserve funds in every part of the country rather than a concentration in one area. The 1913 act also gave the Fed authority to change the percentage of required reserves whenever necessary and to make loans to its member banks under certain conditions.

The importance of the Fed as the nation's primary force for controlling the flow of money and credit, and the organization of the Federal Reserve System and its tools or mechanisms, are discussed at length in Chapter 3.

FEDERAL DEPOSIT INSURANCE

Just as Salmon Chase and his associates could not have predicted the economic changes that would make the Federal Reserve Act necessary, so the lawmakers and bankers who drew up the Federal

Figure 2-4
The Federal Reserve System
Boundaries of Federal Reserve Districts
and Their Branch Territories

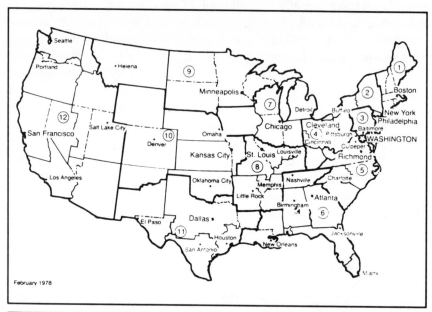

February 1978

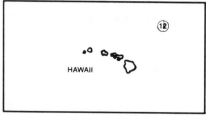

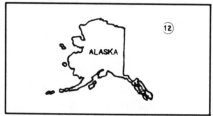

LEGEND

—— Boundaries of Federal Reserve Districts

—— Boundaries of Federal Reserve Branch Territories

⊗ Board of Governors of the Federal Reserve System

⊛ Federal Reserve Bank Cities

• Federal Reserve Branch Cities

SOURCE: *Federal Reserve Bulletin,* May 1978.

Reserve Act could not have foreseen the collapse of the stock market in 1929, the Great Depression, and the banking crisis that resulted. Following the end of World War I, America embarked on an era of wild optimism and unrestrained growth, much of which was financed by the commercial banks. During the "Roaring Twenties" the individual states extended charters to thousands of new banks under the prevailing philosophy that the business boom would continue indefinitely and that the future was limitless. That philosophy was put to rest when the stock market crash of October 1929 caused a decrease of $14 billion in paper values in a single day.

During 1930, more than 1,300 American commercial banks closed their doors, and by 1933 an additional 7,000 had failed. Some $7 billion in deposits disappeared through these bank failures. Many of the banks that were forced out of business were small agricultural banks; however, a single failure in New York City caused the loss of $200 million in deposits. The banks became the hub of a vicious circle. Businesses went into bankruptcy, fired their workers, and defaulted on their bank loans. The nation's unemployment reached 25 percent. Individuals often could not withdraw funds from their banks to meet everyday living expenses because the banks simply did not have cash to distribute.

In 1933, Congress reacted by passing the **Glass-Steagall Act**, also known as the Banking Act of that year. This act significantly altered the operations of commercial banks and did a great deal to restore public confidence in the banking system. The Banking Act of 1933 prohibited banks from paying interest on demand deposits, imposed new restrictions on the issuing of bank charters, separated investment banking from commercial banking by preventing banks from underwriting revenue bonds and corporate stock issues, set limits on the rates of interest that banks could pay on time and savings deposits, and, most importantly, created a system of protecting bank deposits through federal insurance.

A new agency, the **Federal Deposit Insurance Corporation** (FDIC), was established to

- set standards for its members' operations;

- examine them to ensure compliance with standards;

- take action to prevent a troubled bank from failing; and

- pay depositors if an insured bank failed.

National banks, and all other Federal Reserve member banks, are required to join the FDIC; other commercial banks may join if they wish. As an added protection for the individual customer, whose entire life's savings are often entrusted to a savings bank, the act also enabled mutual savings banks to join. Since savings and loan associations are not banks, they cannot join FDIC; however, they have a comparable federal agency, the **Federal Savings and Loan Insurance Corporation** (FSLIC), for the protection of their customers. Today, over 98 percent of all commercial and savings banks in the United States are members of FDIC.

To pay for its insurance coverage, each FDIC member must pay an annual assessment of one-twelfth of 1 percent of its average total deposits. If the fund built up through these assessments should ever prove insufficient to meet its needs, FDIC is authorized to borrow up to $3 billion at any time directly from the Treasury Department; however, such borrowing has never been necessary, even during the period of major bank failures of the 1970s and the problems that occurred in 1980 and 1981. In fact, when the analysis of each year's operations is completed, FDIC usually finds it possible to return a portion of the previous year's paid-in assessment to each member bank as a dividend or rebate. At the end of 1981, the FDIC had a fund of approximately $11 billion available to meet its needs and to provide for emergencies.

The operations of FDIC are directed in Washington by a three-member Board of Governors, of which the Comptroller of the Currency is an ex officio member. FDIC operations are carried out through a network of regional offices, each of which is under the supervision of a local director.

The actions of FDIC and FSLIC to prevent a troubled bank from failing were especially noteworthy in 1981 and 1982. Thrift institutions have always been the nation's largest mortgage lenders. These loans, made primarily for home purchases, traditionally carried interest rates that could not be increased during the life of the loan. In 1981 and 1982, many thrifts found that their financial condition was seriously deteriorating because their interest rates on loans were far lower than the interest rates they had to pay to attract and keep deposits. Their interest expense, therefore, became far greater than their interest income, and thus they showed net operating losses. At the same time, many found that their deposits were decreasing, as customers found other places to put their money at more attractive rates.

To avoid the problems that would result if these banks and savings and loan associations (S&Ls) were allowed to fail, FDIC and FSLIC became very active in mergers, arranging for weaker institutions to be acquired by stronger ones. In doing so, FDIC and FSLIC provided large sums of money as a direct form of aid to the troubled institutions, thus making a merger far more attractive to the acquiring bank or S&L.

During the first 4 months of 1982, eleven mergers of thrift institutions were arranged by FSLIC and six by FDIC. The total cost to the two federal agencies was over $1 billion. However, it was obvious that this was the lesser of two evils. Had the agencies simply allowed the troubled institutions to fail, the total cost would have been far greater because, in that case, direct payments would have had to be made to customers.

THE MONETARY CONTROL ACT

The **Depository Institutions Deregulation and Monetary Control Act** (more commonly known by the last three words of the title) was enacted by Congress in 1980 and has been called the most important single piece of banking legislation since 1933. It was designed to improve the ability of the Fed to control monetary policy and to address the question of competition among financial institutions. Its major provisions include the following:

- Maximum FDIC and FSLIC coverage was increased to $100,000 per account.

- *All* financial institutions offering transaction accounts (those accounts that permit any type of payments to third parties) are now required to keep reserves against their deposits, either with the Fed directly or with banks that are Fed members.

- *All* interest rate ceilings on time and savings deposits are to be gradually eliminated so that all financial institutions can compete freely for these funds.

- A **Depository Institutions Deregulation Committee** (DIDC), consisting of the chairman of the Federal Reserve, the FDIC, the Federal Home Loan Bank Board (which regulates savings and loan associations and some savings banks), and the National Credit Union Administration, together with the Secretary of the Treasury and the (nonvoting) Comptroller of the Currency, was formed. The DIDC was made responsible for the timing and amount of changes in interest rate ceilings on time and savings deposits until their complete phaseout.

- The Federal Reserve's ability to offer loans to member banks was revised so that *all* financial institutions can now apply to the Fed for credit.

- The Fed was directed to implement a system of explicit pricing for all its services to banks, including collecting of checks, making wire transfers, supplying currency and coin, and providing safe-keeping for securities.

- Thrift institutions and credit unions were granted expanded powers to make them more competitive with commercial banks. NOW accounts were authorized for all financial institutions, and all credit unions were authorized to offer share drafts to members.

Effects of the Monetary Control Act

The Monetary Control Act drastically affects every type of financial institution. By imposing reserve requirements on all of them, it prevents attrition from the Fed system and thus gives the Fed additional control over the flow of money and credit. By increasing maximum insurance coverage, it gives depositors at insured banks and S&Ls additional assurance that their funds are safe at a time when many financial institutions have reported losses and other problems. By eliminating maximum interest rates on savings and time deposits, it allows open competition for those deposits among all financial institutions. Federally insured S&Ls that wish to do so may now offer consumer loans and credit cards. They may also make home mortgage loans without restriction as to dollar amount or geographic location. Finally, through its requirement for explicit pricing of Fed services, the act has forced banks to begin passing per-item charges for check collection, wire transfer, and securities safekeeping services along to their customers.

THE GARN-ST. GERMAIN ACT

On October 15, 1982, President Ronald Reagan signed into law the **Garn-St Germain Depository Institutions Act**, fundamentally changing the ground rules for both commercial banks and thrift institutions. The act requires the Depository Institutions Deregulation Committee (DIDC) to authorize banks and S&Ls to offer an entirely new category of deposit account, designed specifically to make those institutions competitive with money market funds. In accordance with the requirements of the act, the DIDC authorized this new form of relationship, effective December 14, 1982; it is commonly known as a **money market deposit account** and has the following characteristics:

- A minimum balance of not less than $2,500, based on an average for a period no longer than 1 month, is required;

- There is *no* interest-rate ceiling as long as the average balance is at least $2,500;

- If balances fall below $2,500, the NOW account rate ceiling applies;

- The account is available to *all* depositors;

- The account is insured by FDIC or FSLIC up to $100,000;

- There are no restrictions on the size or frequency of withdrawals by mail, by messenger, or in person;

- No minimum maturity is required, but depository institutions must reserve the right to require at least 7 days' notice prior to withdrawal;

- Depository institutions may not obligate themselves to pay any fixed or indexed interest rate for a period greater than 1 month;

- Up to six transfers a month are permitted, no more than three of which can be by draft (check);

- Each institution may establish its own minimum denomination for each transaction;

- Loans to meet the minimum balance are prohibited.

The Federal Reserve Board subsequently added another characteristic by exempting this account from reserve requirements if opened as a personal account, and establishing a 3 percent reserve requirement for nonpersonal accounts.

The Garn-St Germain Act also expanded the powers of federally chartered thrift institutions and gave federal regulators additional authority to provide financial assistance to troubled thrifts.

Under the terms of the act, the DIDC acted again in December 1982 and authorized a second type of new relationship, commonly called the **Super NOW** account. This account was made available to customers on January 5, 1983. *With the exception* of the following, the characteristics are the same as those for the money market deposit account:

- The Super NOW account is subject to a reserve requirement of 12 percent;

- It is *not* available to corporations;

- There is *no* limit on monthly transaction volume in the Super NOW account.

At the time of its establishment, the Super NOW account was expected to pay the customer a lower rate than the money market deposit account because of the reserve requirement against it. The Super NOW may eventually replace the traditional checking account for individuals, government agencies, and nonprofit organizations. Conversely, the money market account is viewed as a savings or investment vehicle.

SUMMARY

Banking in colonial times was based on a belief that the highest possible degree of human freedom should be allowed. However, experience proved that banking cannot be granted the same latitude that other businesses enjoy under the free-enterprise system since the actions of banks affect the total economy of the nation.

The legislation of 1863 and 1864, 1913, and 1933 was the result of a realization that certain controls and standards had to be imposed on the banking system but that at the same time management had to be left with some degree of freedom to compete. The dual banking system and the Federal Reserve Act are examples of compromises in legislation to meet various needs and desires among financial institutions.

The legislation of 1980 and 1982 was rather different in that it was designed to remove some of the restrictions affecting the operations of banks and thrift institutions so that they could compete more effectively with nonbank enterprises.

The evolution of American banking is marked by many crises, all of which weakened public confidence in the system. Those crises have, however, been met with solutions that rebuild that confidence. Although bankers and legislators often had strong differences of opinion as to the type and extent of controls that should be placed on banking, their joint efforts over the course of 200 years have helped to build an industry of which its 1 million employees can be justly proud.

QUESTIONS FOR DISCUSSION

1. What problems existed in the banking system in the colonies before 1791?

2. Were the two Banks of the United States improvements over their predecessors and competitors?

3. What caused both Banks of the United States to disappear from the banking scene?

4. What problems did wildcat banking create?

5. List the four major provisions of the 1863–1864 National Currency and Banking Acts.

6. What is meant by the dual banking system?

7. What congressional action forced the discontinuance of state bank note issues?

8. Identify three basic weaknesses that existed in the banking system after 1864.

9. Explain the provisions of the Federal Reserve Act that eliminated those weaknesses.

10. What banking crisis led to the establishment of the FDIC?

11. List four major provisions of the Monetary Control Act of 1980.

12. Identify five characteristics of the money market deposit account authorized under the Garn-St Germain Act.

13. How does the Super NOW account differ from the money market deposit account?

NOTE

1. There are a few exceptions to this general rule (e.g., Bank of California) in the cases of banks that had already established branches across state lines before federal laws on the subject were changed.

Suggested Readings

Calin-Stefanelli, Elvira and Vladimir. *Chartered for Progress: Two Centuries of American Banking.* Washington, D.C.: Acropolis Books, 1975.

Federal Reserve Board of Governors. *The Monetary Control Act of 1980.* Washington, D.C.: August, 1980.

Golembe, Carter H., and David S. Holland. *Federal Regulations of Banking.* Washington, D.C.: Golembe Associates, Inc., 1981.

Klebaner, Benjamin J. *Commercial Banking in the United States: A History.* Hinsdale, Illinois: Drydin Press, 1974.

Timberlake, Richard H. *The Origins of Central Banking in the United States.* Cambridge: Harvard University Press, 1978.

Chapter 3

The Federal Reserve System

LEARNING OBJECTIVES

After completing this chapter, you will have an understanding of

- the distinction between monetary policy and fiscal policy;
- the basic objectives of the Federal Reserve;
- the structure of the Federal Reserve System and the conditions for membership in it;
- the concept of required reserves;
- the basic tools of the Fed for controlling the flow of money and credit;
- the open-market operations of the Fed;
- the basic services provided by the Fed to banks and to the federal government; and
- such terms as discount rate, bank holding company, and fiscal agent.

The Federal Reserve System came into being on December 23, 1913, when President Woodrow Wilson signed the Federal Reserve Act establishing it. His action brought an end to 5 years of detailed study of the nation's financial needs, resources, and problems by the National Monetary Commission, appointed by Congress. The provisions of the Federal Reserve Act also reflected the efforts of its authors to satisfy the divergent viewpoints of many influential legislators, bankers, and businessmen. Wilson himself provided considerable presidential leadership while the act was being written.

The Federal Reserve Act specifically addressed the weaknesses that had been identified in the banking system and provided for decentralized control of local financial affairs and centralized control in matters of national concern. It established an independent agency that was within the structure of the federal government but under private ownership and insulated from congressional and presidential control.

FEDERAL RESERVE POLICY OBJECTIVES

Under the terms of the Federal Reserve Act, the Fed is our primary agency in the area of **monetary policy**. This term is used to describe the actions the Fed may take to influence the nation's flow of money and credit and, therefore, the economic environment. Changes in monetary policy are primarily the assigned responsibilities of the Federal Reserve. At the same time, the economy is also affected by **fiscal policy**. This term describes the activities of the legislative and executive branches of the federal gcvernment in the areas of taxation and spending. For maximum effect, the two policies should work in tandem; however, fiscal policy carries political implications, whereas monetary policy under the Fed is intended to be divorced from those concerns.

Central banks, which perform functions and attempt to achieve objectives similar to those of the Fed, exist in many countries throughout the world. The Bank of France was established by Napoleon I in 1800. The Bank of England has been a major factor in that nation's economic picture since the seventeenth century. In Canada, the Bank of Canada began operations in 1935. However, the Federal Reserve differs from all other central banks in the degree of independence granted to it by the 1913 act. Its private ownership and the fact that its actions do not have to be ratified by the President or Congress make it unique.

Despite the differences, however, the objectives of the Fed are generally consistent with those of the central banks in other countries. It is responsible for regulating the flow of money and credit in order to promote economic growth and stability. Therefore, it endeavors to:

- provide stability in the overall price level and the dollar's purchasing power;

- contribute to a high national level of employment;

- maintain a sound and reasonable system for international balance-of-payments transactions; and

- combat inflationary and recessionary trends as they develop so as to encourage economic well-being.

The actions of the Fed are intended to promote attainment of these four objectives, but many other economic factors also help to determine whether they will be achieved. Nevertheless, the system consistently aims at the same four targets, shifting emphasis from one to the other as conditions dictate.

The four basic objectives are closely tied to each other. An economy can neither grow nor remain prosperous with high levels of unemployment. The large and persistent deficits in our balance of payments encountered in the 1970s and early 1980s affect the international value of the dollar and America's reserve position. During an inflationary cycle, the real value of earned income and accumulated savings is reduced.

Although the Federal Reserve possesses a high degree of independence, it does not operate in a vacuum without any interaction with other policy-making entities of the federal government. The chairman of the Fed's Board of Governors regularly reports to Congress and meets frequently with the President and the chief financial officials of the government. By virtue of his office, the chairman is also a member of the Depository Institutions Deregulation Committee, created under the terms of the Monetary Control Act of 1980. Other members of the Board of Governors maintain constant liaison with those agencies that are chiefly concerned with economic developments and policies.

In the original Federal Reserve Act, the Secretary of the Treasury and the Comptroller of the Currency were ex officio members of the

Board of Governors. However, a 1935 amendment to the act eliminated their membership.

The Federal Reserve, then, while preserving its autonomy, establishes policies and conducts operations within the framework of the national objectives set by the President, the Council of Economic Advisers, the Office of Management and Budget, and other entities within the legislative and executive branches.

FEDERAL RESERVE STRUCTURE

Because the question of ownership and control of any central banking system in the United States has always been so controversial, the Federal Reserve Act very ingeniously combined the interests of the government and the private sector. It specified that ownership of the system would rest with **member banks**, who would be required to purchase Federal Reserve stock in an amount proportionate to their capital and surplus. Then, like the stockholders in any corporation, they would receive dividends as a result of the profitable operations of the Fed. If, after having joined the system, a bank decided to withdraw, it could do so by selling its stock back to the Fed.

Each of the twelve Federal Reserve banks has a nine-member board, six of whose directors are elected by the member banks in that district. The remaining three members are appointed by the Federal Reserve Board of Governors, who, in turn, are named by the President and approved by the Senate. The seven-member Board of Governors in Washington has overall responsibility for supervising the system.

All national banks are legally required to be Fed members; state-chartered banks may join the system if they wish. The terms of stock purchase apply equally to both. Although less than half of all commercial banks are Fed members, the member banks control over 70 percent of all deposits in the banking system.

The ability of the Fed to control the flow of money and credit obviously depends on the extent of bank membership in the system. Since the regulations of the Fed do not apply to nonmembers, any reduction in membership impairs that basic ability. In recent years, Fed membership has actually been declining, and this fact was largely responsible for the enactment of the Monetary Control Act of 1980.

Since 1913, member banks have been required to maintain reserves with the Fed on a non-interest-bearing basis. In exchange, they were given access to various Fed services and enjoyed certain privileges. However, in recent years many banks have determined that they would benefit by withdrawing from the Fed system and thus freeing up reserves to be put to profitable use. The extremely high interest rates of the late 1970s and early 1980s gave them the potential for significant increases in earnings through the use of the freed-up reserve funds, and the services supplied by the Fed could be obtained instead from correspondent banks.

In addition to the requirement that they maintain reserves and purchase Federal Reserve stock, member banks must agree to pay all checks at par, comply with all pertinent banking laws and regulations, and be subject to Fed examination and supervision. In its role as a so-called banker's bank, the Fed provided members with check collection, wire transfer, currency supply, and safekeeping privileges without charge and allowed them to apply to the Fed for credit when necessary.

As was explained in Chapter 2, the Monetary Control Act made significant revisions in the original Federal Reserve Act. It introduced the concept of **transaction accounts**, using the term to describe all relationships with financial institutions that permit transfers of funds to third parties. Table 3-1 shows the dollar deposits in transaction accounts in 1981. The Monetary Control Act also implemented a system of reserve requirements for *all* depository institutions that maintain transaction accounts, required the Fed to institute explicit pricing for its services, and gave all financial institutions access to the Fed as a source of credit.

TOOLS OF MONETARY AND CREDIT POLICY

M_1—defined in Chapter 1 as coin and currency in circulation, most demand deposits at commercial banks, travelers checks of nonbank issuers, and funds withdrawable on demand at other financial institutions— is the basic measure of the United States money supply and is closely watched by the Fed as an indicator of the overall economy. Increasing the money supply is considered to fuel inflation; causing it to grow less rapidly is considered to reduce inflation. As the Fed studies the periodic figures on M_1, and in order to regulate the flow of money and

47

Table 3-1

Deposits of United States Commercial Banks and Thrift Institutions[1]

($ millions)

Depository Institutions	I.P.C. Demand (1)	A.T.S.	Telephone Pre-Authorized Transfer (3)	NOW/Share Drafts	Total NOW/ATS/Share Drafts Amount (5)	Total NOW/ATS/Share Drafts Market Share	Total Transaction Accounts Amount (1+3+5)	Total Transaction Accounts Market Share	Personal Savings Amount	Personal Savings Market Share
Commercial Banks										
December 1980	331,636.9	13,359.1	6,722.8	8,136.7	21,495.8	79.5	359,855.5	96.5	153,038.8	47.6
March 1981	292,084.6	8,994.7	5,490.6	38,360.3	47,355.0	83.4	344,931.0	95.5	147,664.0	47.1
June 1981	293,797.0	8,455.1	5,038.8	42,157.2	50,612.0	82.4	349,448.0	95.2	143,761.8	47.2
September 1981	282,813.1	8,217.1	4,496.8	45,502.1	53,719.2	81.9	341,029.1	95.0	138,700.1	47.5
Mutual Savings Banks										
December 1980	1,708.8	165.3	712.1	1,493.3	1,658.6	6.1	4,079.5	1.1	51,164.8	15.9
March 1981	1,563.4	134.8	696.4	1,631.2	1,766.0	3.1	4,025.0	1.1	50,108.1	16.0
June 1981	1,671.6	127.0	620.8	1,722.0	1,848.0	3.0	4,141.0	1.1	48,175.1	15.8
September 1981	1,709.9	121.7	542.2	1,859.9	1,981.6	3.0	4,233.7	1.2	46,183.4	15.8
Savings and Loans										
December 1980	576.4	165.2	3,084.0	1,041.9	1,207.1	4.5	4,867.5	1.3	99,892.5	31.1
March 1981	585.2	123.3	2,362.6	4,733.3	4,856.0	8.6	7,804.0	2.2	98,242.2	31.4
June 1981	604.1	127.8	2,091.5	5,935.9	6,064.0	9.9	8,759.0	2.4	94,967.6	31.2
September 1981	645.0	126.8	1,727.1	6,783.7	6,910.5	10.5	9,282.6	2.6	89,671.7	30.7
Credit Unions										
December 1980	46.6	1,023.8	1,335.3	1,641.1	2,665.0	9.9	4,047.0	1.1	17,194.4	5.4
March 1981	42.7	983.0	1,513.3	1,839.2	2,823.0	5.0	4,379.0	1.2	17,354.3	5.5
June 1981	48.2	885.8	1,585.5	2,045.7	2,932.0	4.8	4,566.0	1.2	17,516.0	5.8
September 1981	59.0	830.0	1,582.5	2,122.9	2,952.9	4.5	4,594.4	1.3	17,726.1	6.1
Totals										
December 1980	333,968.7	14,713.4	11,854.2	12,313.0	27,026.5	100.0	372,849.5	100.0	321,290.5	100.0
March 1981	294,275.9	10,235.8	10,062.9	46,564.0	56,800.0	100.0	361,139.0	100.0	313,368.6	100.0
June 1981	296,120.9	9,595.7	9,336.6	51,860.8	61,456.0	100.0	366,914.0	100.0	304,420.5	100.0
September 1981	285,227.0	9,295.6	8,348.6	56,268.6	65,564.2	100.0	359,139.8	100.0	292,281.3	100.0

NOTES: These data are reported weekly to the Federal Reserve Banks by commercial banks and thrifts with at least $15 million in total deposits. Since smaller institutions do not report weekly, these data are understated slightly.

NOW deposits are as of December 31, 1980. All other data are averages for the last week in each month.

"I.P.C. Demand" refers to deposits of individuals, partnerships, and corporations.

SOURCE: Walter A. Varvel and John R. Walter, "The Competition for Transaction Accounts," *Sixty-Seventh Annual Report: 1981*, Federal Reserve Bank of Richmond, p. 8. Table originally from *Report of Transaction Accounts, Other Deposits, and Vault Cash* (FR 2900)

credit and thereby affect economic activity in the United States, it employs three fundamental tools or techniques. These are its **open-market operations**, its **discount rate** (the interest rate it charges on loans it grants to banks), and its **reserve requirements**. As a result of the Monetary Control Act, a timetable for phasing in thrift institutions and nonmember banks under the new system of reserves was established, and the ability of the Fed to use reserve requirements as a tool of monetary policy was increased accordingly. The other two instruments, i.e., open-market operations and discount rate changes, should be thought of as being coordinated and employed with a single purpose in mind rather than as independent mechanisms used separately.

Open-Market Operations

The open-market operations of the Federal Open Market Committee (FOMC) constitute the single most important, yet at the same time most flexible, instrument for Fed implementation of monetary policy. The FOMC is made up of the seven members of the Board of Governors, plus the president of the Federal Reserve Bank of New York and four other Federal Reserve bank presidents. By law, all Federal Reserve open-market operations must be directed and regulated by the FOMC, whose basic function involves periodic decisions on the buying and selling of government securities. After each meeting of the FOMC, a directive is issued to the New York Fed, which has been designated as the agent to buy and sell these securities for the accounts of all the Reserve banks.

The volume of transactions handled through the open-market account is in excess of $10 billion per day, with the single heaviest area of trading consisting of U.S. Treasury bills. The account manager at the New York Fed has a staff that is in direct telephone contact with some two dozen securities dealers, many of whom represent major banks.

As an example of FOMC action directly affecting member bank reserves and thus implementing monetary policy, assume that it has directed the purchase of Treasury bills. The reserve accounts of member banks will be credited as each sale is made to the Fed; thus, member banks will be able to put their excess reserves to work and credit will become easier to obtain. This may satisfy the committee's short-term objective of circumventing the stresses imposed by a seasonal or regional shift in the money supply, or it may be intended to have a long-term effect on the overall economy.

The Discount Rate

When financial institutions apply to the Fed for credit and the request is approved, interest is charged at the discount rate, which is set by the Federal Reserve district bank. Each of the 12 banks can change the discount rate whenever it feels such action is appropriate, subject to review by the Board of Governors. Table 3-2 shows the range of discount rates at the New York Fed in recent years; other districts closely resemble this range.

Table 3-2
The Range of Discount Rates at New York
Fed, 1971–1982

Effective Date		Discount Rate (%)
1971	January 1	5½
	December 17	4½
1973	February 26	5½
	May 11	6
	July 2	7
1974	April 25	8
1975	January 10	7¼
	May 16	6
1976	November 22	5¼
1977	October 26	6
1978	May 11	7
	November 1	9½
1979	July 20	10
	October 10	12
1980	December 8	13
1981	December 4	12
1982	May 31	12
	October 22	9½

NOTE: This is a sampling of changes in selected years and does *not* represent a list of consecutive changes. Interim changes were made as necessary.

Borrowing from the Fed is a privilege, not a right. The institution requesting the loan is reviewed according to purpose of borrowing, frequency of loan requests, and amount of existing indebtedness to the Fed. If the loan request is approved, the borrowing institution executes a promissory note and secures it with acceptable collateral.

Loans granted by the Fed are usually made for very short periods of time, such as overnight or 2 days.

Reserve Requirements

Until the Monetary Control Act was passed in 1980, the Fed actively used the system of reserve requirements as a basic tool to control the flow of money and credit. Reducing those requirements freed up funds to meet the needs of the economy and made bank credit easier to obtain; an increase in required reserves had the opposite effect. Prior to the Monetary Control Act, member banks with deposits of over $400 million were required to keep reserves of $16\frac{1}{4}$ percent against demand deposits and 3 percent on savings and time deposits.

The Monetary Control Act, as noted earlier, makes *all* financial institutions subject to requirements on reserves, which may be placed directly with the Fed or with a member bank. A gradual phase-in until 1987 is provided for institutions that were nonmembers in 1980. Maximum reserves will be 3 percent on the first $25 million of transaction account balances and 12 percent of balances above that figure.

FEDERAL RESERVE SERVICES

Under the terms of the Federal Reserve Act, the services of the Fed include supplying currency and coin, collecting checks, making wire transfers of funds, providing safekeeping facilities, and extending credit. These services were originally provided *only* to those banks that were members of the Fed system. As noted earlier, however, the Monetary Control Act of 1980 gave *all* financial institutions the right to apply to the Fed for credit, but it also imposed a system of explicit pricing for services.

In addition to transaction-related services, the Fed also provides a great many economic surveys, tables of statistical data, and financial reports.

Fed services are extremely important to the government as well. The Federal Reserve operates the checking account for the U.S. government; every individual who receives an income tax refund or other disbursement of funds from the federal government by check is actually receiving an instrument drawn on the Fed, and all inflows of funds to the federal government go through the Federal Reserve. The Federal Reserve is also the fiscal agent for the Treasury Department; it is responsble for issuing and redeeming all government obligations and for the safekeeping of all unissued Treasury bills, notes, and bonds. Supplies of unissued currency are kept in Fed vaults, as are the securities and other assets of many foreign countries.

In addition, Federal Reserve examiners regularly conduct examinations of the banks under their jurisdiction to ensure that they are obeying all laws and regulations and accurately showing their financial status. Through this examining function, the Fed helps the federal government maintain a sound banking system.

THE FED AND BANK HOLDING COMPANIES

A holding company is defined as a legal entity that holds a controlling interest in the stock of various subsidiary companies. The holding company itself need not manufacture, sell, distribute, or otherwise engage in any operations of its own; it simply serves as a vehicle for stock ownership. A **bank holding company**, by law, is an organization that holds a controlling interest in the stock of one or more banks. During the 1960s and 1970s, virtually every major commercial bank in the United States converted to the holding-company type of organization, with the bank in each case as the major subsidiary. This action took place so that the holding company, through ownership of nonbank subsidiaries, could engage in various forms of profitable business outside the pure realm of banking.

Under the terms of the Bank Holding Company Act, the Federal Reserve was given authority to supervise and regulate all bank holding companies, regardless of whether the bank components were Fed members. The legislation authorizes the Fed to publish lists of the activities that are permitted or prohibited for all bank holding companies and to make decisions on every request they submit for acquisitions or for the right to engage in various types of business.

FEDERAL RESERVE REGULATIONS

The broad powers of the Fed are illustrated by Table 3-3, which lists the various regulations that apply to all member banks and bank hold-

Table 3-3
Federal Reserve Regulations

Letter Identification	Subject
A	Loans to Depository Institutions
B	Equal Credit Opportunity
C	Home Mortgage Disclosure
D	Reserve Requirements
E	Electronic Fund Transfers
F	Securities of Member Banks
G	Margin Credit Extended by Parties Other Than Banks, Brokers, and Dealers
H	Membership Requirements for State-Chartered Banks
I	Member Stock in Federal Reserve Banks
J	Check Collection and Funds Transfer
K	International Banking Operations
L	Interlocking Bank Relationships
M	Consumer Leasing
N	Relationships With Foreign Banks
O	Loans to Executive Officers of Member Banks
P	Member Bank Protection Standards
Q	Interest on Deposits
R	Interlocking Relationships Between Securities Dealers and Member Banks
S	Reimbursement for Providing Financial Records
T	Margin Credit Extended by Brokers and Dealers
U	Margin Credit Extended by Banks
V	Guarantee of Loans for National Defense Work
W	Extensions of Consumer Credit (revoked)
X	Borrowers Who Obtain Margin Credit
Y	Bank Holding Committees
Z	Truth in Lending
AA	Consumer Complaint Procedures
BB	Community Reinvestment

ing companies. Table 3-4 indexes the regulations by subject matter. These regulations constitute the means by which the Fed carries out congressional policies, and they deal with the functions of the nation's central bank and its relationships with financial institutions, the activities of banks and bank holding companies, and consumer credit transactions. As can be seen, they affect a wide variety of financial activities.

Federal Reserve supervision of member banks begins when banks apply for admission to the system. As members, these banks are sub-

Table 3-4
Federal Regulations by Subject Matter

Subject	Letter Identification
Bank Holding Companies	Regulation Y
Federal Reserve Banks	Regulations A, BB, I, J, N, and V
Foreign Banking Business	Regulations K, M, and N
Interlocking Directorates	Regulations L and R
Other Member Bank Requirements	Regulations F, H, O, P, Q, and U
Consumer Protection	Regulations B, C, E, M, Z, and AA
Monetary Policy	Regulations A, D, and Q
Securities Credit	Regulations G, T, U, and X
Financial Privacy	Regulation S

ject to regular examinations and to all Fed regulations, as well as to the banking laws of other agencies. Annual examinations of national banks are done by the Comptroller of the Currency; however, since all national banks must be Fed members, the Comptroller's staff of examiners gives the Fed copies of all reports of its examinations, and the Fed examiners may conduct additional examinations of their own if they feel they are advisable.

The Fed is also responsible for approving changes in a member bank's capital structure and for approving new branches of member banks when such approval is not inconsistent with state banking laws.

The ever-increasing scope of the international operations of member banks has led the Federal Reserve to assume a much more active role in supervising those operations, always giving due consideration to their impact on the U.S. economy. The Board of Governors takes various regulatory and supervisory actions regarding member banks' global activities, and it exercises control over the lending and investing functions of those banks outside the United States.

SUMMARY

Like much of the legislation that Congress has passed to affect the banking industry, the Federal Reserve Act was born out of crisis. Had it not been for the weaknesses and problems in American banking at the start of the twentieth century, the act might never have been drawn up. The lack of a nationwide check collection system, the failure of the 1863 legislation to anticipate the problems caused by the pyramiding of reserves and an inflexible money supply, and the absence of a central agency in the federal government to control the flow of money and credit were the primary factors leading to the establishment of the Federal Reserve System.

That system, originally designed to provide a means of reform and to address existing weaknesses, has in the intervening years become a vital force, strengthening the entire economy. The rate of growth in the money supply, the domestic rate of inflation, the global fluctuations in the value of the dollar, the balance of payments in America's international trade, and the federal deficit itself are among the major problem areas to which the Fed devotes its attention. The decisions made by the Board of Governors cannot be infallibly effective or universally accepted. Nevertheless, the Federal Reserve remains one of the nation's chief weapons in the ongoing effort to maintain a sound economy and promote general stability and growth.

QUESTIONS FOR DISCUSSION

1. Identify the four objectives of the Fed in regulating the flow of money and credit.

2. How are the members of the Federal Reserve Board of Governors elected or appointed?

3. Which financial institutions are now required to maintain reserves with the Fed?

4. What three instruments or tools does the Fed use to control the flow of money and credit?

5. What purpose does the Federal Open Market Committee serve in the overall operations of the Fed?

6. What is meant by the discount rate? By whom is the discount rate established?

7. Identify three major services the Fed provides to financial institutions, and three services it performs for the federal government.

Suggested Readings

A Guide to Federal Reserve Regulations. Washington, D.C.: Federal Reserve Board of Governors, 1981.

Burke, William. *The Fed: The Nation's Central Bank.* San Francisco, California: Federal Reserve Bank of San Francisco, 1978.

Golembe, Carter H., and David S. Holland. *Federal Regulation of Banking.* Washington, D.C.: Golembe Associates, Inc., 1981.

Historical Beginnings . . . The Federal Reserve. Boston: Federal Reserve Bank of Boston, 1977.

Keeping Our Money Healthy, rev. ed. New York: Federal Reserve Bank of New York, 1977.

Meek, Paul. *Open Market Operations.* New York: Federal Reserve Bank of New York, 1978.

Modern Money Mechanics, rev. ed. Chicago: Federal Reserve Bank of Chicago, 1975.

The Federal Reserve at Work, 6th ed. Richmond: Federal Reserve Bank of Richmond, 1974.

The Federal Reserve System Purposes and Functions, 6th ed. Washington, D.C.: Board of Governors, Federal Reserve System, 1974.

The Four Hats of the Federal Reserve. Philadelphia: Federal Reserve Bank of Philadelphia, undated.

The Monetary Control Act of 1980. Washington, D.C.: Federal Reserve Board of Governors, 1981.

Chapter 4

The Documents and Language of Banking

LEARNING OBJECTIVES

After completing this chapter, you will have an understanding of

- the operation of the barter system;

- the advantages of the credit balances system;

- what is meant by negotiation and delivery;

- the requirements for negotiable instruments;

- the parties to a draft and their roles;

- the distinction between checks and drafts;

- the terms *certified check* and *cashier's check*;

- the four basic types of endorsements; and

- the liabilities of an endorser and the concept of *holder in due course.*

In every industry and profession, a specialized language has been developed to describe whatever is unique to that particular type of work. Accountants, doctors, engineers, and lawyers all have their own terminologies, and they must become familiar with the forms and documents used in their professions. Commercial banking is no different. Bank employees cannot function efficiently if they do not understand the language of banking and the meaning and importance of the documents that are used in it. Trading, buying, selling, and borrowing are as old as civilization itself, and the manner in which these transactions are handled and the terms used to describe them have evolved into the documents and language of banking today.

EARLY METHODS OF EXCHANGE

When primitive people could not produce what they needed or wanted, they learned how to find others who possessed those articles and to establish methods of obtaining them. The earliest of these methods, still in use in some societies, was the simplest. It involved direct, physical exchanging of goods and is known as **barter**. Mutual wants or needs were met through the transfer of merchandise—a satisfactory system as long as its basic weaknesses did not interfere. For barter to take place, it is obviously necessary for the articles of value to be physically brought together and for both parties to agree on their value. An individual who wanted a particular item had to find someone willing to trade and had to arrange a meeting so that the exchange could take place.

Such weaknesses in the system gradually led to the introduction of some form of money as an accepted medium of exchange. However, long before any type of money as we know it had come into existence, various forms of commodities were used whenever two parties agreed on a transaction. Salt, grain, fish or meat, and gunpowder have at one time or another been used as money. The Dutch bought Manhattan Island from the Indians for beads and shiny trinkets. In time, precious metals such as gold and silver came to be accepted as the medium of exchange. In seventeenth-century England, goldsmiths assumed an important role by agreeing to provide safekeeping for their customers' valuables and issuing a receipt. These receipts were used as a medium of payment and are one of the earliest examples of a form of paper currency.

CREDIT BALANCES

Although money offered advantages over the barter system, it nevertheless possessed drawbacks of its own. Whatever the accepted medium of exchange might be, it had to be moved from one place to another, with the consequent risk of loss or theft. As people found new areas of the world containing goods they wished to acquire, distances between buyer and seller posed new problems. The British merchant who wished to import lace from France had to find a method of transporting money to the supplier and could then only hope that it would arrive safely. As commerce grew and as merchants began to expand their operations and to put their faith and trust in other merchants with whom they dealt, a more satisfactory system of payment was developed, and the system of **credit balances** came into being. Credit balances eliminated the risks involved in carrying and transporting money and now form the basis for much of the language and many of the documents of commercial banking.

Under the system of credit balances, merchants agreed that a specific payment would *not* be made for every transaction. The buyer of goods, instead of delivering money to the seller, was told to establish some form of book entry for the sale, thus recording the fact that a certain amount was owed to the seller. The seller would maintain documents providing evidence of the transaction, with the understanding that the credit balances, as shown on the books, could be applied to future dealings between the two parties. In this way, the French supplier of lace had an early form of bookkeeping to substantiate the fact that the buyer in England was indebted for a given amount.

The same French merchant, however, might at some point owe money to another party in England. Could the same system now be used to provide payment to this new, third party? It obviously could. The merchant in England had also kept a record of the amount he owed to the French merchant; if given instructions by the latter, in a secure format so that there could be no dispute, he could pay out part or all of the French dealer's credit balance to the specified third party. For security reasons, the French merchant would have to issue instructions in writing, would have to specify the amount to be paid, and would have to name the party who was to receive the funds.

Certainly, no payments were to be made unless the French merchant specifically authorized them. The origins of today's payment system in banking can be seen in this concept of credit balances.

Using this example, substitute your bank for the English merchant who held the credit balance for you, substitute yourself for the French merchant, and assume that you wish to pay a utility company bill by issuing a check drawn on your personal account at your bank. As the drawer, you issue a dated, signed, written order for payment, naming the utility company as the beneficiary (payee) and specifying the exact amount. The drawee bank, as the holder of the credit balance owed to you, will make the requested payment.

NEGOTIABLE INSTRUMENTS

The system of credit balances offered merchants significant improvements over both the barter method and actual payments in money. Those who knew and trusted their customers were willing to accept written instructions from them to make payments by reducing their credit balances. They could, in turn, employ the same system to pay their own suppliers. All that was necessary was agreement on the language and form of the letter of instructions.

Inevitably, disputes arose among merchants as to whether the payments had been made in exact accordance with instructions, whether the proper party had received payment, whether the instructions had been executed on time and in a proper manner, and so forth. To provide a uniform means of settling these disputes and to establish a system for making payments, lawmakers and courts in various countries gradually agreed on a format and methodology. Safeguards were also written into the laws so that all parties to commercial transactions were protected.

To facilitate the handling of business transactions in the United States, a single statute known as the Uniform Commercial Code (UCC) was drawn up in 1953. This code revised and consolidated many of the laws that had preceded it and has generally been adopted, in part or entirely, throughout the country. It is divided into nine articles, of which Article 3 is the most important for purposes of this discussion.

Article 3 defines the term **negotiable instrument** and sets forth the rights and liabilities of all the parties who deal with checks, drafts, notes, and certificates of deposit. The word **negotiable** is used to describe the quality that enables an instrument to circulate freely and therefore to be accepted in lieu of legal tender in payment transactions. Whenever **negotiation** takes place, an instrument is transferred from one party to another so that the latter becomes the holder. This can be done by delivery alone or by delivery and endorsement. Here the term **delivery** means voluntary physical transfer of possession with the intention of transferring title and rights to the instrument. Instruments that have been lost or stolen are not considered to have been legally negotiated.

Article 3 of the UCC sets forth the following requirements for negotiable instruments:

- All negotiable instruments must be written. No verbal order or promise to pay qualifies.

- They must contain an unconditional promise or order to pay a specific amount of money. The legal term is "a sum certain in money." In this way, there can be no dispute as to the amount of the instrument. A promissory note bearing interest at 10 percent is negotiable; one bearing interest at "the current or prevailing rate" is not.

- Since negotiable instruments are unconditional, they are not governed by or subject to any other agreement involving the parties.

- Negotiable instruments must be *signed* by the drawer or maker. The term **signature** also includes marks and thumbprints, and printed, typed, or stamped signatures are acceptable in addition to handwritten ones.

- Negotiable instruments must be payable on demand or at a definite future time (e.g., "90 days from date" or "on June 28, 19xx"). A demand instrument is payable at sight or on presentation; no time for payment is stated.

- Negotiable instruments must be made payable to **bearer** or to **order.** An instrument payable to "cash" is a bearer instrument; "to order" means payable to a specified party or to anyone to whom that party has transferred the rights to the instrument.

If an instrument does not meet all of the above criteria, it is not a negotiable instrument under the terms of the UCC. The parties involved may still be willing to use and accept it, but the provisions of the code do not apply in that case.

Drafts and Checks

The standard, simplified form for a letter of instructions by which one party ordered the holder of a credit balance to make payment to a third party became known as a **bill of exchange** or, more commonly, a **draft**. A draft is a written order directing that a payment be made.

There are three parties to drafts. The example used earlier in this chapter illustrates this point. The **drawer** issues and executes the instrument. The **drawee**, the holder of a credit balance owed to the drawer, is the party who is instructed to make the payment. The **payee** is the beneficiary of the payment. At the outset, banks were not involved in these transactions; drafts were entirely within the province of merchants and goldsmiths—the latter because they were directed, by means of drafts, to pay out gold or silver to a named payee.

Drafts are still widely used in international and domestic trade. An insurance company may draw drafts on its banks or on itself to honor the claims submitted by its policyholders; a merchant may draw a draft on another merchant; or one bank may draw a draft on another bank. Drafts may be either **time** (i.e., payable at some future date) or **demand** (i.e., payable at sight or on presentation) instruments.

As banks gradually replaced the merchants and goldsmiths as the holders of credit balances, the items drawn on them became uniform and simplified. The demand drafts drawn on banks are called **checks** (Figure 4-1 and 4-2). The drawer of a check gives the drawee bank written instructions to make a payment of funds against an account, exactly as directed.

Of course, it is possible for one party to play more than one role in this system. If Mary Wilson issues a check payable to cash, endorses it, presents it to her bank, and converts part or all of her demand deposit balance into coin and currency, she is both the drawer of the check and its payee.

Every check is a demand draft drawn on a bank. Therefore, every check is a type of draft, but not every draft is a check. Checks must be

Figure 4-1
A Standard Check

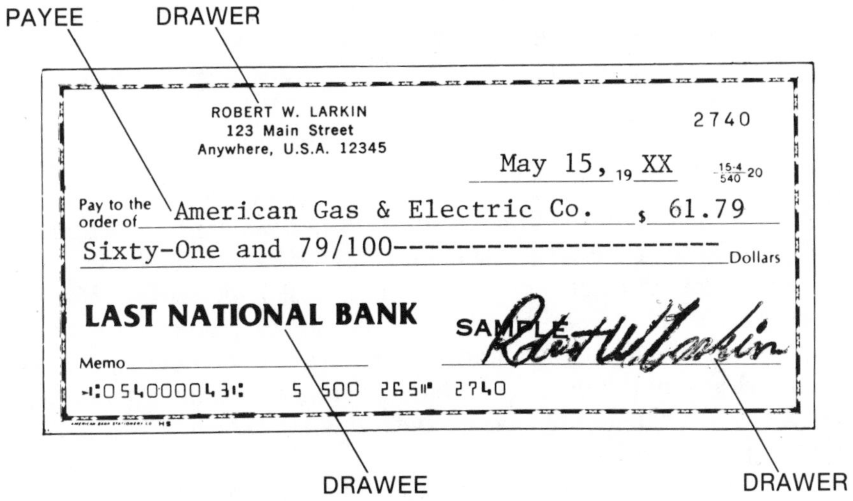

PAYEE   DRAWER

ROBERT W. LARKIN
123 Main Street
Anywhere, U.S.A. 12345

2740

May 15, 19 XX   15-4/540-20

Pay to the
order of American Gas & Electric Co. $ 61.79

Sixty-One and 79/100--------------------Dollars

LAST NATIONAL BANK   SAMPLE

Memo

⑆054000043⑆   5 500 265⑈ 2740

DRAWEE   DRAWER

Figure 4-2
Elements of a Check

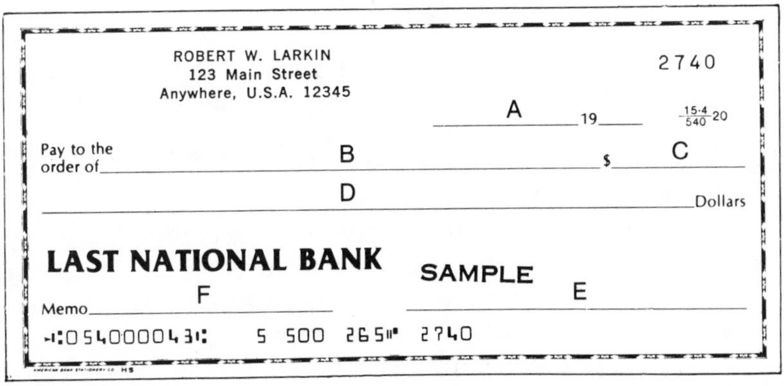

ROBERT W. LARKIN
123 Main Street
Anywhere, U.S.A. 12345

2740

A   19   15-4/540-20

Pay to the
order of   B $ C

D
Dollars

LAST NATIONAL BANK   SAMPLE
F   E
Memo

⑆054000043⑆   5 500 265⑈ 2740

A. Date
B. Pay To The Order Of . . .
C. Amount in Numerals

D. Written Amount
E. Signature
F. Memo . . . (purpose of check)

63

demand instruments, whereas drafts may be either time or demand. Checks must be drawn on a bank; drafts need not be. When all necessary conditions are met, checks must be charged to the maker's account; drafts need not be, since the drawer of a draft can reserve the right to examine and approve it before any charge to an account takes place.

Promissory Notes

Another payment medium, often used in business transactions, is the promissory note. The distinction between drafts and checks on the one hand and notes on the other is most important. Drafts and checks are orders to pay, involving three parties. **Notes** are promises to pay and involve only two parties. Checks are always demand instruments; drafts and notes may be either demand or time. Checks must be drawn on banks; drafts and notes may be executed without the involvement of a bank.

The **promissory note** is one of the essential documents in commercial banking. Every loan made by a bank is supported by some form of note, in which the terms of repayment are spelled out and agreed to by the borrower. The note provides legal evidence of a debt.

Certified Checks

There are many business situations in which the party to whom a check is offered refuses to accept it. Since a check is not legal tender but rather a claim to money, the payee may insist on an instrument that gives greater assurance of actual payment. When people are told that they can take legal title to their new homes as soon as final documents have been signed, or that their new cars are available for pickup, an ordinary personal check may not suffice. A **certified check** will solve the problem.

To certify a check, its drawer presents it to the drawee bank, which immediately verifies that there are sufficient collected funds in the drawer's account to cover it. The amount of that check is usually charged to the account at once and transferred to a special account, *certified checks outstanding,* on the bank's books. By certifying the check, the drawee bank makes itself liable for the amount; therefore, to protect itself it sets aside the necessary funds. When an official bank stamp and signature have been placed on a check (see Figure

4-3), it is converted from the drawer's order to pay into the bank's promise to pay. Certified checks outstanding are part of a bank's liabilities.

Figure 4-3
Certified Check

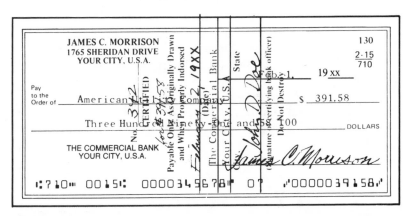

Banks are not legally required to certify checks, but regularly do so, usually for a fee, as a service to customers. The certified check is mutilated or marked in some way so that it will not be charged to the drawer's account again, and the drawee may use some form of perforated impression as part of the certification stamp to prevent any raising of the amount.

While the payee of a certified check assumes that the drawee bank guarantees payment, under special circumstances the drawer may subsequently ask the bank to stop payment on it. If, for example, the item has been stolen or lost, both the drawer's interests and the bank's must be protected. The UCC states that a bank is *not* obliged to accept a stop-payment order on a certified check; however, if the drawer signs an affidavit explaining the problem and indemnifying the bank against claims or losses, the request can be honored.

Cashier's Checks

Another type of negotiable instrument frequently seen in banking is the **cashier's check**, also known as an **official check** or

treasurer's check. These should not be confused with certified checks, where a customer is the drawer. A cashier's check is drawn *by* a bank *on* itself; the bank is both drawer and drawee, and that is why such checks are often called **bank checks** (see Figure 4-4). Banks often use cashier's checks to pay out loan proceeds, to pay suppliers, and make other disbursements. These checks may also be sold to customers when an official bank instrument is needed.

Figure 4-4
Cashier's Check

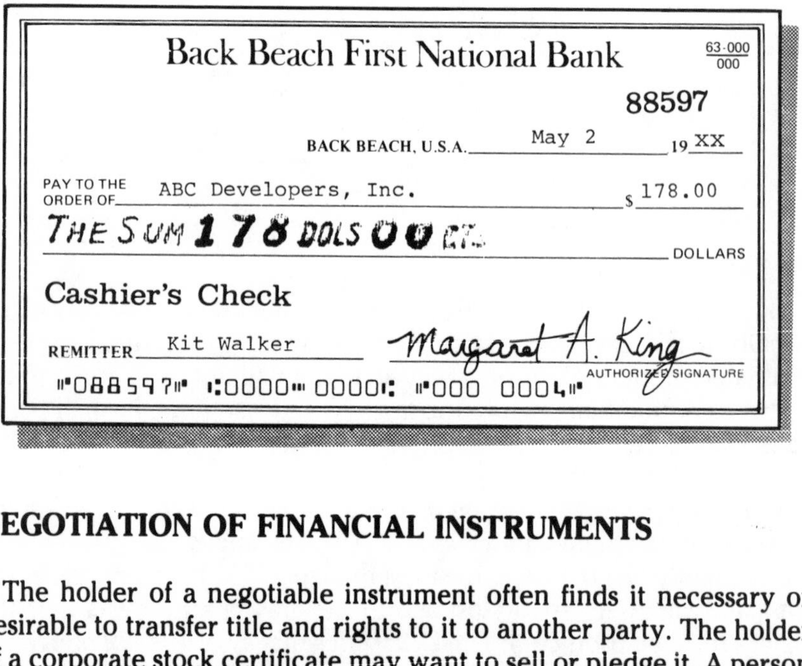

Back Beach First National Bank 63-000/000

88597

BACK BEACH, U.S.A. May 2 19 XX

PAY TO THE ORDER OF ABC Developers, Inc. $ 178.00

THE SUM **178** DOLS **00** CTS _____ DOLLARS

Cashier's Check

REMITTER Kit Walker Margaret A. King
AUTHORIZED SIGNATURE

⑈088597⑈ ⑆0000⑈ 0000⑆ ⑈000 0004⑈

NEGOTIATION OF FINANCIAL INSTRUMENTS

The holder of a negotiable instrument often finds it necessary or desirable to transfer title and rights to it to another party. The holder of a corporate stock certificate may want to sell or pledge it. A person who has received a check may wish to deposit it into a bank account, convert it into coin and currency, or give it to someone else. A merchant who holds a note payable at a future date may need immediate funds and therefore may seek some method of transferring the note in exchange for cash. Each of these transfers of legal right and title is an example of **negotiation**.

Transfers of rights to negotiable instruments, as mentioned earlier, may be accomplished simply by delivery to another party. More frequently, however, **endorsement** is part of the process. There are four principal kinds of endorsements (see Figure 4-5), each of which serves a particular purpose:

- **Blank endorsement**. This consists simply of the signature of the instrument's previous holder.

- **Special endorsement**. The previous holder names the party to whom rights are being transferred—e.g., "Pay to Farmers State Bank"—and signs the instrument.

- **Restrictive endorsement**. In addition to signing the instrument, the previous holder identifies the purpose of the transfer and restricts the use to which the instrument can be put. The most common example occurs when checks are endorsed "For deposit only." Restrictive endorsements are often combined with special endorsements, as when the payee endorses with the words "Pay to Farmers State Bank: For Deposit Only." The UCC affirms that when Farmers State Bank accepts this endorsed check, it is legally required to increase the endorser's account balance and to hold the funds until withdrawal instructions are received.

- **Qualified endorsement**. The purpose of this type of endorsement is to limit the endorser's liability. The words *without recourse,* or words with a similar meaning, are used as part of the endorsement.

Because the volume of checks used has reached such huge proportions and the use of endorsements has become so common, the UCC allows other than handwritten endorsements. Typed, rubber-stamped, or printed endorsements are valid under the code and are widely accepted by banks.

The endorsement on an instrument need not necessarily be applied by the previous holder. Banks frequently provide this by placing a rubber-stamp endorsement on deposited checks, typically using such words as "Credited to account of within-named payee" and guaranteeing the absence of the payee's personal signature and endorsement.

Figure 4-5
Four Types of Endorsements

BLANK ENDORSEMENT

John Q. Public

SPECIAL ENDORSEMENT

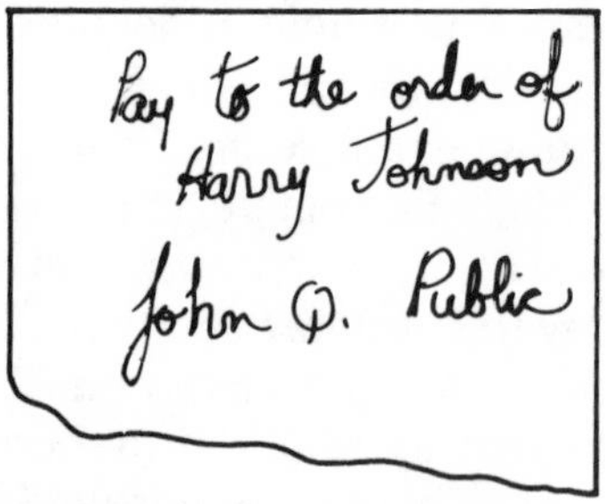

Pay to the order of Harry Johnson

John Q. Public

RESTRICTIVE ENDORSEMENT

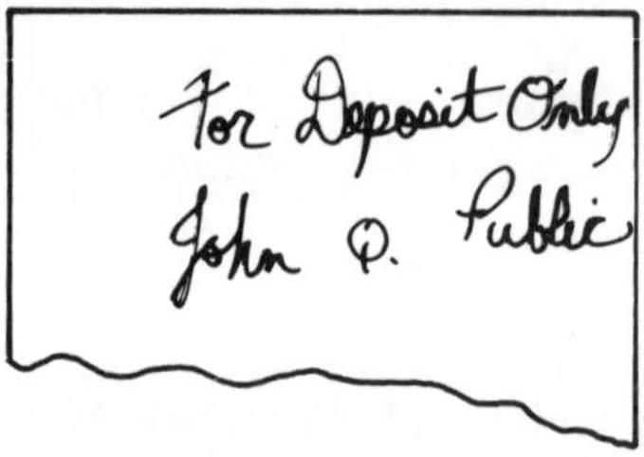

For Deposit Only

John Q. Public

QUALIFIED ENDORSEMENT

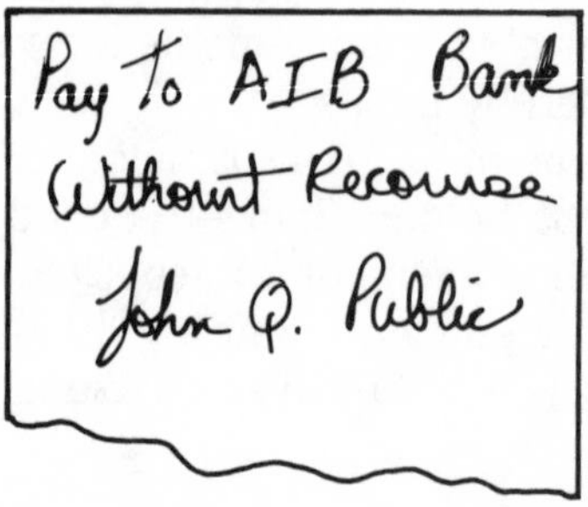

Pay to AIB Bank Without Recourse

John Q. Public

Liabilities of Endorsers

On any given day, millions of checks are endorsed and transferred to banks or other parties, and there is some question as to whether every endorser is fully aware of the legal liabilities that his or her action entails. Obviously, good faith and trust are of paramount importance. An endorser who knowingly transfers rights to a fraudulent check is not acting in good faith, but an endorser who has no knowledge of any defect in, or problem with, the check must still be held liable. All endorsers should understand this concept of liability.

Every endorser of a negotiable instrument assumes the following specific liabilities and responsibilities under the terms of Article 3 of the UCC:

- The endorser warrants that he or she has good title to the instrument or is authorized to obtain payment on behalf of one who has good title, and that the transfer is otherwise rightful.

- The endorser warrants that all signatures are genuine and authorized. (It is recognized, however, that the endorser may not know or be in a position to know that this is true.)

- The endorser warrants that the instrument has not been materially altered and that no defense to payment of any party is good against him or her.

- The endorser warrants that he or she has no knowledge of any bankruptcy proceedings affecting the instrument.

Perhaps most important, the endorser assumes a *general liability*, promising to make good on the item if it is dishonored and if the endorser is properly and promptly notified of that dishonor. This liability is the one that the user of a qualified endorsement seeks to escape.

By endorsing a negotiable instrument, an endorser promises—even though this promise is not specifically stated in every transaction—that he or she will pay the value of that instrument to the next, or any subsequent, party if the instrument is dishonored for any reason. The qualified endorsement is the only instance in which this guarantee of reimbursement does not apply.

The endorser's liability is vital to the efforts of banks to minimize risk. When John Doe presents his endorsed payroll check to a teller and either deposits it or receives cash for it, he is promising the bank that he will make good if the item is returned for any reason. The UCC stipulates that by his endorsement John Doe is stating that the check is genuine and that he has legal rights to it and can do with it as he wishes. The bank can accept the endorsed check from him, secure in the knowledge that it has a valid claim against him if the check is not honored when it is presented to the drawee bank.

Holder in Due Course

The legal protection given to any party accepting an endorsed negotiable instrument is outlined in the UCC under the heading "Holder in Due Course." A bank, individual, or other party that accepts such an item is entitled to this protection and should not be penalized in any way for defects in, or subsequent problems with, the instrument.

To qualify legally as a **holder in due course** and thus to obtain the superior rights conveyed by that title, one must

- receive the instrument for value,

- receive it in good faith,

- receive it under proper conditions of delivery and negotiation,

- receive it without notice that it is overdue or has been dishonored, and

- receive it without notice of any claim against the instrument or defense against it.

If an instrument payable to order is transferred with no endorsement, the concept of a holder in due course does not apply, and the party to whom the instrument was transferred does not have the corresponding legal protection.

When the bank accepted John Doe's endorsed pay check for deposit, or gave him coin and currency in exchange for it, the holder-in-due-course principle applied. The bank acted in good faith, for it surely would not have accepted the check had it known that the instrument was stolen, forged, or otherwise invalid. By crediting his account or giving him cash in exchange for the check, the bank gave

John Doe something of value. As an endorser, John Doe is liable; as a holder in due course, the bank is legally protected.

A holder in due course may recover on an instrument regardless of defenses and disputes that may exist between the prior parties; he or she takes the instrument free from all claims to it on the part of any party with whom he or she has not dealt. A holder in due course would normally seek recovery from the previous or last-named endorser; however, the UCC also gives that holder the right of recovery from the original drawer or maker. In banking transactions, the first-named process occurs far more frequently. If a teller takes an endorsed check on deposit or gives cash for it, and the item is dishonored for any reason, the bank turns to the endorser for recovery. In the case of an item that has been endorsed and deposited, the bank would simply charge the instrument back to the account.

To illustrate the principle, assume that Hazel Adams has purchased a used car from Margaret Jones and has given her a personal check in payment. Margaret, in turn, endorses Hazel's check and gives it to William Crosby to pay a debt to him. Hazel later feels that the car is defective and is not what she contracted to buy. Therefore, she places a stop-payment order on the check at her bank. Crosby, an innocent party to their dispute, is the legal holder in due course. He acted in good faith by accepting the endorsed check, and he gave something of value for it by canceling or reducing Margaret Jones' debt. His legal protection under the UCC consists of a valid claim against the endorser, Margaret. If that claim cannot be satisfied, Crosby may then recover from Hazel, the drawer of the check; he must, however, first turn to the endorser from whom he accepted it.

If our laws did not contain this protective feature, it would be difficult or impossible to induce a bank or other party to accept an endorsed instrument. All forms of commerce and exchanges of property would suffer greatly as a result. The doctrine of holder in due course was intended to provide legal recourse for the transferee.

QUESTIONS FOR DISCUSSION

1. What weaknesses exist in the barter system and in the use of money as a payment medium?

2. What features made the system of credit balances an improvement over other methods of payment?

71

3. Define the following terms:
    a. draft
    b. check
    c. certified check
    d. cashier's check
    e. holder in due course

4. What are the differences between checks and promissory notes?

5. Why is the holder-in-due-course principle important to a bank teller?

6. Identify four characteristics an instrument must have if it is to qualify as negotiable.

7. If an endorsed check is accepted and deposited to an account, what action will be taken by the bank if the item is dishonored?

Suggested Readings

Banking Terminology. Washington, D.C.: American Bankers Association. 1981.

Conboy, James C., Jr. *Law and Banking.* Washington, D.C.: American Bankers Association, 1982.

Donnelly, James H. *A Preface to Banking.* Washington, D.C.: American Bankers Association, 1979.

Farnsworth, E. Allan. *Cases and Materials on Commercial Paper.* 2nd ed. Mineola, New York: Foundation Press, 1976.

Garcia, F. L. *Munn's Encyclopedia of Banking and Finance.* 7th ed. Boston: Bankers Publishing Co., 1973.

Modern Banking Forms. Vol. 2. Boston: Warren, Gorham & Lamont, 1974. Cumulative supplement, 1979.

Smith, Craig. *Negotiable Instruments and the Payments Mechanism.* Washington, D.C.: American Bankers Association, 1983.

Standard & Poor's Corporation. *A Glossary of Financial/Investment Terms.* New York: Standard & Poor's, 1977.

Weber, Charles M. *Commercial Paper in a Nutshell.* 2nd ed. St. Paul's: West, 1975.

Chapter 5

The Deposit Function

LEARNING OBJECTIVES

After completing this chapter, you will have an understanding of

- the importance of deposit function in commercial banking;
- what is meant by the term *cash item*;
- the distinction between a customer's book balance and that customer's collected balance;
- such terms as house check, provisional credit, and float;
- the basic characteristics of cash and noncash items;
- the operations of the night depository and direct deposit systems;
- the actions taken by tellers in accepting deposits; and
- the problem of counterfeit currency.

T he services a commercial bank renders to every segment of the public every day and the work performed by its staff in providing those services are so diverse that it is difficult to single out any particular one as being the most important. Nevertheless, if such a choice had to be made, the **deposit function** would dominate. It is the one banking function upon which all the others rest. Every commercial bank seeks to attract and retain deposits, because they are the raw material that makes it possible for the bank to provide services while generating profits.

As mentioned earlier, most of the funds loaned or invested by banks come from depositors' money, *not* from the banks' own funds. If deposit inflow ceased, the banks would no longer have the funds with which to extend credit; their lending activities would at first be restricted, then eventually eliminated. The American economy, which depends heavily on bank borrowings to finance its expansion and meet its needs, would suffer a serious setback.

The payment function likewise depends directly on the deposit function. Over 100 million checks are in the processing stream on an average day. Customers can issue those checks because they have already deposited the funds to cover them, and payees can accept the items because they, in turn, can deposit them with banks and have them converted into usable funds. The size and scope of the deposit function create the need for an understanding of the procedures banks follow in taking items on deposit and in transforming checks— i.e., claims to money—into funds that customers can use.

Again, the service aspect of the deposit function cannot be overlooked. Consider the case of an insurance company in Milwaukee. Each month it receives thousands of checks in payment of policyholders' premiums. The company assumes that every check is good until and unless it hears otherwise. However, each check is a written set of instructions to a drawee, directing that payment be made. The drawee, wherever located, must make the final decision regarding honoring the item and charging it to the maker's account.

Theoretically, the insurance company could present each check to its drawee, whether that institution was across the street or thousands of miles away. This is obviously impossible, however, in actual practice. Therefore, the company deposits the checks with its Milwaukee banks, which are willing to perform all the work of receiving and processing the deposits because by doing so they provide themselves with the funds needed for loan and investment purposes.

WHAT IS BEING DEPOSITED?

On any given day, a bank teller may conceivably be faced with a rapid succession of customers, each of whom wishes to make a deposit into an account. A critical phase of the teller's work occurs at that point. He or she must never assume that accepting deposits is a simple, routine job, consisting chiefly of counting and examining coin and currency, accepting checks, and issuing receipts. It is essential that tellers understand the nature of the items they are handling and that they know which can properly be accepted at once and which should be questioned further. They must always be aware that a bank, by the mere act of accepting a deposit, exposes itself to serious liability and risk.

Assume that a teller must deal with five customers in sequence who present the following items for deposit:

- A deposit consisting of coin and currency only.

- A deposit consisting of a payroll check drawn on the teller's own bank; i.e., the bank of deposit is also the drawee.

- A deposit consisting of a check payable to the depositor but drawn on another bank in the same city.

- A deposit consisting of a check the customer received from a relative in a distant city.

- A promissory note, payable to the customer.

The teller has been presented with five situations, each different from the others. Not only must the deposit be examined and accepted accurately and quickly, but the teller must also decide whether each item can be handled and must know how to do this.

Cash Items

Any discussion of the language of banking must include a term that often creates confusion, **cash items**. The importance of this term cannot be overemphasized. To the general public, it may mean coin and currency exclusively; in banking it has an entirely different significance. It refers to a position taken by banks because of their belief in the "goodness" of the typical, everyday check.

As mentioned earlier, checks are not money but are claims to money. In each case, the drawee must make a decision as to whether the item can and should be charged to the maker's account. Despite the huge volume of checks that changes hands every day, only one out of every 200 will be rejected; the remaining 199 justify the basic assumption of banks, businesses, governments, and the public that a check is "good" until proved otherwise and therefore can be accepted with confidence.

The entire system operates on an exception basis. When customers deposit the checks they have received, no notification ever takes place unless those checks are returned unpaid for any reason.

Banks, similarly, are willing to assume that the vast majority of checks deposited each day will be honored; therefore, they call these cash items and give them *immediate, provisional* credit at the time they are accepted for deposit.

Both "immediate" and "provisional" have great significance for the bank and the depositor. The word "immediate" describes the fact that the bank gives the depositor an immediate increase in the account balance by crediting the total amount of the deposit on the day it is received. At the same time, the word "provisional" describes the right of the bank to reverse that credit if necessary.

Assume that the ABC Company receives 200 checks today and deposits them with its local bank. The ABC Company's *book* balance will be increased by the total amount of the deposit, and the bank's deposit liability will increase by the same amount.

However, while those 200 checks are in the process of being routed to the drawees, examined, and approved, their dollar total represents uncollected funds, also known as **float**. The ABC Company's book balance, *less* the 200 items that are in the process of collection, is its *collected* balance, i.e., funds that have already completed the check-processing cycle and are known to be good. Because there is always the possibility that one or more deposited items may not be honored, banks, as a general rule, do not allow customers to withdraw uncollected funds.

Because they are uniform and do not require individual, specialized handling, cash items can be processed quickly and cheaply, in large volumes. By treating the typical check as a cash item, banks have been able to develop handling methods that provide speed and efficiency at minimum cost to the customer.

In the example given, the first customer's deposit of coin and currency obviously falls into the cash item category; the teller is dealing with legal tender, so there are no uncollected funds and no reasons for delay in increasing the customer's account balance.

The second, third, and fourth depositors are presenting checks, which will have to be approved for payment by their respective drawees; nevertheless, they are classified as cash items and also increase the account balance on an immediate but provisional basis. The check presented by the second customer will remain within the same bank at which it is deposited. It is called a check **on us** or a **house** check. The third item involves another bank in the same geographic area as the bank of deposit. It is commonly called a **local**, or **clearing**, item. The fourth customer presented a check drawn on a bank in a distant city. This type is known as a **transit** check. Each bank has its own internal policies for classifying checks as local or transit, depending on the geography of the area, the number of banks that serve that area, and the facilities for exchanging and settling for checks.

Each of the three checks is payable on demand, is not accompanied by any documents or instructions that would make customized handling necessary, can be handled quickly and inexpensively in bulk, and is payable in an immediate determinable amount of U.S. currency. All three are cash items.

Every bank uses a variety of techniques to reduce float, since deposited checks that remain uncollected for a period of time have a serious impact on both the bank and its customers. Those techniques are discussed in Chapter 8, which deals with check processing and collection.

Noncash Items

The fifth customer presented the teller with a completely different problem. His promissory note does not meet the tests for cash items, and it will require individual, specialized handling. In this case, the item is classified as **noncash**. The differences between cash and noncash items are listed in Table 5-1.

Table 5-1
Characteristics of Deposited Items

Cash Items	Noncash Items
1. Give customer immediate, provisional account credit.	1. Give customer delayed (deferred) credit.
2. Create float (time lag between account crediting and collection).	2. Do not create float (account not credited until collection is completed).
3. May be payable on demand.	3. May or may not be payable on demand.
4. Must not have documents attached.	4. May have documents attached.
5. Must not carry special instructions or require special handling.	5. Individual, special handling required; may carry customer's or other instructions.
6. Inexpensive; processed in bulk.	6. More expensive to handle.
7. Are payable in U.S. funds.	7. May or may not be payable in U.S. funds.
EXAMPLES	*EXAMPLES*
Checks	Promissory notes
	Drafts with attached documents
	Coupons
	Foreign checks

When customers present noncash items, the teller who accepts them should explain that immediate account credit cannot be given and that an appropriate advice of credit will be sent out as soon as the specialized collection process has been completed; *only then* will the customer's account be credited. There is no immediate credit, and therefore no float. For the same reason, the credit that is finally posted is *not* provisional; the item is known to have been presented and honored.

When a noncash item is dishonored for any reason, as in the case of a promissory note that the maker refuses to accept, no charge-back to the depositor's account occurs, simply because no credit was posted at the time of receipt.

Noncash items are usually handled by a special department within the bank, where they can be given the individual, customized processing that is required. If the volume warrants it, that department may be further subdivided into "city collections" (i.e., those payable locally) and "country collections," which correspond to transit items. Foreign collections make up yet another specialized category because of the different problems they present.

Banks often make exceptions to the arbitrary and strict rules on the classification of deposited items. For example, a customer who is well known to the bank and deposits coupons detached from U.S. government bonds can have those coupons accepted for immediate credit, despite the fact that they would normally fall into the noncash item category. Each bank must establish its own policies.

HOW ARE DEPOSITS MADE?

Historically, most deposits have been made at tellers' windows, at brick-and-mortar facilities of banks. However, to increase and expedite the inflow of deposits and for the greater convenience of customers, banks today have developed many additional ways in which deposits can be made. These are widely used to reduce congestion on the banking floor and eliminate waiting time at tellers' stations—a frequent cause of customer complaints.

Convenience Services

Retail stores, restaurants, theaters, and other businesses that receive currency and checks in payment for goods and services often need to make deposits after banking hours and on weekends. **Night depository** service makes this possible. The customer is given a bag or pouch with a safety lock and a key to a compartment in the bank's wall. He places his deposit in the bag, locks it, and when convenient drops it in the compartment. The deposit will be opened, under special conditions, by bank personnel on the next business day.

Counting and verifying each night deposit is generally done under a system called **dual control**, which involves two bank personnel. Dual control is used in many phases of a bank's daily operations, in addition to the night-deposit processing. Access to vaults and the handling of debit and credit entries usually require the participation of two staff members so that one may verify what another has done. Use of dual control in the night deposit operation helps protect the bank if a dispute arises over whether a deposit was actually made or over the amount of the deposit.

Many banks provide a facility known as a **lobby depository** or **quick-deposit box**. The depositor places his deposit in an envelope, seals the envelope, and puts it in a secure receptacle on the banking floor. In this way the customer avoids waiting for an available teller, and the deposits can be examined and proved—again, using dual control—during nonpeak periods. After each deposit has been examined and verified, receipts are sent to the customers.

Banks also encourage the use of **mail deposits** as another way to reduce traffic in the bank, speed up the handling of deposits, and make banking more convenient for customers. Bank personnel can process the deposits without the pressures created by long lines of impatient customers; thus, errors are reduced. Receipts for mail deposits are sent out after examination and verification.

The **drive-in window** has become a familiar sight in rural and suburban areas, and some banks handle as much as two-thirds of their daily deposit activity through these facilities. Transactions are processed as they would be at any other teller installation, but customers appreciate the convenience of doing their banking while remaining in their cars.

The remarkable world of electronic technology has opened up many additional ways in which deposits to customers' accounts can be made without the need for the depositor to visit the bank and spend time there. **Direct deposit** programs increase in popularity each year; the Social Security Administration has had great success in its efforts to substitute electronic transfers of funds for check disbursements, and direct depositing of payrolls is gaining greater acceptance. Under these programs, information regarding each payment is entered on magnetic tape. The account of the recipient at any financial institution in the country can be credited through the facilities of automated clearinghouses (ACHs), which process the tape and route it to each bank, thrift institution, or credit union. Over 10,000 financial institutions now participate in regional ACHs.

Automatic transfers of funds provide another example of electronic banking. Customers may authorize their banks to charge their accounts and credit the appropriate payees each month to pay insurance premiums, meet loan payments, or handle other expenses. Automatic transfer services also allow banks to move funds from customers' savings accounts to their checking accounts whenever necessary, under a preauthorization form of agreement.

Automated teller machines (ATMs), of which over 20,000 are now in operation at all types of financial institutions throughout the country, offer the most widely used electronic funds transfer services. They allow for cash withdrawals, deposits, account balance inquiries, and transfers of funds between accounts. In the deposit function, they offer the consumer 24-hour service every day of the year.

Preauthorized payments are used by many bank customers as a means of avoiding the time and effort involved in writing and mailing checks and assuming the postage expense. This convenient service overlaps with the concept of automatic transfers of funds. Under the system of preauthorized payments, the customer executes a written agreement under which the bank will automatically create a payment instrument on his or her behalf and enter that instrument into the payment system, exactly as if the depositor had issued it. This system is most effective when a fixed amount of money must be expended at the same time every month.

Transfers Between Banks

Wire transfers represent another way in which deposits can be made to accounts without the involvement of tellers. Billions of dollars move from bank to bank in this manner every day. The Federal Reserve provides a wire network that links the twelve Fed districts and enables banks to make transfers to and from the reserve accounts of member banks, i.e., in so-called **Fed funds**. The use of Fed funds is often requested in large business transactions because the immediate availability of the funds is guaranteed.

In addition to the facilities of the Fed, banks also use the Bank Wire, a private network operated and supported by some 250 major commercial banks that use it to make immediate transfers of funds throughout the country. Assume that a company headquartered in Alabama must move funds to its bank in Detroit, which operates a payroll account for the firm's employees in that area. Upon receipt of proper instructions, the Alabama bank will charge its customer's account and instruct the bank in Detroit, by wire, to post the appropriate credit to the payroll account. This system is rapid and efficient because it reduces the movement of funds to mere bookkeeping entries.

Transfers Within a Bank

A final example of deposits that do not originate with bank tellers can be seen in the multitude of credit tickets prepared each day by departments within a bank. The most common method of paying out loan proceeds is to post a credit ticket to the borrower's account. Sales of securities and foreign collections likewise result in this form of deposit activity.

EXAMINING DEPOSITS

Before a deposit is accepted from a customer, it is essential that an examination process take place so that the bank knows what it is accepting and may properly issue a receipt. The first step in this process removes any noncash items from the rest of the deposit and routes them to the proper personnel for specialized handling. All cash items are then carefully examined.

Counterfeit Currency

Coins and currency pose a special problem for tellers. Counterfeiting has reached record proportions in the United States in recent years, and new and more sophisticated photographic, printing, and copying equipment has made possible the production of large quantities of bogus currency. In many cases, the counterfeiting process results in bills of such a high quality that they are very difficult to detect. Government agencies have expressed great concern over this increasing problem, and an alert teller can be extremely valuable in the effort to reduce counterfeiting.

When a bogus bill is identified in a deposit, the teller should immediately subtract its amount from that deposit and arrange for it to be forwarded to the Federal Reserve, which will, in turn, send it to the Secret Service unit in the U.S. Treasury Department. Under no circumstances should a counterfeit bill ever be returned to the customer, since this would only serve to keep it in circulation. Depositors, in effect, lose the amount of any counterfeit bills that are detected in their currency deposits.

Endorsements

Checks presented for deposit should be examined for endorsement. When a bank insists on proper endorsements, it is serving its own interests as well as those of its customers. Under the principle of holder in due course, the customer who endorses a check and deposits it agrees to make good if necessary. Further, the endorsement provides an audit trail if proof of payment to a particular party is ever required. For example, checks issued by the U.S. government and by many insurance companies require specific endorsements as a means of proving that the funds were paid to the proper beneficiary.

Business Deposits

As a general rule, coins and currency must be counted and examined at the teller's window. However, many business customers make large bulk deposits of coins and currency, making the normal process impossible. Stores, amusement parks, and transportation companies often deposit substantial amounts of rolled or bagged coins and large bundles of strapped bills. Standard bank practice permits the acceptance of these deposits without actual counting and verifying by the teller. In these cases, the bank and its depositor agree that the amount of the deposit is subject to later verification.

EXCESS CASH

The coins and the currency received by a bank in the course of a day are stored in its vaults after proof procedures have been completed. If the bank has an excess of coin and currency on hand, over and above its projected near-term needs, it turns that surplus over to the Federal Reserve to be added to its reserves, or to a correspondent bank, which performs services in exchange for compensating balances. On the other hand, when a bank requires additional coin and currency—for example, for a busy payroll day or during the hectic Christmas season—it obtains a supply from either of those two sources.

Banks should take every reasonable precaution against keeping excess amounts of cash at tellers' stations. Typically, the supply of currency and coin is counted and controlled each day. Should a holdup occur, the loss will be far greater if a teller's cash drawer is overflowing with bills. Also, the mere sight of an overabundance of cash can be a source of temptation to a would-be robber.

In addition to being dangerous, it is also wasteful to have excess cash on hand. Surplus funds, turned over to the Fed or a correspondent, release other funds for loan and investment purposes and thus contribute to the bank's earnings.

PROBLEM SITUATIONS

One of the challenges that every teller faces in the course of a day's work requires dealing with those customers who try to take advantage of a momentary lapse in concentration or the pressures of an especially hectic hour, when lines are at their longest and the teller inevitably becomes fatigued. Banks are often defrauded in this way, even when what appears to be nothing more than a routine cash item is involved.

The **split deposit** is a common technique used to defraud the banks. A customer opens an account and later presents a check to a teller, with the request that part of it be deposited and the remainder be paid out in cash. The teller who grants such a request is assuming a very real risk. Establishing a bank account does *not* give a customer the right to use it as an automatic medium for cashing checks. The check used in this type of banking transaction may have been stolen or may be dishonored by the drawee for some valid reason. If the depository bank is unable to recover the funds from the depositor, as is often the case, it suffers a direct loss.

Another common fraud involving the deposit function uses a technique known as **kiting**. Here, the customer establishes accounts with two or more banks and uses a check on one, drawn against nonexistent or uncollected funds, as a means of obtaining cash from another.

Other problems in the acceptance of cash items often involve the exact designation of the named payee and the bank's responsibility to accept instructions only from that payee or from another party to whom the named payee has transferred his or her rights. A check payable to a corporation, an estate, a business name, or another form of legal entity should never be accepted on deposit for an individual account unless there are strong reasons for doing so as an exception. Also, when a check has been prepared in error and the payee's name misspelled, it is proper and customary for the teller to ask that it be endorsed both ways. Again, this provides an audit trail and legal evidence of the receipt of the funds.

SORTING AND PROVING DEPOSITS

Depending on their size, the volume of deposited items they handle each day, and the extent to which they have automated their systems, various banks have designed their own individual methods of sorting and proving the deposited checks after the customer has left the teller's window. The most widely used method is known as **batch proof**. It is based on the theory that if the necessary sorting work on all deposited items and other items is done correctly, and if accurate totals have been derived for each sorting category, the sum of the totals of the categories must equal the total amount processed for the day. Even though counter errors may take place, the batch proof system more than compensates for that by making it unnecessary for every individual deposit to be proved separately.

Whether the batch proof or another system is used, and regardless of the bank's size or volume of activity, two steps must be completed after all deposits have been received at tellers' windows:

1. The deposited amount must be proved; and

2. Separate, accurate control totals must be developed, showing the destinations to which deposited checks are sent and the amount that has been sent to each.

Deposited and cashed checks are sorted into three groups: on-us, local, and transit. The totals for these groups must equal the tellers' activity for the day after cash substitution tickets, accounting for currency and coin, are included.

Figure 5-1 shows the check-processing flow in those banks with a daily deposit volume large enough to warrant a centralized department. In smaller banks, the sorting and routing work may be done directly by the tellers. Chapter 8 covers the details of check process-

Figure 5-1
The Check-Processing Workflow

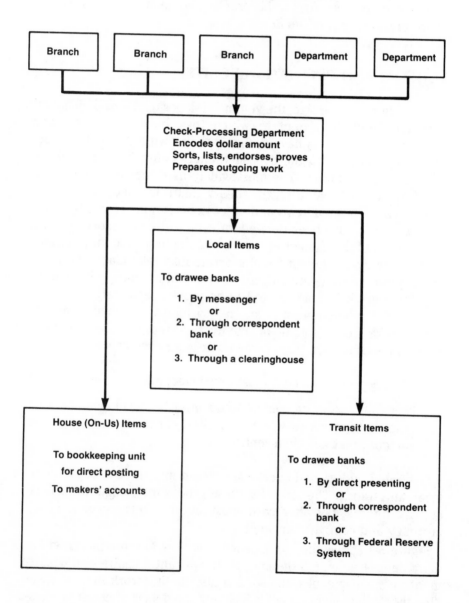

ing through the next logical point, i.e., the sending of checks to their drawee banks.

SUMMARY

Accepting deposits simultaneously serves the best interests of banks and their customers. If it were not for the check-handling capability developed by banks, the economy would suffer tremendously because each payee would have to assume the entire task of sorting and routing every check. By rendering this service, banks also provide themselves from the daily inflow of raw material that they need in order to generate profits.

Deposits are received in many ways, but regardless of the method—tellers' windows, through an ACH, night drop, lobby depository, or ATM—the bank must be able to recognize the nature of the deposited items, screen out the noncash items, and process the work with speed and accuracy. Speed is important because float has no real value, either to a bank or to its customer. Accuracy is essential because customers demand and expect this.

No teller should ever feel that receiving deposits is a simple process that creates no risk or liability for the bank. On the contrary, each teller must be aware of the need to understand and apply the criteria for immediate credit, the holder-in-due-course principle, and the potential for loss resulting from his or her actions. Tellers must constantly be on guard to protect the bank against those who would try to defraud it.

QUESTIONS FOR DISCUSSION

1. What is the relationship between a bank's deposit function and its credit function?

2. What is the significance of the words "immediate" and "provisional" when they are applied to the depositing of cash items?

3. Define the term *float*. How is float created? Do noncash items create float?

4. What is a "house" check? A clearing item? A transit check?

5. In addition to daily activity at tellers' windows, identify five other ways in which deposits may be made to customers' accounts.

6. Explain the difference between a customer's book balance and his or her collected balance.

7. Identify five criteria of cash items. What is the most common example of a cash item?

8. What actions should a teller take when a counterfeit bill is identified in a customer's deposit?

9. What purposes are served by making sure that each deposited check has been properly endorsed?

10. Is the batch proof system used in your bank? How does this system operate?

11. Give two reasons why the amount of cash at tellers' stations should be kept to a minimum.

Suggested Readings

American Bankers Association. *A Guide to Interest-Bearing Transaction Accounts.* Washington, D.C.: American Bankers Association, 1978.

American Bankers Association. *Loss Prevention* (Seminar). Washington, D.C.: American Bankers Association, 1980.

American Bankers Association. *Retail Deposit Services Report.* Washington, D.C.: American Bankers Association, 1982.

Friedman, David H. *Deposit Operations.* Washington, D.C.: American Bankers Association, 1982.

Chapter 6

Bank Relationships
with Depositors

LEARNING OBJECTIVES

After completing this chapter, you will have an understanding of

- the extent of the competition faced by commercial banks today;
- the operations of credit unions and thrift institutions;
- the nature of the contract between a bank and its customers;
- the importance of identification and legal right when a new account is being opened;
- the terms *attorney-in-fact* and *rights of survivorship*;
- the distinction between the nature of a proprietorship and that of a corporation;
- the importance of a corporate resolution;
- the role of savings and time deposits in commercial banking;
- the importance of interest expense to banks; and
- such terms as All Savers Certificate, Keogh and IRA plans, and Form 1099.

A lthough its traditions stretch back for 200 years, banking in the United States has changed more in the post-World War II period than in its entire previous history. As domestic and international economies grew, as new technologies were developed and new industries formed, and as changing markets began to display changing financial needs, commercial banks reacted by revising many of their time-honored attitudes. Many became, for the first time, aggressive marketers. A bank account is no longer the symbol of a well-to-do individual, nor is the use of bank services restricted to a few selected customers. Banks today have become the supermarkets or department stores of finance. On any given day, any one of them may be offering a service, such as a bank card, a bank-by-telephone system, a certificate of deposit, or a loan to finance a boat or a cooperative apartment, that did not exist 30 years ago.

THE COMPETITION

Competition in the financial marketplace has grown, both in quantity and in type, at an incredible rate since World War II. The share of the total assets in that marketplace held by commercial banks has shrunk at an alarming rate. Customers who in the past were forced to go to commercial banks for financial services now have far more freedom of choice. Areas that were once the exclusive domain of the banks have now been opened up to competitors, and sophisticated customers show no hesitation in moving money from one financial intermediary to another, whenever and wherever advantages and benefits can be found.

Credit Unions

Credit unions historically were organized to offer certain limited financial services to employees of a firm or individuals who were bound together by some type of social, fraternal, or religious bond. Today, they are far more loosely organized, and virtually any common ties among individuals suffice for chartering and operating this type of institution.

During the 1950s credit unions doubled in number and increased their total assets sixfold. In the 1960s they again doubled their membership and tripled their assets. The most recent figures show that over 22,000 credit unions exist in the United States, with assets of over $66 billion.

Credit unions enjoy exemption from taxes on their income, and their operating expenses are low because their physical facilities are often donated by the sponsoring company or agency of government. Because of these advantages, they are able to pay higher interest on deposited funds and charge lower interest on loans than the commercial banks.

Credit unions fall under the umbrella definition of financial institutions offering transaction accounts; therefore, they are directly affected by the Monetary Control Act of 1980. They are required to keep reserves, either directly with the Fed or with a commercial member bank. The same legislation gave them access to the Fed for borrowing purposes, and they may offer NOW accounts, credit cards, and mortgage loans. Credit unions also can provide their members with share drafts to be used instead of checks as a payment medium.

Savings and Loan Associations

Savings and loan associations (S&Ls) were originally formed as building societies, providing a source of home mortgage credit to individuals. Today there are over 4,600 S&Ls in the United States, with total assets of over $629 billion. They remain the largest lenders in the home-mortgage field. In addition, the Monetary Control Act, while subjecting them to reserve requirements, also gives them additional lending powers and a right to offer NOW accounts. S&Ls enjoy a competitive advantage over commercial banks in that they have been given more extensive branching privileges, and in many cases they operate across state lines.

Money Market Funds

Because the commercial banks did not offer forms of investment specifically aimed at the smaller investor who had a limited amount of money to put to work, **money market funds** (MMFs) were first organized in 1972. Since that time, they have displayed phenomenal growth (see Figure 6-1); assets of money market funds exceeded 216 billion as of December 1982. By pooling the funds of large numbers of individuals, MMFs can obtain higher yields on their investments than the average investor. They have become major competitors of both commercial banks and thrift institutions. Many MMFs give their cus-

Figure 6-1
Growth of Money Market Funds

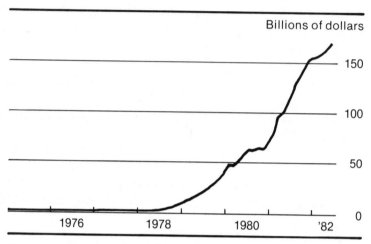

SOURCE: *Federal Reserve Bulletin*, July 1982, p. 394

tomers check-writing privileges, a credit card for cash advances and other uses, and the right to borrow at any time, up to the full dollar value of the individual investor's stake in the fund.

Other Competitors

No discussion of the competitive financial marketplace would be complete unless such organizations as Sears Roebuck, Merrill Lynch, and American Express were mentioned. These institutions have publicly stated their intentions of becoming the financial supermarkets of the future. They have been able to expand, often by acquiring other companies, without being restricted by the regulations that affect banks. Sears Roebuck, for example, owns a major insurance company, owns one of the country's largest S&Ls, owns a major brokerage firm, has over 25 million active cardholders whose installment debt to the company exceeds $7 billion, and has announced plans to install ATMs in its stores throughout the nation. Merrill Lynch, in addition to its role as America's largest brokerage firm, offers a wide range of MMFs and is entering the commercial lending field. American Express Company acquired the nation's second-largest brokerage firm, Shearson Hamill, in 1981 and thus enhanced its ability to offer a broad range of financial services, including travelers' checks and credit cards.

MEETING THE COMPETITION

Throughout much of their history, commercial banks neglected the "retail" market—i.e., services to consumers—and concentrated exclusively on dealing with businesses, agencies of government, and correspondent banks. Their competitors capitalized on that neglect and offered as many financial services as possible to individuals. Savings and loan associations, savings banks, credit unions, and money market funds all came into existence to fill a financial need that the banks had ignored.

Banking today reflects an entirely different approach. To meet the ever-increasing competition, banks offer new and better services. Their success in gaining new customers, however, carries with it a serious problem. Establishing a relationship with a new customer may now require more care and skill on the bank's part than was needed in the past. As commercial banks try to cope with the competition by dealing on an expanded scale with individuals, with every size and type of business, and with authorities and agencies of government, their desire to attract deposits should never cause them to relax their standards. There are fundamental precautions that should be taken at the beginning of a relationship with a customer and throughout its life cycle. If they are faithfully observed, these precautions will lessen the bank's risk and will guarantee that both parties are fully aware of the obligations they are undertaking.

Any bank employee who is involved in opening new accounts must be prepared to deal with completely unknown individuals. These individuals may be unsure of the type of relationship they want to establish and unaware of the banking laws that apply to each type of account, the individual bank's policies, and the answers to a whole series of "what if?" questions. It is essential that depositors understand what they and the bank can or cannot do in each type of deposit relationship. Thus, understanding should be established at the time the account is opened.

Full-Service Banking

As mentioned earlier, one major change that has taken place in commercial banking involves the basic shift in marketing approach and philosophy. Most banks today offer a combination of "wholesale" and "retail" banking—that is, they offer their services to every segment of the marketplace and cater to individuals as well as to businesses, agencies of government, and other banks. One example of this change can be seen in the wide variety of demand and time deposits now available at banks.

Traditionally, commercial banks viewed themselves as the nation's reservoir for demand deposits—i.e., checking account money—and generally left the entire field of savings and time deposits to the savings banks and S&Ls. For many years this policy worked very well. However, the credit function depends on the deposit function. In the period following World War II, the commercial banks were faced with a steadily increasing demand for credit as the economy and population grew. Yet their deposit growth—which would have furnished the funds needed to meet that credit demand—suffered because of competition from other institutions. It became apparent that new methods of attracting funds would have to be developed. Entire new areas of bank marketing opened up, and expansion of all forms of deposit relationships was emphasized.

Today, the basic deposit structure of commercial banks throughout the country shows far more in time and savings deposits than in demand deposits. The banks remain as the principal depositories for checking-account funds, but their customers increasingly demand some form of interest-bearing relationship and quickly move money from demand deposits into various types of accounts that will give them an attractive rate of return. Balances in checking accounts are monitored very closely by these customers and generally are kept to a minimum.

Demand deposits are volatile; that is, the rate of turnover is very high. On the other hand, savings and time deposits are not meant for current or near-term use and tend to stay with the bank for longer periods of time. The traditional lines separating the two types of deposits have been relaxed in recent years. NOW accounts and those providing automatic transfer service give customers the best of both worlds; they can issue checks while simultaneously earning interest. In mid-1982 NOW account balances were $87 billion.

Within the two basic categories—demand deposits and time and savings deposits—banks offer a wide range of services to suit the wants and needs of every type of customer. Checking accounts can be opened for one or more individuals, for every type of business, for nonprofit or unincorporated societies and associations, for correspondent banks, for governments, and for trust relationships. The range of savings and time deposits includes the basic savings account, the NOW account, the certificate of deposit, Christmas, Vacation, and Hanukkah Club accounts, and money market certificates.

The actions of the Depository Institutions Deregulation Committee in 1982, under the terms of the Garn-St Germain Act, allowed commercial and savings banks and savings and loan associations to offer two additional new types of accounts, commonly referred to as the "money market deposit account" and the "Super NOW" account, so that they could compete directly with money market mutual funds in attracting deposits. The former is available to all types of depositors; the "Super NOW" account cannot be offered to corporations. Interest-rate ceilings do not apply to either of these new types of accounts, and both types are covered by the Federal Deposit Insurance Corporation or the Federal Savings and Loan Insurance Corporation for the customer's protection.

ESTABLISHING IDENTITY AND LEGAL RIGHT

Before a bank can open its doors and accept its first deposit, it must obtain a charter from either the Office of the Comptroller of the Currency (if it is a national bank) or from state banking authorities. That charter gives the bank the legal right to enter into contractual arrangements with customers. A contract is a legal agreement that can be enforced; a bilateral contract is one in which both parties agree to certain terms and conditions.

Thus, regardless of whether a demand deposit, savings account, or time deposit relationship is being opened, one standard principle applies in every instance. The bank is entering into a contract, and the representative who opens the account is presumed to be acting on its behalf and to have the legal authority to do so. At the same time, the new customer is also agreeing to the terms of that contract. The bank *must* satisfactorily identify the party or parties with whom it is dealing *and* verify their legal right to enter into the contract.

Identification

How can a bank determine that the individual who wishes to open an account is the person he or she claims to be and is one with whom the bank would normally want to do business? This can only be determined on a "best efforts" basis. In the majority of cases a driver's license, automobile registration, credit cards, or other form of identification will be produced. Of course, a forger could counterfeit all of those documents. The individual acting on behalf of the bank must simply use his or her best judgment in evaluating whether the identification can be properly accepted.

References from another commercial bank or thrift institution or from the individual's employer may be used as an additional form of identification. Some banks also use a form of fingerprinting when opening an account and have found this effective in turning away those who have reasons to object to it. Bank personnel who open accounts must be especially wary of those people who take exception to any of the methods of establishing suitable identification. The bank must know its customer and must be satisfied that it is opening an account for a party with whom it can deal in confidence.

Consider this hypothetical situation. A man of whom the bank has no prior knowledge whatever approaches a bank representative and asks to open a personal account with a substantial amount of cash. As soon as he is asked to produce identification and furnish references, he loudly objects, claiming that this is an invasion of his privacy and that his personal affairs are none of the bank's business. He says that he is giving the bank a large amount of genuine currency as evidence of his own good faith and threatens to go to another bank unless the new account is opened on his terms.

An inexperienced staff member could easily be intimidated by this. Faced with the loss of a potential new account, he or she might give in to the stranger's demands and open the account without following standard procedures. Could there be serious consequences for the bank as a result? Obviously, any number of unpleasant and costly situations could occur.

The initial cash deposit might consist of money obtained illegally; in this case, the bank could become the subject of unfavorable publicity and involved in claims and lawsuits. The individual might subsequently deposit stolen checks that he has endorsed; as a holder in due course the bank would rely on the endorser to make good on any problem check, but in this case the endorser might have withdrawn the funds and left town. Banks *can* and *must* be selective in opening accounts. They are under no compulsion to establish relationships with those who fail to meet their criteria.

Legal Right

Establishing the legal authority of a person to enter into a contract with the bank poses a different set of problems. Charles Jackson may produce a satisfactory set of documents that establish his identity. However, if he claims to be an officer of a corporation or a member of a partnership, or if he states that he is the executor of an estate or the agent for a musician or athlete, the bank must be satisfied that he can act on behalf of that business entity or individual. The forms and documents obtained at the opening of the account will vary, based on the nature of the legal authority that must be obtained in each situation.

DEMAND DEPOSIT RELATIONSHIPS

Checking accounts are opened whenever there is a need for a means of paying business or personal expenses and bills. The customer's intention is not to have the balance accumulate; rather, the customer wants the safety and convenience of a relationship that will provide for regular and frequent inflows and outflows of funds. The simplest of these is the personal checking account.

Individual Accounts

In opening a checking account for the use of one person alone, the bank is less concerned about legal right than it is about the customer's identity. If the individual's identification and references meet its standards, the bank may usually assume that he or she has the authority to enter into a contractual agreement with it.

Each new depositor should sign a set of signature cards. These remain with the bank and may be used to verify signatures on checks, loan applications, transfer instructions, and the like. Signature cards (see Figure 6-2) usually outline the general rules and regulations of the bank.

A person who is opening a checking account might ask that a supply of checks be provided at once so that he or she could begin issuing them. Again, to comply with this request could cause serious problems for the bank unless the person has been positively identified. It is far more prudent to advise the customer that the initial supply of checks will be available in a few days, by which time the investigative procedures should have been completed.

An individual depositor, since he or she has the legal right to issue instructions to the bank on all matters pertaining to the account, also has the right to authorize another person to act on his or her behalf. This is done by executing a legal document called a **power of attorney** (see Figure 6-3). This form, when properly signed and completed, allows the authorized party, the **attorney-in-fact**, to do anything that the principal would do. Therefore, the attorney-in-fact can sign checks, apply for credit, and the like. The rights of the attorney-in-fact continue in effect until the principal dies or cancels them.

If a power of attorney has been properly executed and filed with the bank, the signature cards on the account must be revised to show that the attorney-in-fact now has signing powers.

Joint Accounts

Two or more depositors may share a single checking account, in which case they are referred to as **joint tenants**. The most common example of this type of account involves a husband and wife. Legally, neither party has exclusive rights to the account; both are considered to have equal rights to it. Therefore, in most cases either party may sign checks and otherwise issue instructions to the bank. The signature cards must clearly show that this is the case.

Joint accounts may be opened with **rights of survivorship**. Unfortunately, this term is not always understood clearly. It does not always automatically mean that, upon the death of one party, the other has a

Figure 6-2
Signature Card with Typical Bank Deposit Contract

Social Security Numbers

1. _Walter Baker_   2/20/19XX   1. 123 45 6789
      Signature   *Date*

2. _____   _____   2. _____
      Signature   *Date*

3. _____   _____   3. _____
      Signature   *Date*

All accounts requested shall be subject to, and the above-signed will be bound by, the applicable Terms and Conditions governing such accounts, in effect on the above date and as modified from time to time by ABC Bank & Trust Company. A copy of Terms and Conditions are acknowledged as being received.

In receiving items for deposit or collection, this bank acts only as depositor's collecting agent and assumes no responsibility beyond the exercise of due care. All items are credited subject to final payment in cash or solvent credits. This bank will not be liable for defaults or negligence of its duly selected correspondents nor for losses in transit, and each correspondent so selected shall not be liable except for its own negligence. This bank or its correspondents may send items, directly or indirectly, to any bank including the payor and accept its draft or credit as conditional payment in lieu of cash. It may charge back any item at any time before final payment, whether returned or not, the bank shall have until midnight of the next business day after receipt within which to honor or refuse payment of any item drawn on it if deposited during regular business hours, and any item received after regular business hours shall be deemed received at the opening of the next business day, and each branch or office of this bank shall be deemed a separate bank. In making this deposit the depositor hereby assents to the foregoing conditions.

Figure 6-3
Power of Attorney Form

✓·	DEMAND ACCOUNT
	SAVINGS ACCOUNT
ACCEPTED BY *(gm)*	OFFICE 17

𝔎𝔫𝔬𝔴 𝔞𝔩𝔩 𝔐𝔢𝔫 𝔟𝔶 𝔱𝔥𝔢𝔰𝔢 𝔓𝔯𝔢𝔰𝔢𝔫𝔱𝔰

THAT_____ I, TERRENCE O'NEIL _____

do make, constitute and appoint_____ GABRIEL ROMERO _____

_____ true and lawful attorney for____ me ____ and in____ my ____

name:

1. To withdraw all or any part of the balance in_____ my _____

account number 2345678 ____ in

THE INSTITUTE NATIONAL BANK

by drawing checks, if a demand account; or, by giving the required prior notice and by executing the proper withdrawal order or receipt if a savings account.

2. To endorse notes, checks, drafts or bills of exchange which may require____ my ____ endorsement for deposit as cash in, or for collection by said bank.

3. To do all lawful acts requisite for effecting any of the above premises; hereby ratifying and confirming all that the said attorney shall do therein by virtue of these presents.

This power of attorney shall continue in force until due notice of the revocation thereof shall be given in writing.

*In witness whereof*____ I ____ have hereunto set____ my ____ hand and seal this____ 10th ____ day of ____ April ____,
one thousand nine hundred and____ seventy-nine ____

SIGNED, SEALED AND DELIVERED
IN THE PRESENCE OF

George W. Williams *Terrance O'Neil*

complete claim, free of any complications, to any and all funds that are in the account. Both the bank and the parties to the account should understand that state laws may govern this relationship. In some states, the survivor must pay all state taxes on the account balance before the bank is allowed to permit withdrawals from the account.

It is also possible to establish a joint checking account that does not carry rights of survivorship. Such accounts are called **tenants-in-common** relationships. They usually require that both parties must sign checks or other documents addressed to the bank.

In those states with community property laws, banks must be governed by the laws applying to joint accounts. The foregoing general information must then be modified accordingly.

Proprietorship Accounts and Fictitious Names

It is a common practice for individuals to own and operate businesses under names other than their own. To identify the nature of his business in the minds of his customers, Harry Cole may devise some eye-catching, easily remembered trade name, or he may simply choose to have the business known as Harry's Travel Agency. An individual who operates a business as its sole owner is a **proprietor**, and the business is then known as a **proprietorship**.

If the proprietorship is being operated by Harry Cole under his own name, a bank would simply require identification, references, and signature cards in order to open an account for him. However, when a fictitious name such as Harry's Travel Agency is being used, it is essential that the link between the owner and that trade name be legally established.

For this reason, many states require that a proprietor who uses a fictitious name register it with state or county authorities. The bank should obtain a copy of this form, which is usually called a Business Certificate or Certificate of Registration of Trade Name (see Figure 6-4), and file it permanently. The term "D/B/A" (doing business as) is often used in connection with this type of relationship; that is, Harry Cole *is* Harry's Travel Agency and is conducting a business under that name. Therefore, he can sign checks on an account in the business name, can endorse checks on that basis, can enter into legal contracts using the fictitious name, and can sue or be sued as a business entity.

101

Figure 6-4
Business Certificate

𝔅usiness 𝔠ertificate

I HEREBY CERTIFY *that I am conducting or transacting business under the name or designation* of PRIDE INSTALLERS

at 4200 Trinity Place
City or Town of New York   *County of* New York   *State of New York*

My full name is Solomon S. Miller
and I reside at 6200 Riverdale Avenue, Bronx, New York 10471

I FURTHER CERTIFY *that I am the successor in interest to*

the person or persons heretofore using such name or names to carry on or conduct or transact business.

IN WITNESS WHEREOF, *I have this* tenth *day of* June *1979, made and signed this certificate.*

COUNTY
CLERK'S
SEAL

Solomon S. Miller

- Print or type name
- If under 21 years of age, state "I am _____ years of age."

STATE OF NEW YORK
COUNTY OF   New York   } *ss.:*

On this tenth *day of* June *1979, before me personally appeared*

Solomon S. Miller

to me known to me to be the individual described in and who executed the foregoing certificate, and he thereupon has duly acknowledged to me that he executed the same.

NOTARY
STAMP

J. Smith

Notary Public

Partnership Accounts

When two or more individuals enter into a business venture together, a **partnership** is frequently formed. The business may be operated under the names of the individual partners (e.g., Mitchell and Wilson; Brown, Walker, and Brown), or a trade name may be adopted. Partnerships are widely used in American business. Many major accounting firms, law firms, and brokerage houses are partnerships. Most states have adopted laws pertaining to the conduct of this type of business and the rights and obligations of each partner. These laws have a direct bearing on the commercial banks in their relationships with the partnership.

Typically, a legal document called a **partnership agreement** is drawn up whenever a partnership is formed or amended. It states the contributions each partner has made to the business, the nature of the business, and the proportions in which each partner will share in profits or losses. Any one member of a partnership may be empowered to act for all the others, so that the actions of one are legally binding on all.

In opening an account for a partnership, a bank should obtain signature cards showing the signatures of those who will be authorized to issue checks, apply for loans for the partnership, and otherwise deal with the bank. It should also obtain a copy of the agreement covering the partnership, either on a standard bank form or as originally executed by the partners. If the partnership is to operate under a fictitious or trade name, registration of that name with state or county authorities is required and the bank should have a copy of the registration form in its files.

Generally speaking, partnership law provides that the death of any partner terminates the partnership. However, it is also recognized that it would create a hardship and be unreasonable to all parties if the business were to be dissolved immediately. Therefore, provision is made for the business to continue and to be reorganized by the surviving partners. The rights of those survivors include the authority to handle all partnership assets, including balances on deposit with banks. The estate of a deceased partner cannot take control of a partnership bank account. Whenever death of a partner occurs, the bank of account must revise all its documents accordingly.

Corporate Accounts

The third type of business venture for which a bank may open a checking account is the **corporation**—an entirely different type of legal entity. A corporation, regardless of its size, is legally owned by its stockholders, who have contributed their capital to it and have been given shares of stock in exchange. No corporation can legally exist without stockholders. It may be as small as a husband-and-wife business or as large as one of the industrial giants with sales of many billions of dollars, but the same legal principles apply. In the first case, the husband and wife are the only stockholders; in the second, there are thousands.

Most commercial banks in the United States are chartered under the corporate format. The incorporators of a new bank contribute their capital, apply for a charter, issue shares of stock, and establish an entity under the law. One of the smallest banks may have only a handful of shareholders, often consisting of members of the family that originally founded the institution. On the other hand, the largest banks in our money market centers have 70,000 or more stockholders.

From the banking standpoint, there are essential differences between the nature of a corporation and that of other types of businesses. While the stockholders are the legal owners of the corporation, they are not usually liable for its debts. A corporation is not affected by the deaths of any stockholders or officers; legally, it can exist forever. In addition to having stockholders, corporations must also have **directors** (who are elected by the stockholders) and **officers** (who are named by the board of directors); neither of these terms is used in connection with partnership or proprietorships. A corporation has the same legal status as a person in that it can sue or be sued.

The directors, elected by the stockholders, are the active, governing body of the corporation and are responsible for the conduct of the business. They can be held responsible for negligence and for any and all acts of omission or commission. Should the corporation fail and go into bankruptcy, its directors may be sued individually or collectively for what they did or what they failed to do.

It is only through the directors of a corporation that the legal right to open and operate a bank account can be established. Therefore, the basis for all such accounts is a form known as a **corporate reso-**

lution (see Figure 6-5), a certified copy of which is filed with the bank. This legal document, signed and sealed by the corporate secretary, gives evidence that the board of directors met on a certain date, approved the opening of an account with the named bank, and authorized certain corporate officers to sign checks and borrow on behalf of the corporation. Many banks have their own standard corporate resolution forms and supply these to customers to be executed, signed, and sealed. If a corporation wishes to use its own form instead of the bank's, care must be taken to ensure that it meets all of the bank's legal requirements.

Every corporation must operate under the terms of a charter, which is granted by the state and gives the corporation its legal right to do business. A set of bylaws usually supplements the charter; these are adopted by the stockholders and describe the purposes of the corporation and the nature of the business, the duties of individually titled officers, and other business matters. In establishing a corporate account, a bank may ask for copies of the charter and bylaws of the corporation.

A corporation may be formed by two people, who then are the only stockholders and are also the officers and directors. On the other hand, a major industrial firm may have hundreds of corporate officers: a chairman, a president, vice chairmen, executive and senior vice presidents, vice presidents, a treasurer, a secretary, a comptroller, and numerous assistants to these titles. The fact that an individual has been given an official title by the corporation does not necessarily give him or her the right to transact business with the bank on the corporation's behalf. Only those individuals designated by the board of directors can do so. Therefore, whenever the corporation resolution and/or bylaws mention official titles, the bank must have on file the names and the signatures of those who hold those titles and who will be conducting business with the bank on the corporation's behalf. The signature cards on file for every corporate account must show the title and specimen signature of each designated officer or other authorized signer. If the corporation names new officers who are authorized to deal with the bank, or if an existing signer dies, resigns, or retires, new signature cards must be obtained. An official notice of the election of new officers should be executed by the corporate secretary under seal and filed with the bank.

Figure 6-5
Corporate Resolution

CORPORATE RESOLUTION

ACCOUNT NUMBER	7764625
OFFICE	20
ACCEPTED BY	(JM)
DATE	5-17-19XX

Anchor Broadcasting Co. Inc.
(account title)

"RESOLVED, that an account in the name of this Corporation be established or maintained with the INSTITUTE NATIONAL BANK and that all checks, drafts, notes, or other orders for the payment of money drawn on or payable against said account shall be signed by any __two (2)__ (indicate number) person or persons from time to time holding the following offices of this Corporation.

President   Treasurer   _____

Secretary   _____   _____

Indicate title only; not individual's name.

FURTHER RESOLVED, that said INSTITUTE NATIONAL BANK is hereby authorized and directed to pay all checks, drafts, notes and orders so signed whether payable to bearer, or to the order of any person, firm or corporation, or to the order of any person signing the same.

The undersigned Secretary of __Anchor Broadcasting Co. Inc.__ (name of corporation) hereby certifies that the above is a true and correct copy of a resolution regularly adopted by the Board of Directors of the Corporation at a duly called meeting of the Board held on __5-10-19XX__ (date), at which a quorum was present and voting throughout; and that said resolution is presently in full force and effect.

I further certify that the persons named below are those duly elected or appointed to the Corporate Office or capacity set forth opposite their respective names.

NAME	TITLE
John Little	President
Arthur Burnstein	Secretary
Rose Mary Forest	Treasurer

In Witness Whereof, I have hereunto set my hand and affixed hereto the Corporate Seal of this Corporation

(Corporate Seal)

Arthur Burnstein
Secretary

Dated: May 15, 19XX

Through mergers or acquisitions, corporations often change their official names to reflect new or expanded activities. The XYZ Machine Tool Corporation, for example, may amend its existing charter (with the approval of its stockholders) or apply for a new charter so that its name becomes XYZ Industries, Inc. In this way, it publicizes the fact that it is no longer merely a tool manufacturer. Documentary evidence of the new corporate name must be certified by state authorities and furnished to the bank.

A corporation can be identified, as distinguished from other types of businesses, by its name. When it obtains its charter it is legally required to use *Inc., Corporation, Incorporated,* or *Limited* as part of its official, legal title. For this reason, every corporation is considered to be operating under a fictitious name. If Harry Cole were to apply for a corporate charter, the name of his business would have to reflect this; for example, it could become Harry's Travel Agency, *Inc.*

Fiduciary Accounts

The word **fiduciary** comes from the Latin word meaning faith or trust. It is used in banking terminology to cover a variety of relationships in which one party is handling assets and property for the benefit of another. Fiduciary accounts may be extremely simple and informal, as in the case of an account established in trust for a minor child, or far more complicated and formal, as when an executor or administrator is handling all the details of a substantial estate. Fiduciary accounts must be opened and handled with at least the same degree of care as checking accounts.

Suppose, for example, that Matilda Henderson presents herself as the relative of a newborn child and wishes to open an account on the child's behalf, with herself as trustee. Her identity is subject to the usual checks; however, her legal authority is self-established, for she is voluntarily creating a relationship for the benefit of the infant, who cannot execute any legal documents giving her the right to do so. The tendency among banks is to handle these **informal trusts** (also called **"Totten trusts"**) without trying to obtain detailed legal documentation.

On the other hand, if James Wilson, according to the terms of the will of a deceased person, has been made the **executor** of an estate, he is responsible for certain actions affecting that estate. The bank's approach to opening an account for him in that capacity will be quite different from Mrs. Henderson's case. As executor, he is responsible for determining the total value of the estate, paying all debts, taxes, and claims, and then distributing the remainder. The bank must obtain some proof of his right to act for the estate, in addition to signature cards. Similarly, if an individual has been appointed a **trustee**, **guardian**, or **conservator** by the action of a court or the signing of a legal agreement, the bank of account would have to obtain the necessary documents establishing this authority—and again, signature cards would be necessary.

The questions of identity and legal right as they apply to fiduciary accounts clearly depend on the type of account being opened. Many states have adopted the **Uniform Fiduciaries Act**, which contains the provisions that legally apply to fiduciary accounts and gives banks guidelines on the type and extent of documentation that should be obtained. It also outlines the steps the banks should take in maintaining and policing these accounts.

Examples of the documents that a bank might need in the case of a formal, complex fiduciary relationship would include a certified copy of the court decree that appointed the fiduciary, letters testamentary, or a copy of the agreement that gave one party the right to handle the property of another.

Public Funds Accounts

Thousands of types and levels of government authorities and agencies must receive and disburse funds on behalf of the communities and citizens they serve. The Internal Revenue Service collects taxes for the federal government and issues refund checks; a turnpike authority collects tolls, pays suppliers, and uses checks to pay employees; a local government receives revenue-sharing payments from Washington and makes its own disbursements. Government entities have debt service, payroll, and public assistance payments to make. All these activities require bank accounts. Because in most instances the funds involved are regarded as belonging to the public and are to be used for the public's benefit, the general term **public funds accounts** is used to describe these relationships. They are opened for any department, agency, authority, or other entity of any federal, state, or local government or political subdivision (e.g., a school district).

The unit of government must officially appoint the banks with which it wishes to open accounts. State and local laws usually prescribe the procedures that must be followed in each case. The bank that opens a public funds account must be guided by these laws.

Generally speaking, all such accounts must be secured by specific, segregated assets in the bank's possession; that is, the bank must set aside U.S. government obligations or other assets of unquestioned value as a form of collateral protecting the deposits. This provides an additional guarantee that public funds will never be lost. If the bank does not have in its possession, or cannot obtain, enough government securities or other satisfactory assets that can be pledged, it must decline to accept a new public funds account.

Informal Relationships

The final category of checking accounts is an extremely broad one that includes accounts established for social or fraternal groups, unincorporated or other not-for-profit associations, and other informal types of relationships. A bowling league accumulates funds during the year through members' payments of dues. An employee group raises money to hold a testimonial or retirement dinner. A community committee is formed to accept contributions on behalf of a family that has suffered some calamity. Such groups can hardly be expected to provide the bank with legal, formal documents and agreements.

Because such organizations are not listed in state or local government records, the bank that establishes an **informal account** must rely largely on its knowledge of the parties with whom it will be dealing. Signature cards obviously are needed. Beyond that, each situation will dictate what additional letters, agreements, or special documents should be obtained. The bank's legal staff should be consulted to ensure proper documentation.

TIME DEPOSITS

Although the intention of the savings or time depositor is quite different from that of the checking account customer, and while the impact on the bank of the time or savings deposit is also different, the bank still must establish, beyond reasonable doubt, the *legal right* and the *identity* of the parties with whom it is dealing. Basic requirements cannot be relaxed simply because a savings account is being opened or a CD issued. Many of the frauds that have been perpetrated on banks began with the opening of a modest savings account that was taken for granted and on which the bank's standard procedures were not followed. Like its demand deposit counterpart, the savings account or time deposit creates a contractual agreement between customer and bank. The bank must be satisfied with the agreement, and it must know who is authorized to withdraw or receive funds. The customer must be aware of the terms and conditions of the relationship.

Savings Accounts

As mentioned earlier, savings accounts were part of the "retail" type of business that commercial banks traditionally neglected, and the funds represented by savings were almost exclusively deposited with thrift institutions. The money set aside by individuals for some future purpose—education, travel, vacation—with the objective of steady growth and the benefit of earned interest did not represent the type of deposit that commercial banks wanted to attract, and it is interesting to note that this attitude existed in early colonial times and prevailed until the period immediately following World War II. Many savings banks were opened in New England in the late seventeenth and early eighteenth centuries to encourage thrift and provide depositories for the small saver, and those savings banks operated side-by-side with the commercial banks of that period. Similarly, the savings and loan associations came into being to fill two needs that the commercial banks had neglected: They accepted deposits from individuals of modest means and used those funds to extend home mortgage credit.

In the years since World War II, the emphasis on savings accounts at the commercial banks has increased as the banks have come to realize that these accounts represent a valuable source of funds and give the individual depositor additional convenience. Savings accounts also constitute more stable relationships—that is, they do not fluctuate rapidly as demand deposits do. Because they are less volatile and can be expected to stay with the bank for longer periods of time, savings account balances traditionally have been used by both commercial banks and thrift institutions as the basis for long-term loans such as home mortgages.

Savings accounts are typically opened for individuals; jointly, for two or more depositors, with either party permitted to make deposits and withdrawals at any time; for fiduciaries; and for unincorporated or nonprofit organizations. In addition, the Federal Reserve changed its regulations in 1975 and allowed corporations to open savings accounts with member banks, with a limit of $150,000 on these corporate savings accounts. This action was taken to make commercial banks more competitive with thrift institutions, since the latter had been offering savings accounts to corporations for many years.

In every case, at the time the savings account is opened the identity of the customer(s) must be clearly established, signature cards must be obtained so that all requests for payment of funds can be authenticated, and any necessary supporting documents must be filed. As an additional safeguard, many banks ask the depositor to supply some highly personal piece of identifying data, such as mother's maiden name. The "scrambled signature" system has also become widely used. This system builds a special pattern into a camera lens so that the depositor's signature is distorted and cannot be read by the naked eye. When a withdrawal slip or other document is presented, it is inserted into a camera equipped with this type of lens so that a comparison can be made.

Traditionally, the identifying characteristic of each savings account was the passbook. Many customers still insist on being given a passbook as proof of the existence of the account; they insist on seeing each deposit, withdrawal, and interest credit posted. Of course, it is gratifying to a customer to see the steady growth of an account by looking at a passbook, but with today's technology the passbook itself is entirely obsolete. Modern automation methods make it possible for banks to dispense with passbooks completely and to place the entire savings account function on computer. Many banks have installed on-line systems so that any teller at any branch has access to immediate information on the status of an account. Instead of passbooks, the bank provides each savings account customer with quarterly statements showing every transaction, including interest credits. Some banks include this information on the same computer statement that shows checking account activity.

Many of the safeguards and procedures discussed with regard to checking accounts also apply here. When accepting deposits to a savings account, tellers must watch for noncash items, examine currency to detect any counterfeits, and insist on proper endorsement of all deposited checks so that the bank is protected as a holder in due course.

Signature cards govern the operation of savings accounts as they do demand deposits. The signature card actually constitutes the contract between the bank and its depositor. Figure 6-6 shows a specimen card for savings accounts.

Certificates of Deposit

As the banks' competitors have become more numerous, more aggressive, and more successful, federal regulatory authorities have attempted to help by giving the banks authority to offer an increasingly wide range of time deposits. It is useful here to restate the basic difference between savings and time deposits: The former have no fixed maturity date, whereas each type of time deposit carries a specified term. Time deposits grow in importance in the commercial banking system each year and represent the largest component of the banks' total deposit structure, as seen in the figures in Table 6-1.

The most important single development in the change of the deposit structure from a demand to a time base occurred in 1961, when the **negotiable certificate of deposit** was introduced. This instrument is commonly referred to as the CD and has displayed the most rapid growth of any instrument in the history of American banking. In mid-1982 over $136 billion in large CDs (i.e., those issued for $100,000 or more) had been placed with the nation's large commercial banks. The figure of $136 billion includes *only* those CDs issued by banks that had domestic assets of $750 million or more; additional billions of dollars in CDs were outstanding at smaller commercial banks and at thrift institutions.

No interest rate ceiling exists on negotiable CDs issued for $100,000 or more; the rate quoted to a customer depends entirely on money market conditions and on the bank's particular need for funds on a given day.

The basic certificate of deposit had existed in the banking system for many years and was used as a convenient instrument for business or personal investing. *Any* CD is an official receipt issued by a bank, stating that a specified sum of money has been left with that bank,

Figure 6-6
Sample Signature Card
FRONT

CHECKING-ACCOUNT NAME   ☐ CK STORAGE   ACCOUNT NO.
                                                       ☐ BONUS CK
                                                       ☐ YES CHECK

This agreement concerns a CHECKING account with us. This is an ☐ INDIVIDUAL ☐ JOINT ACCOUNT. The words "you" and "your" mean everyone who has signed this agreement. "We," "our," and "us" mean First National Bank.
WE MAY:
Handle your deposits according to our usual rules for this kind of service which may change from time to time. Charge our usual fees which may change from time to time. Take funds from the account to pay our expenses and lawyers' fees if there is a dispute about your account, but only if the dispute is not our fault. Take funds from the account to pay any signer's debts to us even if we have collateral for the debts. Endorse checks for you which we receive for deposit. Deposit all checks payable to any signer of this agreement when endorsed by any of you or one for the other. Pay out funds with any of the signatures below. But we may require all your signatures if there are conflicts among you. ☐ MAIL ☐ HOLD all your statements and other notices. Mail them to you if you do not call for them in 30 days. If they are returned to us undelivered, we may destroy them after 2 years. We may do any of the things listed above without giving you notice.
YOU UNDERSTAND:
We keep our records by microfilm or other copying. If one of your checks cannot be copied at reasonable cost, we do not have to accept the check or pay it. We will send you bank statements and may send you cancelled checks. You promise to look at them promptly and let us know if there is any mistake or anything wrong. We are relying on the information and promises in this agreement. Each of you must pay in full if we suffer any loss because the information is wrong or the promises are broken, but we can never collect more than the amount of our loss and our lawyers' fees. You or we can close this account at any time.
IF ONE OF YOU DIES:
The other signers will let us know in writing immediately. The other signers can withdraw as much of the funds as the law allows. If there is more than one signer of this agreement, each one will keep all the promises.
☐ ATM Card: You have asked that we issue you an ATM Card to access our automatic teller machines. You have received a copy of the ATM Agreement and agree to follow its rules.

_____   _____   _____
Signature (1)   Date   Social Security No.

_____   _____   _____
Signature (2)   Date   Social Security No.

BACK

MAIL
ADDRESS _____
                                                                          /   /
      CITY   STATE   ZIP CODE   DATE
EMPLOYER   POSITION   PHONE
(1) _____   _____   _____ BUS. _____

                                                                   HOME _____
(2) _____   _____   _____ BUS. _____

                                                                   HOME _____
   MOTHER'S MAIDEN NAME   MOTHER'S BIRTHPLACE
(1) _____   (1) _____
(2) _____   (2) _____
   BANK REFERENCES   FROM   TO
(1) _____   _____ _____   _____ _____
                                          MO.   YR.   MO.   YR.
(2) _____   _____ _____   _____ _____
                                          MO.   YR.   MO.   YR.

FOR BANK USE ONLY
I.D. TYPE _____ NO. _____ UNI-CK. _____

ROUTING _____ SERVICE CHG. _____ CYCLE _____ DATE OPEN _____

FED. RES. _____ DEPOSIT $_____ BON. CKG. _____ CK. STOR: _____

ATM CARD _____ SAVINGS NO. _____ OPEN BY _____ REV. BY _____

Table 6-1
Deposit Structure: All U.S.
Commercial Banks

Category	Dollar Amount in Billions
Demand Deposits	315.4
Savings Deposits	227.6
Time Deposits	701.0
Total Deposits	1244.0

SOURCE: *Federal Reserve Bulletin*, June 1982, p. A17

usually for a stated period of time at a specified rate of interest. However, the CDs issued before 1961 were nonnegotiable; the holder could not readily transfer his rights to the instrument prior to maturity. The change to a *negotiable* type of certificate transformed American banking. Corporate treasurers, affluent individuals, financial officers for institutions and agencies of government, and the public in general quickly realized that they could turn surplus funds over to their banks and receive, in exchange, a certificate that was a guaranteed obligation of the issuing institution, was completely or partially insured by FDIC, bore interest at a higher rate than passbook savings, and could easily be transferred to another party before maturity. A broad secondary market exists for negotiable CDs, so that the holder is never forced to hold one until its maturity date.

Largely because of the huge amount of CDs that have been issued by commercial banks, interest expense has become by far the most significant single cost factor in their annual operations. It exceeds such other expenses as salaries and wages, benefits, taxes, and equipment and occupancy costs. It is now the largest, fastest growing, and least controllable expense item. Customers today realize that banks must depend on them for deposits and that the banks are willing to pay a competitive price to obtain the funds they need. The ratio of time to demand deposits climbs each year, and the banks' interest expense rises accordingly. Table 6-2 shows this trend.

Money Market Certificates

In 1978 federal regulatory authorities allowed commercial banks and thrift institutions to offer, for the first time, a new instrument

Table 6-2
Interest Expense at Commercial Banks

Year	Interest Expense As a Percent of Total Operating Expenses
1975	45.5
1976	49.5
1977	49.3
1978	51.1
1979	54.3
1980	57.3
1981	61.0

SOURCE: "Profitability of All Insured Commercial Banks, 1979," *Federal Reserve Bulletin*, September 1980, p. 691; and "Profitability of Insured Commercial Banks," *Federal Reserve Bulletin*, August 1982, p. 463.

called the **money market certificate** (MMC). As of December 1982, MMCs required a minimum investment of $10,000, with a 26-week maturity, and were not negotiable. The interest rate offered each week changes according to the rates on the most recently issued 6-month U.S. Treasury bills. Purchasers of MMCs are guaranteed the interest rate that was in effect at the time of purchase. These certificates proved immediately popular and are widely offered by commercial banks today as a means of attracting deposits.

All-Savers Certificates

As of October 1, 1981, all financial institutions were authorized to begin offering federally insured savings certificates on which the interest—unlike that on other forms of savings and time deposits—was *exempt* from federal income tax, up to $1,000 for an individual or $2,000 for a married couple filing jointly. The All-Savers Certificates were introduced in an effort to encourage individual savings and carried the following provisions and restrictions:

- The certificates could be issued throughout the year 1982; authorization after 1982 would take place through congressional action.

- The certificates were issued for 1 year and carried substantial penalties for early withdrawal.

- Interest rates were equal to 70 percent of the yield on the most recent issue of 1-year Treasury bills.

- Interest income from these certificates was exempt from federal income tax and might also be exempt from state and local taxes, according to the laws of those entities.

Financial institutions held a total of $42.5 billion in All-Savers Certificates at year-end 1981, of which commercial banks held $17.4 billion.[1]

Other Time Deposits

In their quest for additional deposits, commercial banks now offer a wide variety of other forms of time deposits. These include time accounts with fixed ceiling interest rates and those with variable rates. The fixed-rate category includes time deposits for 7 to 89 days; 90 days to 1 year; 1 to 2 years; 2 to 2½ years; 2½ to 4 years; 4 to 6 years; 6 to 8 years; and 8 years or more.

Banks are also authorized to offer variable-rate time deposits for 91 days, 6 months, 12 months, and 30 to 41 months. In many cases, minimum deposits are specified for the various forms of time deposits that can be offered.

Keogh and IRA Relationships

Since the era of the Great Depression in America, increasing emphasis has been placed on the need for some form of retirement security to protect every category of worker. The federal social security program covers some 150 million individuals, and about 30 million workers also enjoy the benefits of pension plans established by their employers. However, millions of Americans did not have the advantages of private pension plans because the firms they worked for did not provide such benefits; the self-employed were at a similar disadvantage. To remedy this, Congress enacted the Employee Retirement Security Act in 1962 and ERISA (the Employee Retirement Income Security Act) in 1974. These acts allowed qualified individuals to establish their own personal, tax-sheltered plans with banks or other financial intermediaries.

The two types of plans are known as **Keogh** accounts for the self-employed and **Individual Retirement Accounts** (IRAs). Originally, IRAs were available *only* to those who had employment income not covered by a qualified pension or retirement plan. In 1981, new federal laws expanded the eligibility criteria for IRAs and also increased the maximum allowable annual contributions to Keogh accounts. The salient features are now as follows:

- All self-employed persons can contribute up to 15 percent of annual income to a Keogh plan, with a maximum of $15,000 per year.

- Individuals who have income not covered by a qualified pension or retirement plan may place $2,000 per year in an IRA, or $2,250 if the spouse is not employed. As of January 1, 1982, IRAs can also be used by individuals who *do* have a qualified pension or retirement plan. The same limits on annual contributions apply. Therefore, an individual may have *both* an IRA and a pension plan.

- All money contributed to a Keogh or IRA is deductible for federal tax purposes. Interest accruing on that money is exempt from taxes until withdrawn.

- The minimum age for withdrawals is 59½. Withdrawals must begin during the year when the individual attains the age of 70½. Payouts from IRA and Keogh accounts then represent taxable income.

In addition to thrift institutions, brokerage firms and insurance companies compete aggressively for Keogh and IRA activity.

Effective December 1, 1981, all depository institutions were authorized to offer time deposits with no interest-rate ceilings for use in connection with Keogh and IRA accounts.

Club Accounts

Various types of club accounts are offered by commercial banks to assist individuals who wish to set aside funds regularly throughout the year. The purpose may be to provide for the holiday season (Christmas and Hanukkah Club accounts), for a vacation, or for educational expenses. These club accounts are relatively simple and informal.

Club account customers usually execute a signature card and agree to make regular deposits. The bank mails or delivers a check for the balance at the end of the specified period. Interest may be paid on all deposits, at the option of the bank. The flow of money from banks to consumers during the Christmas/Hanukkah season contributes to the vast increase in spending that occurs in the American economy at that time of year.

LEGAL RESTRICTIONS ON DEPOSITS

As part of the overall pattern of regulation and supervision of banking, it has been customary for state and federal authorities to draw specific lines of demarcation separating the time deposit from the demand deposit functions and to place restrictions on the payment of interest to customers. This has been especially true since the era of the Great Depression. Before that, it was common practice for banks to offer interest on demand deposits. This led to aggressive competition that often took the form of bidding wars, so banks found their interest expense steadily increasing despite the fact that they were not offering time deposits or savings accounts to any appreciable extent.

The increased interest expense could be offset only by making loans and investments to maximize income. The greater the emphasis that was placed on increasing income, the more likely it was that normal credit standards would be lowered and loans of lesser quality granted.

When the economy collapsed during the Depression, banks found themselves holding a great many worthless promissory notes representing substandard loans they had approved. This cause-and-effect cycle of paying interest on checking accounts and making lower quality loans to derive additional interest income was a major factor in the wave of bank failures in the early 1930s.[2] Each federal and state agency concerned with commercial banking reacted to this problem by establishing various regulations regarding payment of interest to depositors.

Since 1933, Federal Reserve Regulation Q has been the principal control over interest payments at member banks. The Glass-Steagall Banking Act of 1933 expressly prohibited payment of interest on demand deposits. The Fed then implemented Regulation Q, which sets a maximum rate of interest that member banks may pay on savings and time deposits. Any member bank that wishes to offer a lower rate may do so, but it will undoubtedly find that this places it at a competitive disadvantage.

Under the terms of the Monetary Control Act of 1980, Regulation Q is to be phased out by March 31, 1986. The Depository Institutions Deregulation Committee (DIDC) established by that act must meet at least once each quarter to decide on interim steps.

Regulations of the Federal Deposit Insurance Corporation, practically identical with those in Regulation Q, apply to all insured non-member banks, including mutual savings banks. In the relatively few cases of banks that belong to neither the Fed nor the FDIC, individual state laws apply, and they are very similar to those of the two regulatory agencies. The substance of all these regulations is as follows:

- No savings or time deposit is payable on demand. Only in the NOW account can a customer execute a demand instrument against such a deposit.

- Any bank has the legal right to insist on advance notice of any withdrawal from a savings account. This preserves the nature of the relationship as not being payable on demand. Of course, banks do not regularly exercise their right to advance notice in actual daily practice; the important point is that they *could* do so at any time, as long as they applied the same rules to all depositors without discrimination of any kind.

- A contract exists in the case of all time deposits, under the terms of which the customer agrees to leave funds with the bank for a specified period of time. If the customer finds it necessary to withdraw funds before the maturity date, a substantial penalty *must* be assessed. Figure 6-7 shows the type of statement to cus-

Figure 6-7
Sample Customer Disclosure Explaining
Federal Regulations

C A U T I O N
There are substantial penalties
if you make an early withdrawal
from a Certificate

F.D.I.C. Regulations say that you may not withdraw all
or any part of your money from a certificate account
before the maturity date, except with the consent of the
Bank. The Bank's consent may be given only at the time
you ask to withdraw money. If the Bank does give its
consent, it must impose a penalty. The F.D.I.C. Regulation says:

Penalty for Early Withdrawals. Where a time deposit
with an original maturity of one year or less, or any
portion thereof, is paid before maturity , a depositor
shall forfeit an amount at least equal to three months
of interest earned or that could have been earned, on
the amount withdrawn at the nominal (simple interest)
rate being paid on the deposit, regardless of the length
of time the funds withdrawn have remained on deposit. Where a time deposit with an original maturity
of more than one year, or any portion thereof, is paid
before maturity, a depositor shall forfeit an amount at
least equal to six months of interest earned, or that
could have been earned, on the amount withdrawn at
the nominal (simple interest) rate being paid on the
deposit, regardless of the length of time the funds
withdrawn have remained on deposit.

In other words, the minimum penalty is the loss of **3**
months interest if the certificate is for 1 year or less, and
loss of 6 months interest if the certificate is for more
than 1 year. Payment of the penalty may result in a reduction of the principal amount you originally
deposited.

This penalty provision does not apply in the event of the
death of an owner of a time deposit, or to certain pre-
mature withdrawals of time deposits of an Individual
Retirement Account.

Member: FDIC

tomers that makes this clear. It must also be noted that a bank has the legal right to refuse payment of any time deposit before its stated maturity date, if it wishes to make this a matter of policy.

The increased scope and complexity of time deposit relationships has led to a corresponding increase in the detailed regulations regarding interest that may be paid on each type.

Tax Reporting

As the amount of interest paid to bank depositors has steadily increased, the Internal Revenue Service has naturally become concerned over the reporting of this interest as income. Therefore, *all* commercial banks, thrift institutions, credit unions, and other organizations that pay interest of $10 or more to any recipient in a calendar year must report that payment to IRS. Payments must be identified by the recipient's social security or corporate identification number. The dollar amount of interest paid must be clearly shown, and a copy of the reporting form, known as a Form 1099, must be sent to the recipient of the interest as a reminder that the amount must be shown on that recipient's tax return.

Legislation passed by Congress in mid-1982 requires that banks paying interest to customers and corporate payers of dividends *must* withhold required taxes before making the actual disbursements. Recipients who claim an exemption from the provisions of this legislation must file an appropriate form with the bank or corporation.

SUMMARY

The initial meeting between a representative of the bank and a new customer sets the tone for all their future dealings. If a favorable impression is created at the outset, the image of the bank is enhanced and the new customer is likely to tell others about the reception and treatment he or she received. On the other hand, if the initial encounter leaves a poor impression in the customer's mind, it is unlikely that the bank will ever improve its image as far as that customer is concerned.

At the same time, the bank can never lose sight of the fact that the same initial contact may involve the establishing of a legal contract.

The desire to make a good impression on the customer at the outset must be secondary to the need for doing whatever is appropriate to protect the bank. The identity of the customer, the nature of the relationship, the customer's legal right to enter into a contract, and the legal restrictions and bank policies that apply to each account must be clearly established and understood at the time an account is opened. The bank must know at all times with whom it is dealing and from whom it can properly accept instructions pertaining to any phase of the handling of the account. At the same time, the customer must be made aware of any conditions or restrictions that apply. Banks can avoid a great deal of trouble by exercising diligence and care at the start of a relationship as well as throughout the life of that relationship.

QUESTIONS FOR DISCUSSION

1. What benefits or advantages do credit unions and money market funds offer to a customer?

2. How can a bank justify demanding identification and references from a person who merely wants to deposit cash to open an account?

3. What is the difference between the principle of identity and the principle of legal right or authority?

4. What rights does an attorney-in-fact possess in the handling of a principal's account? What document conveys those rights? How long do the rights last?

5. What is the difference between proprietorships and partnerships?

6. Identify the three groups that are involved in the operation of a corporation.

7. What is the essential nature of a fiduciary account?

8. What forms or documents should be obtained in connection with each of the following types of new account relationships?

   - A fictitious-name proprietorship

- A partnership
- A corporation
- A church society
- An agency of government

9. What is the difference between a savings deposit and a time deposit?

10. What are the characteristics of money market certificates?

11. What benefits were offered to individuals through the introduction of All-Savers Certificates?

12. What is the difference between Keogh accounts and IRAs?

13. What tax reporting problems do savings and time deposits create for banks?

NOTES

1. "Banks' Share of All-Savers Revised Up," *American Banker*, June 3, 1982, p. 2.

2. Paul S. Nadler, *Commercial Banking in the Economy*, New York, Random House, 1968, p. 61.

Suggested Readings

American Bankers Association. *Developing Bank Services* (Seminar). Washington, D.C.: American Bankers Association, 1982.

American Bankers Association. *Knowing the Competition* (Seminar). Washington, D.C.: American Bankers Association, 1982.

American Bankers Association. *New Accounts* (Seminar). Washington, D.C.: American Bankers Association, 1980.

American Bankers Association. *New Deposit Instruments* (Seminar). Washington, D.C.: American Bankers Association, 1981.

American Bankers Association. *Selling Bank Services* (Seminar). Washington, D.C.: American Bankers Association, 1980.

Bank Administration Institute. *Opening New Accounts.* Rolling Meadows, Illinois: Bank Administration Institute, 1975.

Compton, Eric N. *Savings and Time Deposit Banking.* Washington, D.C.: American Bankers Association, 1982.

Hamilton, Dee. *Successful Business Development for the Community Bank.* Washington, D.C.: American Bankers Association, 1978.

Herrick, Tracy G. *Bank Analysts Handbook.* New York: John Wiley & Sons, 1978.

Staats, William F. *Money and Banking.* Washington, D.C.: American Bankers Association, 1982.

Chapter 7

Paying Teller Functions

LEARNING OBJECTIVES

After completing this chapter, you will have an understanding of

- the difference between *paying* and *cashing* checks;
- the tests that can be applied in paying;
- the risk a teller assumes when cashing;
- the actions tellers should take during holdup attempts; and
- the importance of a bank's tellers in their dealings with individuals who present checks.

Whenever a teller is handed any check and is asked to give coin and currency in exchange for it, two delicate factors are involved: customer goodwill, on the one hand, and sound banking policies and

125

practices on the other. Every teller is expected to be fast and accurate, particularly on those hectic days when lines are long and tempers short. The customer who presents a check to a teller, only to be told that there is some problem that requires time and effort to resolve, is especially prone to complain about being needlessly questioned and delayed. All too often, the customer does not understand why a particular check cannot be immediately converted into legal tender and why it requires the approval of an officer or other authorized person. A large segment of the population believes that any commercial bank is the logical place to present any check.

To enhance its public image, a bank might wish to do everything possible to shorten the lines of waiting customers and to hand over coin and currency, in exchange for checks, with a minimum of delay and inconvenience. However, if it neglects any of the basic steps in the decision-making process and fails to appreciate the risk that may be involved, losses will invariably result. All tellers must understand the serious responsibilities they assume whenever they handle the paying and cashing of checks.

PAYING AND CASHING CHECKS

The use of the two verbs, pay and cash, is intentional. To the general public, one of them would have sufficed; if people are asked why they are going to the bank, they will invariably answer that they need to have a check *cashed.* The likelihood is that they have never, in their entire history of dealing with banks, said that they want to have a check *paid.* In fact, there is a world of legal and technical difference between the two terms, and every teller must be aware of that difference.

Paying a check is a legal obligation of the drawee bank if all tests and requirements are met. *Cashing* a check is a service that is performed as a courtesy or accommodation. Banks are legally required to pay checks; there is no obligation of any kind requiring them to cash checks. While the two terms may be misunderstood by the public, they should never be misunderstood by a bank. Each of the two terms involves different rules and different risks.

Paying Checks

A check is not money but is a claim to money; it is an order to pay, addressed to the drawee. In Chapter 9, the point will be made that *nine* tests can be applied to determine whether a check should be honored; at the teller's window, an on-us check can be subjected to all nine of these tests, and if the answers to the questions raised by those tests are satisfactory, the drawee bank must honor the instructions given to it and give coin and currency in exchange for it. The Uniform Commercial Code specifically mentions that under these circumstances the check in question has been legally *paid*. While it is true that the check will eventually have to be processed through bookkeeping, the funds it represents have already been paid out. Therefore, the process of paying a check is equivalent to posting it to an account.

This type of situation most commonly involves an individual checking account. Depositors regard the funds on deposit with a bank as immediately convertible into cash. When the need for funds arises, they issue checks (often payable to "cash") and present them to tellers. This ease of conversion again illustrates the point that coin and currency and checkable deposits are treated on the same basis when the nation's money supply is being calculated.

In examining a check, payable to cash or to the named party presenting it and presented to its drawee bank, a teller can apply the nine tests referred to previously, making sure that the check is drawn on an open account that has a sufficient available balance; that the drawer's signature is both genuine and authorized; that the check is properly dated and has not been altered; that there is no stop-payment on it; that there is no "hold" on the account; and that the check has been properly endorsed. In this situation, the teller has ready access to all the necessary data and the decision is relatively easy to make. The use of on-line terminal systems, in which tellers' windows are directly connected to the bank's computer, assists in this process.

Paying checks is further simplified and expedited through the use of personalized identification cards, usually containing the customer's signature and account number. A photograph of the depositor may be included. These cards are particularly valuable at banks that operate a network of branches. A customer can maintain a personal account at one branch and cash personal checks drawn on that account at any other branch without having to obtain official approval. The same cards may also be used to identify bank customers to merchants, thus helping to facilitate purchases for them.

Legally, checks payable to cash are bearer instruments and are presumed to belong to the person who presents them for encashment. A teller who is presented with such a check has every right to ask that it be endorsed at the window. The endorsement provides the only valid record of where the funds went.

Cashing Checks

When a teller *pays* a check, his or her bank is the drawee and all the necessary information is available so that a decision can be made. In paying the check, the teller is following the maker's exact, written instructions. This is not the case in *cashing* checks.

On any business day, large volumes of payroll and dividend checks, public assistance and tax refund checks, and simple personal checks are presented to tellers with the request that they be cashed. The verb *cashed* is used in this case because the checks in question are drawn on other banks. Tellers assume a far greater risk in giving coin and currency in exchange for these checks, simply because all the necessary information regarding them is not readily available. The teller has no way of determining if the account on which the check is drawn is open and cannot verify the maker's signature. He or she has no knowledge of a stop-payment order that may have been placed on the item, or of any "hold" that exists on the account. Perhaps most important, the teller is entirely unaware of the balance in the maker's account; it may be insufficient, or the check may be drawn against uncollected funds. The teller can *only* examine it for correct date, alteration, and proper endorsement.

Because of this lack of information, checks are cashed only when there is a valid reason for doing so and when the teller is satisfied that the bank will be able to recover the amount if necessary. The payee's endorsement is of prime importance in this respect. It makes the paying bank a holder in due course. A teller who cashes a check should make sure that it is endorsed exactly as payable, and may also note, under the endorsement, the identification that was presented.

If, as stated, the risk in cashing checks is far greater than the risk incurred in paying, why do banks frequently cash checks at all? The answers lie in the need for providing services. The risks are assumed simply because there are valid reasons for doing so.

Assume, for example, that the XYZ Corporation carries its main corporate account at Bank A but also maintains a payroll account with Bank B. The corporation asks Bank A to cash payroll checks presented to it with proper employee identification and signs an agreement indemnifying Bank A against any losses. XYZ's employees are then told that they can, if they wish, cash their salary checks at Bank A. If Bank A had refused the corporation's original request for check-cashing services, it would have jeopardized the relationship with a valued customer and possibly led to the loss of an account.

In a second everyday situation, a depositor who is well known to the teller and has maintained a satisfactory account with the bank presents a check drawn on another bank and asks that it be cashed. Discretion, tact, and good judgment are the keys to this situation. The teller technically has every right to insist that the check be deposited and that the customer wait to draw against it until the funds have become collected and available. Because that legal right exists, however, does not mean that it must be automatically exercised in every case. A teller may be handed a dividend check for $25, payable to an individual who has had an account with the teller's bank for many years; because the dividend check is drawn on another bank, the teller curtly refuses to cash it. That single injudicious act, even though the teller is technically right, can destroy the good will that has been built up over a period of years. As a service to the depositor, the teller should cash the check and note the customer's account number on the back as an audit trail.

Many depositors believe that their bank account automatically means that they can cash checks against it. Obviously, from the bank's standpoint, this is not true. Cashing actually represents giving someone the use of the bank's funds and incurring risk. The bank account should be considered as the vehicle for depositing checks, not as the automatic justification for cashing checks. In some cases, banks have established and publicized a policy of allowing check cashing *only* when the party presenting an item has an available balance sufficient to cover it.

The question of tellers' authority to cash checks is obviously one that each bank must address as it sees fit. Generally, the latitude given to tellers to handle these situations reflects their length of experience and possibly their record of past performance. Dollar limits may be established for each teller who has check-cashing authority; these limits can be raised if the teller's performance warrants it. Inevitably, however, situations arise in which a person who presents a check for cashing must be referred to an officer, a customer service representative, or some other authority. If this is done tactfully, so that the individual is made aware of the reason for the referral, no ill will need be created.

In this connection, it must be explained to the party presenting the check that it is not necessarily the "goodness" of the check that is being questioned in any particular case. For example, individuals who present U.S. government checks to a convenient bank and automatically expect to receive cash for them cannot be led to believe that the maker does not have funds on deposit to cover the checks. Rather, it must be emphasized that the bank has no legal obligation whatever to cash any check. Whenever a bank agrees to give coin and currency for a check drawn on another bank—even when the check in question was issued by the U.S. Treasurer and drawn on the Federal Reserve—it does so on the basis of limited information and because there is a sound reason for doing so and a means of recovering the funds from the payee if necessary. A letter of indemnification from a business to which check-cashing privileges have been extended or a "hold" on the account of a depositor for whom a check has been cashed are examples of the protection that the bank should have if it is to render this service.

As the use of automated teller machines increases and customers use ATMs as a means of withdrawing funds directly from accounts, instances of *paying* will become less numerous. However, the problems inherent in *cashing* cannot be resolved by a machine. The good judgment and prudence of tellers will still be required, and the image of the bank created by their actions will be improved or tarnished accordingly.

HOLDUPS

In the annual crime statistics published by the Federal Bureau of Investigation, one of the most distressing figures shows the number of bank holdups that have been committed. Each FBI report shows an increase in the frequency of this type of crime, despite all that the banks have done to make holdups difficult to commit and unprofitable to the perpetrators.

Every banking office is a source of temptation to the would-be robber. This temptation is compounded when the bank has not taken the proper measures to keep tellers' supplies of coin and currency to a workable minimum or when there is some other obvious lack of proper security measures. Law enforcement agencies have repeatedly said that certain banks have virtually invited robberies to take place by ignoring the essentials of internal security.

Even when supplies of cash are rigorously controlled, however, holdup attempts still take place with alarming regularity. One basic responsibility of every bank is obviously the protection of depositors' funds; however, that protection is not the personal responsibility of each teller when lives are at stake. The general rule for tellers is that, during holdups, individual displays of heroism are *not* expected and should *not* be contemplated or encouraged. Bank robbers are unpredictable, often irrational, and frequently desperate. Tellers who put up a show of resistance during a holdup are risking not only their own personal safety but the safety of other bank personnel *and* customers as well.

Most banks are required by law to equip their premises with cameras and burglar alarms. In those neighborhoods where the number of holdups has been high, many banks have installed bullet-proof plastic shields in front of each teller's station. Many banks have armed guards on duty on the premises. Nevertheless, the teller is the first line of defense, and no type of security system can be more effective than the actions he or she takes during a holdup. Every teller training program, while stressing the fact that physical resistance is not expected, should also stress the positive actions that can be taken. These actions will materially assist the law enforcement agencies in their work. Every robbery of a bank automatically constitutes a federal offense, and tellers can help the authorities in apprehending the criminals by following certain basic procedures.

For example, tellers should make every effort to remain calm during a holdup, taking note of the physical characteristics of the bandit. Height and weight, scars, and other identifying features can be observed (see Figure 7-1). Silent alarms can be activated by a pedal or

Figure 7-1
Physical Description Form

COLOR CAUCASIAN SEX MALE NATIONALITY EUROPEAN (NORTH) AGE 25-30 HEIGHT 6' WEIGHT 170

BUILD HUSKY - WELL-BUILT COMPLEXION LIGHT HAIR BLONDE - WAVY EYES GREEN - LARGE
(THIN, STOCKY, ETC.)   (LIGHT, DARK, RUDDY, ETC)   (COLOR, WAVY, STRAIGHT, LONG, SHORT, HOW COMBED, ETC.)   (COLOR, SMALL, LARGE, ETC.)

NOSE MEDIUM EARS MEDIUM GLASSES NONE MUSTACHE OR BEARD SMALL MUSTACHE
(LARGE, SMALL, BROAD, PUG, ETC.)   (PROMINET, SMALL ETC.)   (DESCRIBE FRAMES)   (COLOR, SHAPE, ETC.)

MASK OR FALSEFACE NONE SCARS OR MARKS SMALL MOLE ON LEFT CHEEK
(TYPE, COLOR, ETC.)   (TATOOS, BIRTHMARKS, FACIAL BLEMISHES, ETC.)

DISTINGUISHING CHARACTERISTICS CONFIDENT MANNERISMS: WELL-DRESSED: PROFESSIONAL
(HOW WOULD YOU PICK THIS PERSON OUT OF A CROWD?)

CLOTHING
(DESCRIBE COLOR, TYPE OF MATERIAL, STYLE, ETC.)

HAT NONE
OVERCOAT NONE
RAINCOAT NONE
JACKET BLUE BLAZER
SUIT NONE
TROUSERS BLACK
SHIRT LIGHT BLUE
TIE NONE - OPEN COLLAR
SHOES BLACK
OTHER CLOTHING NONE

MISCELLANEOUS

WEAPON EXHIBITED SATURDAY NIGHT
(REVOLVER, AUTOMATIC, KNIFE, ETC.)
SPECIAL - CHROME COLOR

SPEECH EDUCATED: CLEAR -
VERY PRECISE IN DIRECTIONS

ANY NAMES USED NONE

MANNERISMS LEFT HANDED
(RIGHT OR LEFT HANDED, UNUSUAL WALK OR CARRIAGE
CHEWING ON TOOTHPICK
NERVOUS HABIT, ETC.)

PROMPTLY FILL OUT THIS FORM AS ACCURATELY AND AS COMPLETLY AS POSSIBLE AND GIVE IT TO BRANCH MANAGER.

button on the floor or a device in the cash drawer. Decoy or marked money can be given to each teller to be handed over during a holdup, in the hope that this money can be traced to the robber. Anything given to the teller, such as a note, should be kept so that fingerprints or other identifying evidence can be checked. Some banks have prepared bundles of money, to be given out during a holdup, containing an exploding device filled with a conspicuous dye.

Every holdup is a traumatic experience for the bank personnel involved. Thorough training in the recommended procedures to be followed during holdups is absolutely necessary. Even though there is no way of predicting the reactions of either the teller or the robber, the importance of remaining calm cannot be overemphasized. There are many recorded instances in which a simple, calm approach thwarted the holdup attempt completely.

In one incident, a person who had staged a holdup early in the day returned to the same teller in the afternoon for a second attempt. Law enforcement officials happened to be questioning the teller when the robber made his second appearance. She was able, calmly and quietly, to point him out, and he was apprehended at once. In other situations, tellers have kept their poise and, by questioning the bandit on the details of a note, have attracted the attention of bank guards who have captured him on the spot.

By endeavoring to remain calm and collected, by avoiding any attempt to use physical force, and by following those procedures that will help authorities to apprehend the criminal, every teller can play a part in protecting the bank, its staff, and its customers.

FRAUDULENT SCHEMES AND PRACTICES

Just as the nature of banking makes banks likely targets for holdups, so it also provides swindlers, thieves, and confidence men and women with a constant target for their fraudulent practices. A teller's course of training cannot end with graduation from the bank's program; it must be continuous, because the criminals who look upon banks as a favorite prey are often highly skilled, are constantly developing new methods to deceive banks, and may be thoroughly familiar with a particular bank's procedures.

The split deposit, discussed earlier, is one of the most frequently used methods of illegally obtaining funds. Another technique forges an officer's initials on the back of a check to show that it has been approved for cashing; the teller who does not verify this assumes a real risk. Frequently, an individual at a teller's window will engage the teller in a steady stream of subjects in the hope of creating a distraction. The telephone may be used to give a teller instructions on a payroll to be prepared or a check that will be presented for cashing; again, there is a constant need for tellers to be on the alert at all times.

Customers of banks may be the unwilling and unwitting victims of various types of frauds. In one of these, individuals claiming to be bank examiners have contacted depositors and have indicated that they are attempting to apprehend a dishonest teller. The customer is asked to withdraw a substantial sum of money and to turn it over to the "examiners," who subsequently substitute paper for it and return a sealed envelope to the depositor. By the time the substitution is detected, the thieves have long since departed. The best defense against this confidence scheme is an announcement by the bank to its customers that any contact by individuals who claim to be conducting an examination should be reported to the bank and to police at once.

In addition, every bank should, as a matter of policy, advise its tellers and platform personnel of the types of fraud that can be perpetrated. An awareness of the methods that are being used to defraud banks will materially assist in the effort to reduce losses.

SUMMARY

Years ago, the work of tellers was subdivided; one group, called receiving tellers, handled deposits only, while paying tellers were responsible for all paying and cashing functions. Today, it is far more common to find individuals serving as unit tellers, with both functions combined. This gives each teller a far more diversified set of tasks to perform every day. The changeover, coupled with the increased activity that all banks have experienced, intensifies the need for comprehensive teller training.

Any list of required teller attributes would necessarily include accuracy, total honesty, courtesy, and the ability to work well under pressure. Tellers must be able to handle a variety of transactions and make decisions promptly and efficiently; they are the "front line" of banking, and banks are often judged entirely on the basis of the professionalism and attitude toward customers displayed by their tellers.

Every teller must clearly understand what *paying* and *cashing* involve. They must be able to balance the need for establishing and maintaining customers' good will with the simultaneous need for protecting the bank's and depositors' assets. The manner in which they treat requests for conversion of checks into money is vitally important. A curt refusal and an inflexible attitude can have unfortunate consequences; an overemphasis on not offending anyone can result in substantial losses.

All banks are natural targets for every form of larceny. It is only through education that a state of constant vigilance can be established and maintained.

QUESTIONS FOR DISCUSSION

1. Why is a bank legally obliged to *pay* checks presented to it?

2. What risks does a teller assume in *cashing* checks? What tests can be applied in these situations?

3. Should a bank be willing to cash every check that is presented to it by its own depositors?

4. What actions should a teller take during a holdup attempt?

5. If a check has been made payable to cash, why should a teller ask that it be endorsed by the individual who presents it?

Suggested Readings

American Bankers Association. *Bank Teller Basics: An On-The-Job Training Program* (Seminar). Washington, D.C.: American Bankers Association, 1981.

American Bankers Association. *Loss Prevention* (Seminar). Washington, D.C.: American Bankers Association, 1980.

American Bankers Association. *Professional Teller Training Series* (Seminar). Washington, D.C.: American Bankers Association, 1983.

American Bankers Association. *Teller Training* (Seminar). Washington, D.C.: American Bankers Association, 1978.

American Bankers Association. *Training for Productivity* (Seminar). Washington, D.C.: American Bankers Association, 1981.

Chapter 8

Check Processing and Collection

LEARNING OBJECTIVES

After completing this chapter, you will have an understanding of

- the importance of speed and cost in the systems used for routing and collecting checks;

- the distinction among book, collected, and available balances;

- the objectives of check processing systems;

- the use of transit numbers and check routing symbols;

- the ways in which local checks can be presented to drawees;

- the advantages of membership in a clearinghouse association;

- the role of correspondent banks in the collection of transit checks;

- the concept of Fed availability and how it compares with the availability schedules of banks; and

- such terms as explicit pricing, nonpar item, and RCPC.

N o business venture can hope to succeed for any length of time if it offers the public certain goods or services and is then unable to cope with the volume of business that its marketing efforts have generated. In no industry is this truer than in commercial banking. All of the recent advertising campaigns, promotions for new branch openings, offers of more attractive forms of deposit relationships, and other techniques banks have used in the post-World War II era have brought about a tremendous increase in the number of depositors and the resulting volume of paper that must be handled. The use of checks in America now averages 100 million per day, and despite the introduction of various forms of EFTS, the volume continues to grow. It would be ironic and tragic if the banking industry, having succeeded in attracting so many new customers, found itself incapable of handling the activity they create and, as a result, lost their business. The techniques developed to aid in the rapid and efficient processing and collecting of checks are all aimed at resolving this problem.

Many bank customers today take advantage of ATMs, and in this way reduce their own use of checks. Others pay for purchases by using their bank cards, so that the goods and services they buy are directly charged to their bank accounts; again, their need for checks is reduced. Still others avail themselves of bank-by-phone systems, so that their banks pay bills for them through direct debiting, or they authorize their banks to make certain periodic payments for them automatically. Through all these examples of new technology, the United States is moving to a "less-check" society. However, a completely "checkless" society does not appear attainable. Checks, and the processing problems they create, will remain fundamental in the payments system, and, in the face of escalating labor costs, the banks must be prepared to handle those checks quickly and efficiently.

CREDIT BALANCES AND CHECK PROCESSING

In its simplest terms, banking's existence depends on the ability to attract and retain funds in the form of deposits and to put those funds to work to earn profits. Deposits, however, consist largely of checks, and before those checks can be converted into usable funds for profit purposes, they must undergo a process that can be traced directly back to the concept of credit balances discussed in Chapter 4.

A bank named as drawee on a check is obligated to follow the exact orders for payment given to it by the drawer (maker). [In strict legal terminology, **makers** issue promises to pay (notes); **drawers** issue drafts (checks). In everyday, common usage, however, the issuer of a check is known as the maker, and that term is used throughout this text. The reader should keep in mind that the maker of a check is actually drawing a demand draft on a bank.] It can pay out funds from accounts *only* in exact compliance with the instructions given to it. In some circumstances, however, the drawee cannot honor a specific check. Whenever this happens, and a check has to be returned unpaid to the presenting bank, the drawee must act promptly. To delay the process would be to render a disservice both to the presenting bank and to the person who deposited or cashed the item.

If a drawee were allowed to take as much time as it wished to decide whether it should honor checks sent to it, the amount of float—uncollected funds, consisting of deposited checks that have not yet been honored—in the banking system would rise to entirely unacceptable levels. Customers who had deposited checks drawn on other banks would never be exactly sure of their collected balances. Banks themselves would suffer from such delays; their increased float would restrict their loan and investment capabilities and therefore decrease their income and profits.

The Uniform Commercial Code, Federal Reserve regulations, and local clearinghouse rules all contain specific provisions concerning the time frame within which a drawee must act on all items presented to it. If a drawee violates these rules and tries to return a check unpaid to the presenting bank after the stated time limit, it may find that the presenting bank will not accept it and that its right to dishonor the check has been lost.

Banks are willing to give immediate but provisional credit for deposited checks, since they act in the belief that most items will be honored by the drawees. The system operates on an exception basis. Notification on cash items is sent to customers *only* when a check is returned. If banks were to notify every customer of the fact that deposited checks had been presented to, and honored by, the drawees, the present volume of paperwork would double, creating an impossible situation. Both the presenting bank and its depositor are anxious to use the funds represented by deposited checks; in the absence of contrary information, both assume that the process of presenting and collecting those checks has been completed satisfactorily.

A related banking principle states that the more quickly a check is presented, the more likely it is to be honored. At the time a check was issued, funds may have been on deposit to cover it; however, other checks may have been presented in the interim and paid against the account, thus leaving insufficient funds.

All these points emphasize the need for *speed* in the check collection process. However, speed cannot be the sole determinant; it must always be balanced against *cost*. These two factors generally determine the method or channel that will be used to collect checks, and they must be considered together. The fastest method is often the most expensive, whereas the cheapest method is usually the slowest.

Assume that a bank in Vermont accepts on deposit a check drawn on a Missouri bank. If speed alone were being considered, the Vermont bank could have a messenger fly to Missouri, physically present the check to the drawee, obtain some form of acceptable settlement for it, and fly back to Vermont. This might well be the quickest method, but the expense involved could not be justified unless the size of the check made it advisable.

Conversely, a Los Angeles bank that accepted on deposit a check drawn on a bank in Boston could, if it wished, send that check to the drawee by regular mail. No expense other than postage would be incurred; costs would be kept to an absolute minimum. The time required under this method, however, would make it unacceptable to both the California bank and its depositor. Neither one could afford the luxury of waiting for several days to find out if the check had been honored.

All banks analyze speed and cost together so that maximum speed is achieved without incurring excessive expense.

BALANCES

The term *balance,* as used to refer to the status of an account, can be very misleading. Much more specific terminology is needed to give an accurate picture for both the bank and its customer.

The **book** (=**ledger**) balance is the amount on deposit as shown on the bank's books on any given day. Deposited items receive immediate credit; therefore, the book balance at any time may include a substantial amount of float. A major corporation, correspondent bank, or agency of government may have a book balance in seven figures, but float may constitute a large part of that balance.

If the total amount of float is subtracted from the book balance, the result is the **collected balance.** When no float exists in an account, the collected balance and book balance are identical.

The **available balance** in an account represents the funds that the bank would permit to be withdrawn if the account were to close out on that day. Depending on the bank's policies regarding availability of funds to customers, the available balance may be lower than the collected balance.

Under the U.S. banking system, the deposit figures reported by commercial banks are mere paper entries, and funds are represented as being in two places at the same time. This occurs because deposited checks, since they are treated as cash items and are given immediate credit, increase the depositor's book balance at once while their dollar amount is still on deposit in the accounts of the makers. A corporation may issue hundreds of checks in a single day, but its bank balance will not be reduced until those checks have been presented back to its bank and posted to the account. At the same time, the same checks have been deposited by their payees, whose own book balances have been increased by the deposits.

THE OBJECTIVES OF CHECK PROCESSING

When a bank discusses with its customer the level of balances in an account, or when it prepares detailed analyses of an account relationship for purposes of extending credit or other services, it must always identify the amount of daily float. Uncollected funds have no value to the bank for loan and investment uses, or to the customer, who usually is not permitted to draw against them. For these reasons, two basic objectives of check processing and collection are defined:

1. To ensure that all deposited or cashed checks will be presented to drawees with speed and accuracy; each drawee must then decide whether to honor the checks sent to it and must return any unpaid items within strict time limits.

2. To reduce the daily amount of uncollected funds in the banking system, so that both the banks of deposit and their customers can have available working capital.

AIDS TO CHECK SORTING

In the early years of the twentieth century, the growth of the banking system and the corresponding increase in check volume created a need for a uniform, nationwide program of bank identification so that the process of sorting checks according to drawee banks could be expedited. Prior to 1910, many of the banks in money market centers, which served networks of correspondents, had developed their own uncoordinated numbering systems to identify those banks to which they sent checks most frequently.

The American Bankers Association resolved this problem by developing and implementing a national numerical system, identifying every commercial bank in the United States. In 1911, the ABA published the first so-called Key Book, which lists the **national numerical system number** (also known as the **transit number**) assigned to each bank. This book, formally titled *Key to Routing Numbers 19xx,* is the most frequently used reference work for identifying a bank or determining its geographic location. It is updated regularly as new banks are formed and others go out of existence; the 1982 version was the 64th edition.

The Transit Number

The ABA plan specified that the transit number for each bank would be printed in the upper right corner of all checks drawn on that bank. The transit number is always in two parts, separated by a hyphen. The prefix (preceding the hyphen) uses numbers 1 through 49 to identify cities, 50 through 99 to identify states, and 101 to identify territories and dependencies. Prefix numbers for cities were assigned on the basis of population; thus, all New York banks have prefix number 1, Chicago 2, Philadelphia 3, and so forth. The suffix (following the hyphen) identifies the individual bank in that city, state, or territory.

If a check has been mutilated in processing and the drawee's name is no longer legible, the Key Book immediately identifies the drawee through the transit number. A check drawn on 77-613, for example, can be identified as belonging to Sargent County Bank in Forman, North Dakota, as quickly and readily as a check drawn on 2-221 can be identified as belonging to Sears Bank in Chicago. Tellers are often trained to enter the transit number of each deposited check directly on the customer's deposit slip. This allows the bank of deposit to trace a specific check, if necessary.

The Check Routing Symbol

Until 1945, the transit number was the sole means of identifying drawees, aside from their printed names on each check. However, as check use continued to grow, it became apparent that an additional sorting aid was needed. The American Bankers Association, with the aid of the Federal Reserve Committee on Collections, therefore introduced the *check routing symbol* as a method of sorting checks according to their destinations. This has proved to be of immeasurable help in check processing.

The ABA recommended that the check routing symbol and the transit number be combined in fractional form and printed clearly in the upper right corner of every check. The check routing symbol is the denominator of the fraction; the transit number is the numerator (upper portion). The routing symbol always consists of three or four digits and is assigned *only* to those banks that participate in the Federal Reserve's check collection system.

The check routing symbol is not intended to identify a particular bank; rather, it gives information as to the Federal Reserve facility to which the check should be sent and indicates whether the Fed will give a presenting bank immediate or deferred credit for it.

The United States is divided into 12 Federal Reserve geographic districts. Typically, the check routing symbol's first digit (if the symbol consists of three digits) or first two digits (in the case of four-digit symbols) identify the drawee bank's district. All drawee banks in Ohio, for example, are in District 4 and have a symbol beginning with that digit. Banks in California are in District 12, and the check routing symbol therefore begins with those two digits.

The next digit in the check routing symbol shows the Federal Reserve Bank or Branch that serves the drawee bank. The final digit indicates the availability that the Fed will give the sending bank *if* the item is sent to it within a stated time frame. If the final digit is a zero, the check is given immediate credit by the Fed; all other digits indicate deferred (=delayed) credit. Fed availability and the variations in the format of the check routing symbol that have been introduced in recent years are discussed in detail later in this chapter.

Magnetic Ink Character Recognition

While the use of transit numbers and check routing symbols was of great help in expediting check processing, they both required reading by the human eye. Even further improvements became necessary in order to make the checks readable by modern data processing equipment— improvements required by the steady growth in check volume and increases in labor costs. The American Bankers Association, collaborating with check printing firms, equipment manufacturers, and other specialists, set out to develop a technique to meet this need. In 1956 the ABA Bank Management Commission announced the development of a common machine language using **magnetic ink character recognition (MICR)**. The MICR system made it possible for checks and other encoded documents to be read directly by data processing equipment. An individual design for each of the numerals from 0 through 9 was prepared (see Figure 8-1); the quantity of magnetized particles in the ink used to print each character varied, so that the machines used to read the information could never mistake one numeral for another. Specifications for banks were also designed; these contained guidelines for the placement of all MICR information and required that all checks be within a specified size range (see Figure 8-2).

The acceptance and implementation of the MICR system in the ensuing years eventually brought about a Federal Reserve regulation that unencoded checks would *not* be accepted by the Fed as cash items.

Each bank today uses its own system of assigning account numbers to its customers. Each new check issued to a depositor is pre-encoded with the necessary MICR data—the bank's combined transit number and check routing symbol and the customer's account number. The

Figure 8-1
Magnetic Ink Characters

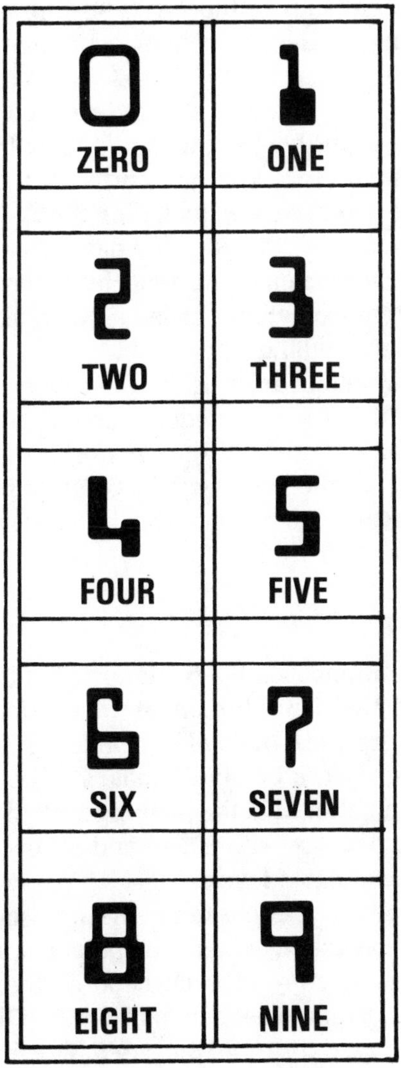

0 ZERO	**1** ONE
2 TWO	**3** THREE
4 FOUR	**5** FIVE
6 SIX	**7** SEVEN
8 EIGHT	**9** NINE

sequential check number may also be encoded; this is useful in the preparation of computer-generated bank statements and in the customer's own bookkeeping system.

As seen in Figure 8-2, the MICR-encoded transit number and check routing symbol combination contains nine digits. The first eight of these contain the essentials of those two sorting aids; the ninth is a check digit, enabling the data processing equipment to verify that the first eight are correctly encoded.

The *first* bank to receive a check as a deposited item or give cash for it is generally responsible for encoding the dollar amount in magnetic ink in the area in the lower right corner of the check. Once this has been done, every other bank, including the Fed, that has modern reading equipment can use the encoded data for sorting, processing, and posting. If a check cannot be read by a bank's equipment, it becomes a reject item (sometimes called a non-machinable item) and must receive special handling.

Under the MICR system, banks also began supplying customers with deposit slips on which their individual account numbers were pre-encoded. When debit and credit tickets are prepared by various departments within the bank, the necessary encoding of MICR data must be performed so that these documents can be processed electronically and posted to accounts.

Electronic Sorting

In previous generations, when a bank accepted a check on deposit it usually recorded the depositor's name and information as to the check amount and drawee bank by hand on ledger sheets. Today, the sheer volume of daily work obviously makes this method obsolete. It is only through automation that the banking system can process some 100 million checks per day with speed and accuracy while keeping handling costs to acceptable levels.

In a large bank today, all deposited items are usually sent to a central processing department—often in batches at various times throughout the day. A copy of each deposit slip accompanies the checks. If coin and currency made up part or all of the deposit, a cash substitution ticket is used for proof purposes. The first step in the process ensures that every item is fully and correctly encoded with all the necessary MICR data.

Figure 8-2
Placement of MICR Data on Checks

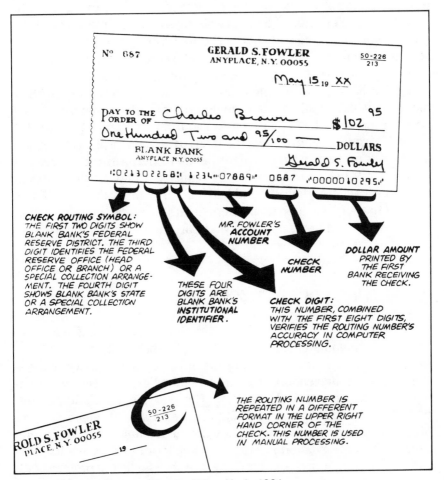

Source: Federal Reserve Bank of New York, 1981.

Once all the work has been fully encoded, high-speed sorter-readers can handle 1,000 or more checks per minute on the basis of predetermined computer programs. For example, every deposited check belongs in one of the three categories mentioned earlier; it is an on-us item, a clearing item according to the depository's definition of that term, or a transit check. Each sorter-reader can be programmed to read the transit-routing field, sort deposited items into these three groups, and then fine-sort them. The fine-sorting process can batch checks by individual drawee, by Federal Reserve district, or in some other grouping, according to the depository bank's needs.

The MICR program has not eliminated all previous check-sorting methods; it has supplemented them and made electronic processing possible for those banks wishing to use it. Many commercial banks, instead of purchasing or leasing their own data processing equipment, rely on their correspondent banks to perform the processing for them. By the same token, many banks still find it convenient to use proof machines that sort and batch items without the use of MICR data. In these cases, a proof machine operator reads the information on all checks and uses manual keys to sort the items and record their totals.

PRESENTING LOCAL CHECKS

During each business day, checks that have been classified as local items are accumulated by tellers and departments, then proved and sorted either by proof machine operators or by MICR sorter-readers. Every check is then endorsed by the presenting bank and listed according to its drawee bank destination. The endorsement is important, since by placing its stamp on outgoing items a bank guarantees all previous endorsements and makes the next bank a holder in due course. The abbreviation P.E.G., meaning "prior endorsements guaranteed," is commonly used for this purpose. The listing process compares the total dollar amount of checks for each individual drawee to the dollar total for the entire sort.

Local checks may then be presented to drawees in one of three ways:

- By messenger (also known as **direct presenting**);
- Through a correspondent bank; or
- Through the facilities of a local clearinghouse.

This listing is in order of historical development and also of relative importance. Direct presenting of checks by bank messengers was the first system used. Correspondent bank services became more widely used with the passage of time and the increase in check volume. For most major banks in money center communities today, local clearinghouses handle by far the largest volume.

By Messenger

Messenger presentation is an excellent system in those situations where check volume is low and in those communities having relatively few banks. It may also be justified when an especially large check has been taken on deposit and messenger service provides the fastest means of presenting that item to the drawee. Again, speed and cost must be considered together to determine whether this method is desirable in a particular case.

Through Correspondents

Correspondent banks, in exchange for account balances, provide a variety of services, of which the collecting of checks is the most traditional and perhaps the most widely used. A commercial bank that maintains a relationship with a larger correspondent often relies on it to present and collect checks. Similarly, thrift institutions use their commercial bank correspondents for this purpose.

In performing the work of check processing and collection, correspondent banks simply accept the day's deposited items and treat them as they do all other deposits; that is, they credit an account, sort the items, and present them to the drawees.

Through a Clearinghouse

A clearinghouse association is entirely voluntary. No federal or state laws or banking regulations require that such an association be formed or that any particular bank join one. However, because of the benefits they offer to members, clearinghouses are very popular and have been implemented in many cities throughout the country. Use of a clearinghouse has proved to be the quickest and most economical method of

- *presenting* local checks and

- *obtaining settlement* for those checks from the drawees.

The history of the New York clearinghouse may be cited as an example. In the mid-nineteenth century, New York City was the site of 57 commercial banks. Each of these used messengers to present checks to local drawees and obtain some form of settlement for them. As the volume of checks grew and the importance of timely presenting increased, each bank found that more messengers, making more individual trips, were required to complete the day's work.

The establishment of the New York clearinghouse in 1853 eliminated the need for a continual stream of bank messengers going to and from the individual banks. It provided a central meeting place at which presentation of checks and settlement among the banks could be quickly and conveniently performed. Today, 12 of New York City's largest banks process almost $4 billion of checks through the clearinghouse on an average business day with a degree of speed and efficiency that could not be achieved under any other conditions.

In a typical clearinghouse operation, each member bank sends a messenger and a settlement clerk to the daily settlement clearing. The messenger delivers batches of sorted, listed, and endorsed checks to each of the other members; the settlement clerks record the dollar amounts of checks presented to their banks by each of the others. The total dollar amount of checks taken to the clearings by any one bank must prove to the dollar totals for each of the batches it is delivering to the other banks.

Members in a clearinghouse *do not* settle with one another individually, nor is cash used as a means of settlement. Rather, each bank typically maintains a settlement account with the local Federal Reserve Bank or with a correspondent.

If a bank delivers a dollar amount of checks at the clearings larger than the dollar amount of checks presented to it, it is owed money. If it is presented with a dollar amount of checks larger than the total it delivers to the other members, it owes the clearings.

When the daily volume warrants it, a clearinghouse may provide for members to deliver checks and noncash items several times during each business day. At the New York City clearinghouse, for example, four exchanges of checks, one of return items, one of matured bonds and coupons, and three of stock certificates occur each day. The settlement clearing takes place at 10 A.M.; at that time all the transactions for the preceding 24 hours are brought into proof and the final computation of each bank's credit or debit is made.

Clearinghouse members in each community establish their own agreements on times of exchanges, methods of settlement, and the amount of annual assessment to be levied on each member to support operating expenses.

Banks that do not belong to a clearinghouse generally use the services of correspondents to present and collect local checks.

PRESENTING TRANSIT CHECKS

The problems of presenting those items that have been classified as out-of-town, or transit, are far more complicated. The geography of this country is such that a bank may cash or accept on deposit checks drawn on banks thousands of miles away. The sorting and routing process is further complicated by the fact that thousands of other banks are the drawees, rather than the relatively few local institutions. For a bank in Washington, D.C., one transit item may be drawn on a bank a few blocks away across the District line whereas another may be drawn on a bank in Oregon, Texas, South Dakota, or Florida. The bank in Washington must be prepared to deal with both types of transit items, and the two governing factors of speed and cost become even more critical in view of the distances and the number of possible drawees involved.

As in the case of local items, there are three available methods for presenting and collecting transit checks. Again, they are listed in order of historical development and relative importance. Transit items may be collected

- By direct presenting to drawees;

- Through correspondent banks; or

- Through the facilities of the Federal Reserve.

By Direct Presenting

Although direct presenting was the earliest method, it is the least used today. Sometimes it may be the quickest method; at the same time, it is likely to be the most costly. Its use is generally restricted to situations in which the expense can be justified when measured against the cost. Typical circumstances in which direct presenting is used might include the following:

- When a particularly large check has been received and the increase in available funds resulting from use of the quickest method offsets the expense involved.

- When an item includes special instructions from the depositor, to whom the expenses of direct presenting will be charged.

- When the sending bank finds that it cannot meet the local Fed schedule for delivery of checks to a specific destination.

Through Correspondent Banks

Correspondent banks handle a significant portion of the total transit check volume, and before the Federal Reserve's check collection system was established they were the most widely used agency for this purpose. In many cases the correspondent arrangement is reciprocal; that is, each bank maintains an account with the other, and each uses the other to collect transit items for it. An example might involve a mutual correspondent agreement between a bank in St. Louis and one in Richmond. The St. Louis bank sends all checks drawn on banks in the Richmond area to its correspondent and receives account credit for them, just as any other depositor would. At the same time the Richmond bank batches all checks drawn on banks in the St. Louis area and forwards them to that bank.

In other cases, unilateral arrangements exist. A bank that has implemented sophisticated, rapid systems for check collection actively markets that service and acts as a transit check collection agent for various correspondents throughout the country. For example, a Chicago bank, priding itself on the flexibility and speed of its collection system, receives checks from other banks and presents them at the clearinghouse in Chicago or uses helicopters to deliver checks to other drawees in the Chicago area and outlying sections of Illinois.

Banks wishing to expand their correspondent network often stress their check collection capabilities as a reason for other banks to establish a relationship with them. In many cases, their prompt and efficient transit operations give the presenting banks, which had originally cashed the checks or accepted them on deposit, better availability than could be gained through the Fed.

Through the Federal Reserve System

The lack of a nationwide check collection system before 1913 was mentioned earlier as having been one of the post-1863 weaknesses. The Federal Reserve System addressed this weakness by establishing the world's largest system, which now handles some 35 million checks per day with a dollar value of some $20 billion. The Federal Reserve Act provided that each of the 12 Federal Reserve banks would serve as a center for check collection in its area and that transit work would flow quickly and efficiently among all 12 districts. Each of the district banks has established branches within its district. Federal Reserve banks pay each other for the dollar results of each day's transactions by settling net balances through the Interdistrict Settlement Fund, maintained at Fed headquarters in Washington.

A bank with a modest volume of transit work might use its local Federal Reserve bank exclusively. In this case, it would forward unsorted work, destined for any or all of the 12 districts, to that local Fed facility. On the other hand, banks with large volumes of transit items must sort their transit work according to the 12 districts before sending the items to the local Fed. As previously noted, all transit checks sent to the Fed must be fully encoded in MICR if the checks are to be treated as cash items.

Suppose, for example, that a woman living in Dallas buys some merchandise from a dealer in Sacramento and pays for it with a check drawn on her Dallas bank. The merchant deposits her check in his local bank, and it is forwarded by that bank to the San Francisco Fed, which in turn sends it to the Federal Reserve bank in Dallas. From that point, the check is delivered to the drawee so that it can be examined and, if honored, charged to the maker's account. The drawee bank pays the Dallas Fed for the check; the Dallas Fed reimburses the San Francisco Fed; and the latter credits the account of the Sacramento bank.

FEDERAL RESERVE AVAILABILITY

The reserve accounts that member banks must keep with their district Federal Reserve bank serve many purposes, including the access they provide to Fed funds transactions, money transfers, and supplies of currency. Perhaps most important, those accounts are used to credit sending banks for the transit work they have sent to the Fed for collection.

Each of the 12 Federal Reserve banks prepares and publishes a check **availability schedule** applicable to the sending banks in its district. This schedule tells the sending bank how soon its account(s) at the Fed will be credited for transit work *if* checks are sent out in accordance with a detailed timetable. All transit items sent to the Fed are classified as *same-day* (=*zero-day*), *1-day*, or *2-day* availability.

A zero-day item sent to the Fed is classified as immediately available to the sending bank, whose reserve account is credited on the day the Fed receives the item. This, of course, assumes that the item has been received by the Fed within the limits of its timetable. If a bank fails to meet that timetable and delivers the check to the district Fed after the deadline, it loses the benefit of zero-day availability.

All zero-day items credited to sending banks by the Fed immediately increase the reserve account positions of those banks. All federal government checks, since they are drawn on the Federal Reserve, are zero-day items, and the zero that appears in the check routing symbol on each of them indicates this.

For check collection purposes, the Fed also carries a **deferred account** on its books for the sending banks, and all 1-day and 2-day items are posted to that account when received. Each day, the Fed automatically moves the dollar amount of these items from one category to the next; that is, today's 1-day item becomes an available item tomorrow, when the Fed transfers its dollar amount to the sending bank's reserve account. The 2-day item, posted to the sending bank's deferred account today, will become a 1-day item tomorrow and will be credited to the sending bank's reserve account on the next business day.

The fact that the Fed gives credit to sending banks in a maximum of 2 days creates a float position that is similar to that created by those banks in giving credit to their own depositors. It is physically impossible for the Fed to present each transit check to the drawee and have that drawee examine and honor the item and settle with the Fed in 2 days or less. However, just as the banks of deposit post credits to their customers' accounts before they know whether the deposited items will be honored, so the Fed acts on the assumption that most of the check volume is "good" and the accounts of the sending banks are credited accordingly.

However, there is one significant difference. A local bank can restrict its depositor from drawing on uncollected funds, even though his book balance has been increased through the depositing of checks. As will be described later, it can establish its own availability schedule and refuse to honor checks that are drawn on it if they are presented "early." The Fed does not have this restrictive feature. Every transit check sent to the Fed receives account credit for the sending bank on the same day, in 1 day, or in 2 days; thereafter, its dollar amount becomes part of the sending bank's reserve account and can be put to work at once.

On a typical business day, the Fed has a total float position of approximately $2 billion, since it has given the sending banks credit for items that have not, at that time, been presented and honored. A blizzard, an airline strike, or some other emergency that prevents the prompt delivery of checks to drawees enlarges that float position even further. Depending on the respective geographic locations of the sending bank and the drawee, 3, 4, or even more days may be required for the Fed to complete the presenting and collection process.

In an effort to reduce its daily float position, the Fed has implemented three major changes in its check processing systems and regulations. The first of these reduced the amount of time allowed to a drawee to decide whether an item should be honored. Under the revised schedule, any drawee bank presented with checks by the Fed must either pay for those checks or return them within 24 hours. Payment is most commonly made by a debit to the sending bank's own account at its district Fed.

The second major revision took into account the large geographic areas that many Fed districts embrace and the number of potential drawees within each district. For example, the Sixth Federal Reserve District has its headquarters in Atlanta, with branches in Jacksonville, New Orleans, Birmingham, Nashville, and Miami. Each branch must serve a great many widely separated drawee banks in the six states that make up the district. To speed up check collection and reduce Fed float, the Federal Reserve is establishing special new facilities, called RCPCs (Regional Check Processing Centers), in each of the 12 districts. These are strategically located check collection points to which transit work can be sent directly for prompt handling. Each RCPC, in turn, will sort the checks sent to it and deliver them to the respective drawees. The Federal Reserve plans to establish approximately 40 RCPCs.

The original format of the check routing symbol has necessarily been revised to give effect to the introduction of RCPCs. Check routing symbols now show the RCPC nearest to the drawee bank; thus a sending bank, through its sorting procedures, can determine the RCPC to be used and send transit checks directly to that point.

The third revision, which the Fed has implemented on an experimental basis, changes the traditional concept that stated that every check had to be physically sent to its drawee for examination and honoring. In the case of large checks, the Fed has introduced a system that forwards electronic information to the drawee banks, instead of physically routing the items. Obviously, the largest checks are also those on which decisions are sought at once; electronic presentation meets this objective.

Assuming this system is used, suppose, for example, an Atlanta vendor receives a $100,000 check from a Minneapolis corporation and deposits the check in an Atlanta bank. That bank converts the payment instructions to magnetic tape and follows the same procedure for other large checks received on the same day. The magnetic tapes from all the Atlanta banks then go to the Atlanta Federal Reserve bank, which sorts the payment instructions by destination and sends them to the appropriate Fed district. The Federal Reserve banks in each district then instruct the drawee banks to create debits to the accounts of the original makers. This system of electronic presentment virtually eliminates float.

The long-standing concept that every check had to be physically presented to its drawee is also affected by new systems of photocopy transmission. Banks in some major cities are experimenting with sending a photocopy image of checks over telephone lines to drawee banks. Again, this system can eliminate float, since the drawee can make an immediate decision on whether to honor the item, and the bank of deposit can be guided accordingly.

BANK AVAILABILITY SCHEDULES

A problem frequently encountered by bank customers involves the waiting period imposed on them before they can draw against deposited checks. A man who banks in New Orleans, for example, and gives his bank a check drawn on a bank in Utah may be aware that the Fed will credit his bank in a maximum of 2 business days; yet the New Orleans bank may add several days to the Fed figure and tell the depositor that the funds are not available to him until that time frame has ended.

Every commercial bank, as a matter of policy, sets its own availability schedule for customer purposes, which is not always identical with the Fed timetable for availability. The primary reason for this is that the bank of deposit must consider the possibility that a deposited check will be returned. The Fed cannot physically present and collect every check in 2 days, despite the fact that it gives the sending bank credit on that basis. A period of time over and above the Fed availability schedule must be added by the bank of deposit. If a check is returned, the Fed will reverse the provisional credit it gave the sending bank and the latter, in turn, must charge the amount back to its depositor. Recovery of the funds may be difficult or impossible if the depositor has already been allowed to withdraw them.

In enforcing their own availability schedules, banks naturally differentiate among the various types of accounts. A large corporation that has maintained a substantial account and established its credit standing will be granted availability privileges far different from those accorded to the individual who keeps nominal balances in his or her account.

The right of banks to establish a waiting period on deposited checks and to implement their own particular availability schedules has been upheld in several court decisions.

EXPLICIT PRICING

Until 1981, the Federal Reserve provided services to member banks without charge (except for the discount rate on loans). In the area of check collection, all the tasks of presenting checks to drawees, obtaining settlement, and transferring funds from deferred to reserve accounts each day were handled for member banks free. At the same time, member banks were required to maintain substantial reserve accounts with the Fed.

The Monetary Control Act of 1980 completely changed both these systems. It made *all* financial institutions subject to reserve requirements and reduced the amount of those reserves. At the same time, it placed all Fed services on a direct-charge basis. Under the terms of the act, the Federal Reserve was required to implement a system of specific pricing for every check sent to it for collection; thus the sending bank must now pay those charges and, in turn, must recover them from the depositor.

RETURN ITEMS

Although most checks will be honored when presented, there will always be a small minority that the drawee cannot or will not honor. The most common reason for a refusal to pay is "insufficient funds." All dishonored items are called **return items.** By law and tradition, any dishonored check must be returned promptly to the sending bank so that the provisional credit originally given to it can be reversed and the depositor notified. Generally, return items flow back to presenting banks by the same method used to direct them to drawees. The reason for dishonor of a check must be clearly shown by the drawee, usually through use of a "return slip" that specifies the nature of the problem.

NONPAR ITEMS

An extremely small number of American commercial banks, as nonmembers of the Fed, create a further problem in the check collection system by refusing to honor checks drawn on them for the face amount; they deduct a settlement or exchange charge from each item as it is presented to them. Federal Reserve regulations require that all member banks honor checks at their par (face) value; hence, these nonmember banks are called **nonpar banks** and the checks drawn on them are **nonpar items**.

A bank accepting a nonpar check on deposit treats it as a cash item and gives the depositor credit for the face value shown on it. However, when the check reaches the nonpar bank it will be settled for a lesser amount. The difference, representing the settlement charge, must be charged back to the depositor. This creates additional bookkeeping work and clerical expense for the bank.

Furthermore, Federal Reserve regulations stipulate that all checks processed through the Fed must be paid at par. Nonpar items cannot be sent to the Fed and must be presented through correspondent banks or sent directly to the drawees.

Both the number of nonpar banks and the volume of checks drawn on them are very small. From time to time Congress has considered legislation that would eliminate the nonpar system and require all banks to pay at par; however, this legislation was never enacted.

CASH LETTERS

A **cash letter** resembles a deposit slip and is used to list outgoing batches of cash items sent to the drawee, correspondent, Federal Reserve bank or branch, or RCPC. It lists every check in each batch and shows the dollar amount. Cash letters are used for proof purposes by the sending bank and the receiving bank or Federal Reserve facility.

It has become standard practice for sending banks to prepare and retain a **microfilm** record of all cash letters sent out and of the individual checks contained in each shipment. If the checks themselves are destroyed or lost, the microfilm makes it possible to reconstruct the shipment. Copies of cash letters and checks can be made from the microfilm and accepted by the drawees.

SUMMARY

By implementing the concept of cash items, the commercial banks have provided a major service to their customers. At the same time, they have imposed on themselves the monumental task of processing some 100 million checks per day and presenting those checks to the proper drawees. The drawees, in turn, must decide promptly whether to honor or return each check.

Throughout history there have been continual efforts to expedite this process and to cope with an ever-increasing check volume in a timely and efficient manner, at minimum cost to the depositors. The creation of transit numbers, check routing symbols, MICR programs, and new systems of electronic presentment illustrates these efforts to sort, route, and collect deposited items with the proper combination of speed and cost.

Checks may be presented to drawee banks directly or through correspondents, clearinghouses, or the Fed. Each bank of deposit must analyze its check volume and determine which method of presentation provides the best solution.

The Monetary Control Act directly affects the check collection system since it requires that the Fed impose a system of explicit pricing and collect a direct charge from the sending banks for every check it handles.

QUESTIONS FOR DISCUSSION

1. What is the relationship between a bank's daily float position and that bank's income and profits?

2. Explain the differences among the terms book balance, collected balance, and available balance.

3. What are the two factors to be considered in choosing the channel or method for collecting deposited checks?

4. What information, useful to a sending bank, is found in the check routing symbol?

5. What are the advantages or benefits of bank membership in a clearinghouse association?

6. Identify two situations in which a bank might choose to present transit checks directly to their drawees.

7. How and when do sending banks receive credit for transit checks they have sent to the Fed?

8. Why do banks refuse to permit customers to draw against deposits according to the Fed availability schedule?

9. What problems do nonpar checks create for the banks that accept them as deposits?

Suggested Readings

American Bankers Association. *Check Processing: A Programmed Training Unit.* Washington, D.C.: American Bankers Association, 1975.

American Bankers Association. *Education in Personal Economics Program: Checking Accounts Management.* Washington, D.C.: American Bankers Association, 1980.

American Bankers Association. *Key to Routing Numbers 1982.* Chicago: Rand McNally, 1982.

American Bankers Association. *Loss Prevention—Checks.* Washington, D.C.: American Bankers Association, 1976.

American Bankers Association. *Routing Number Excerpts from the Final Report ABA/FRS Check Digit Task Force.* Washington, D.C.: American Bankers Association, 1977.

American Bankers Association. *Routing Numbers: Specifications and Guides.* Washington, D.C.: American Bankers Association, 1976.

Bank Administration Institute. *Exception Item Recommendations.* Rolling Meadows, Illinois: Bank Administration Institute, 1978.

Bank Administration Institute. *Industry Procedures for Adjustment Resolution.* Rolling Meadows, Illinois: Bank Administration Institute, 1978.

Chapter 9

Bank Bookkeeping

LEARNING OBJECTIVES

After completing this chapter, you will have an understanding of

- the distinction between a bank's bookkeeping unit and its general ledger department;

- the sources from which a bookkeeping unit receives its daily work;

- the basic functions of the bookkeeping department;

- the advantages and disadvantages of dual posting systems;

- the information contained on the daily transaction tape;

- the nine tests that can be applied to checks as part of the overall bookkeeping function;

- the difference between genuine and authorized signatures; and

- the advantages of the cycle statement system.

When the system of credit balances was first substituted for the physical exchange of money or other articles of value, the goldsmith or merchant who held those balances had to be able to maintain accurate and timely records of every transaction. As banks gradually assumed the handling of credit balances, they also necessarily assumed the task of recordkeeping and the responsibility for knowing the status of each account relationship at all times. In addition, they found themselves faced with the need to furnish customers periodic reports on all transactions.

A bank must be able to handle the deposit and payment functions efficiently and promptly and at the same time guarantee to its depositors that every transaction affecting an account will be properly recorded. The end product of this entire operation, i.e., the monthly bank statement, is vital to the customer's relationship with, and image of, the bank. Errors, mispostings, delays, or other problems in this area cause strong and immediate customer dissatisfaction and reflect on the bank's ability to handle the volume of business it has sought to generate.

The term "bookkeeping" can be traced directly to the introduction of the credit balances system. A holder of those balances maintained some form of "book" or ledger for each client and carefully recorded all deposits and payments for that client in it. Today, the word bookkeeping may conjure up an image of a person, perhaps wearing a green eyeshade and seated on a high stool, whose job it was to enter, in meticulous pen-and-ink script, each day's activity. Indeed, in the early days of American banking, that image was accurate; banks maintained staffs of people who literally "kept the books" and performed all the tasks that had been the responsibility of the merchants and goldsmiths.

As the number of bank customers and the daily volume of deposits and payments increased, the work of posting and maintaining detailed, accurate sets of books demanded new and improved technology. Just as the *manner* in which the work was performed was revised to meet the increased requirements of both the banks and their customers, so the *name* given to the function was changed. Many banks today no longer have or refer to a **bookkeeping department**; far more often, the term **demand deposit accounting** (DDA) is used to describe the system and the department through which the work of examining checks, posting them to accounts, and rendering statements is performed. However, for purposes of uniformity, the traditional term, *bookkeeping,* will be used throughout this chapter to describe the function and the unit.

A distinction must be made here between the bank department commonly called **general ledger** or **general books** and the bookkeeping unit itself. The general ledger department coordinates all the figures from each department and branch within the bank and prepares a daily financial statement that shows all assets and liabilities for the entire institution. Included in the statement is a caption for **demand deposits**; that figure results from the work done in the bookkeeping department, which has posted all the transactions affecting each customer's account and has arrived at a closing balance in each case. The sum total of those closing balances appears as a single entry on the bank's daily balance sheet.

SOURCES OF BOOKKEEPING WORK

Every instrument that affects a customer's balance in any way must be processed through the bank's bookkeeping department. Deposit slips and other credits must be posted to increase the account balance. Checks must be examined to determine if they should be honored and then posted to reduce the balance. Data from the bank's ATMs must also be entered, and electronic debits and credits are also part of the processing flow. The *posting* process performed by bookkeeping can also be referred to as the *paying* of checks; the net effect on a customer's balance is identical, whether he or she has received cash from a teller or has issued checks that will be charged to an account.

All the items that bookkeepers receive each day come from a variety of sources. Automated clearinghouses forward electronic posting material. Deposit slips originate with tellers. Debit and credit tickets are prepared by many departments—e.g., securities, loan, trust, and collection. Checks are presented by clearinghouses, the Federal Reserve, and directly by other banks, in addition to those cashed or taken on deposit by tellers.

Although it is true that posting involves the entering to accounts of both credits and debits, the stress in this chapter is on the debit activity, i.e., the reducing of account balances. Each day, commercial banks settle with each other for billions of dollars on the basis of the authority contained in the pieces of paper called checks. The most important single function of the bookkeeping unit is to examine all checks presented. This involves ensuring that the customer's instructions are followed exactly—no more and no less. Those items that meet all the examining tests are charged to accounts; those that should not or cannot be debited to accounts must be returned promptly to the presenters.

BASIC BOOKKEEPING FUNCTIONS

When all checks and debit and credit tickets have reached the bookkeeping department, the unit can perform its essential daily functions. To prepare and maintain up-to-date, accurate records on every checking account, a typical bookkeeping unit must

- examine all work presented to it to ensure that proper account numbers and dollar amounts appear;
- post all debits and credits to the proper account;
- arrive at a new closing balance for each account;
- return those items that are dishonored;
- render statements to customers;
- generate internal reports for the information of various units within the bank; and
- answer inquiries from outside sources as to the status of accounts.

Preliminary Examination

It is not the purpose here to suggest that every bank, if it has not already done so, should adopt a fully automated system of demand deposit accounting. One of the functions of bank management is to determine how much money and effort should be spent on automation. Many banks do not find it necessary to install the expensive and highly sophisticated computer systems that are found at larger, more active institutions. This is not to say that these banks are behind the times; rather, they have chosen the type of bookkeeping operation that will meet their objectives while keeping expenses within budgeted figures.

Regardless of the degree of automation that a particular bank elects to provide, there are certain basic procedures that can be followed. Checks can be examined visually or by machine to determine if all the necessary MICR data have been properly encoded. If information is missing, it can be encoded before the items move to any further processing. Similarly, all checks presented to a bank can be examined to ensure that they actually belong to that bank. **Missorts** can and do occur, whereby items are sent to the wrong bank; these must be screened out at once and returned to the presenting unit. Debit and credit tickets must also be examined for complete and accurate encoding.

Posting and Computing New Balances

For banks that employ nonautomated bookkeeping systems, a typical procedure might entail sorting all debits and credits by account name or number, obtaining from a file of statements or ledger cards those that must be posted, making the actual posting entries, and calculating the new balance in each case. If this is done by a single person, there are many possibilities for error. A debit or credit on which a sorting error was made might be posted by a bookkeeper who did not detect the original mistake, or a ledger card for John Smith might be pulled from the file and posted with work intended for William Smith's account.

The Dual Posting System. In an attempt to reduce these possibilities for error and improve the accuracy of the bookkeeping function, a system called **dual posting** was developed. It requires that a ledger file (for the bank's use) and a statement file (for the customer's use) be prepared and maintained on each account and that two operators post all work and prove to each other. One operator posts debits and credits to the ledger, while the other posts to the statement. Since two people are unlikely to make the same mistake, dual posting provides greater accuracy. However, since every item must be posted twice, it is also far slower and more expensive. The benefits must be weighed against the costs.

Partially Automated Systems. In an attempt to achieve the accuracy of dual posting while simultaneously reducing their expenses, many banks have implemented systems that combine nonautomated and partially automated features. These systems require that every checking account have its own identifying number and that equipment be used that can "read" information encoded in magnetic strips on the back of each ledger sheet. Several firms have marketed these systems to banks under their own trade names. The common feature is an ability to make a comparison of the information encoded on the ledger sheet with the information encoded on the posting work. This eliminates many of the common types of human error. In some cases, the equipment can read the previous closing balance in the account and compute a new balance after debits and credits have been posted.

Automated Systems. All computerized bookkeeping systems require a completely implemented MICR program. If the work to be posted has been fully encoded with account number and dollar amount in magnetic ink, today's data processing equipment can perform not only the basic bookkeeping functions but a whole host of other tasks at speeds that would have been unthinkable with older, less sophisticated systems.

There is scarcely any limit to the amount of data that can be stored in the memory of a large, modern computer. Every type of relevant data on an account can be entered and readily accessed. For example, the master file on the ABC Corporation payroll account might show the account number, the fact that ABC maintains other accounts with the bank, the industry code assigned to ABC by the government to identify its type of business, the branch or other area of the bank in which the account is domiciled, the identity of the bank officer responsible for the relationship, and other useful information. Depending on their computer capabilities, banks can design programs containing any of this in addition to whatever other information they feel is needed. The master file may be on discs, magnetic tape, or other media tailored to the particular type of computer.

In fully automated bookkeeping, all debits and credits typically are passed through a MICR **sorter-reader**, which captures the information encoded on each item and prepares a magnetic tape called the **daily transaction tape** or **entry run**. This tape is prepared in account-number sequence. It lists the account number, the dollar amount of every transaction, and a code to indicate the type of debit or credit.

Depending on the bank's size and its volume of daily activity, the transaction tape may be prepared in a single run after the close of business or may represent an accumulation of several separate entries. For example, a large bank may receive a substantial number of checks at the morning exchanges in the local clearinghouse and may make the initial tape entries as soon as those checks are received and examined. Later in the day, the same bank may receive additional checks presented to it by the Fed and directly by other banks. The entry run can be adjusted as these batches of work reach the bank. If the bank has many departments and branches that originate debit and credit tickets, it may wait until a very late hour before finalizing the transaction tape to reflect all these transactions.

When all entries to the entry-run tape have been made, the next step, called **merging** or **updating**, takes place. This procedure combines the transaction tape for that day with the **master file** that was the result of the previous day's posting; in other words, the closing balances on each account, as of the close of business on the previous day, are now adjusted to give effect to the new debits and credits. This process accomplishes two closely related objectives: It creates a new master file tape for use in the next business day's processing; at the same time, it creates a new summary figure, reflecting the closing balance in each account and providing a demand deposit total for use in the general ledger department. The master file that is the result of each day's posting therefore becomes the basis for all of the next day's bookkeeping work.

Examining Checks

One of the most important elements in every drawee's daily bookkeeping is the detailed examination of every check presented to it. No volume increases or changes in technology can absolve a bank from its obligation to scrutinize each check to ensure that it can and should be posted to an account. Every check is a written set of instructions to a drawee, which has an inescapable duty to comply with those instructions *if* the item meets a series of examining tests.

Traditionally, the bookkeeping procedure involved examining all checks *before* they were posted to accounts. If a check met all the tests applied to it, it was charged to an account after having been examined. In some cases the check was referred to an officer, who quickly decided whether it should be posted; based on that officer's judgment, it was either debited to the maker's account or returned unpaid.

Today's automated bookkeeping systems have reversed this procedure. Whatever examinations are performed take place *after* the checks have been posted to accounts by the computer. There is a logical, sound reason for this. The percentage of checks to be returned is relatively small, and it is far simpler for the drawee to post every item without examining it first. Any necessary adjustments can be made subsequently.

Just as the concept of cash items resulted in a system of provisional credits, whereby deposited items increased a customer's balance at once but could be charged back later if necessary, so the system of fully automated bookkeeping has created a system of provisional debits, whereby checks are automatically posted to accounts. If an item must be returned unpaid for any reason, the original debit is reversed and a credit is posted. Automated bookkeeping does not change the drawee's obligation to examine checks; it merely changes the stage of the bookkeeping cycle at which the examining process takes place.

Whether that examination is performed before or after posting, there are nine tests that can be applied to every check to determine whether it should be charged to the maker's account. If an item fails to pass any of these nine tests, it *may* be returned unpaid. Many banks assume a calculated risk by eliminating some of these tests. In doing so, they must recognize that there is a potential for serious loss whenever a drawee honors a check that should have been returned.

The nine validity tests can be subdivided into five *visual* tests, performed through an examination of the check itself without reference to any other sources of information, and four *nonvisual* tests, in which the check itself does not provide sufficient information and other files, computer information, or records must be consulted. The visual tests answer these questions:

1. Is the item an actual check, drawn on an open account with our bank?

2. Is the drawer's signature genuine *and* authorized?

3. Has the check been altered?

4. Is the check properly dated?

5. Has the check been properly endorsed?

Visual examination of the check is all that is needed for these five tests. Even the determination of genuine and authorized signatures may be made without reference to other sources, since some banks have personnel who are so familiar with the signature files that they can tell at a glance whether the check meets this test.

The four remaining tests require that bank staff members refer to information other than that appearing on the check itself. These non-visual tests answer the following questions:

1. Has a stop-payment order been placed on the item?

2. Has a hold been placed on the account?

3. Is there a sufficient balance to cover the amount of the check?

4. Is the account balance available to the drawer?

At its discretion, a drawee may elect to honor a check even if it does not meet all nine tests. If the drawee does so, it should always have a valid reason for its action. Generally speaking, however, all nine conditions must be met if a check is to be charged to an account.

Actual Check on Our Bank. The first step is designed to ensure that the item is, in fact, a valid check on which the bank is the drawee. It must be drawn against an account at the bank that permits check withdrawal. Missorts sometimes occur; in other cases, an instrument is presented that purports to be a check drawn against a demand deposit but is actually drawn against some other form of relationship. A check may also be drawn against a closed account. All such items should, of course, have been detected and screened out during the original entry run.

Genuine and Authorized Signatures. Each signature on a check must be both genuine and authorized. If the bank's signature card files show that two signatures are required, *both* must meet this test.

A **genuine** signature is one that is not forged; it is an actual, valid signature of the maker. However, a genuine signature is not necessarily an **authorized** one. The bank must determine whether the signer has the legal right to issue instructions to it. John Jones may sign his own name on a check drawn against the account of the Morrison Trading Company; his signature is genuine, but the drawee must also determine whether he has been given the authority to act on the company's behalf. The same criteria apply to individual accounts. Kevin Wilson may establish a personal account in his name only. If his wife, Lucy Wilson, signs a check drawn on that account, her signature *is* genuine but *is not* authorized, and the checks cannot be honored. Drawees can honor *only* those checks signed by parties who have the right to instruct that payment be made.

Businesses that issue large quantities of checks find it convenient to use facsimile signatures, which are machine-generated or rubber-stamped replicas. This saves the time-consuming, burdensome task of having each check signed individually by an authorized party. If a bank is to honor checks bearing facsimile signatures, it must have on file a properly executed authorization from the maker.

Alterations. The test for alteration reflects the principle that a drawee is authorized *only* to follow the maker's exact instructions. If the maker drew a check for $10 and someone raised its amount to $100, the drawee would be expected to detect the alteration and reject the item because it did not conform to the maker's instructions. If the drawee failed to do so and the account was charged for the raised (larger) amount, the drawee would be liable for the error.

However, there is one exception to this general rule. If the depositor's own lack of diligence and care in issuing the check made it easy for an alteration to take place, the bank *may* be able to escape its normal liability. The burden of proof would then be on the bank to show that it exercised its proper role in examining the check and that the alteration was due to the negligence of the maker.

Dates. Checking the date on each item is an important part of the examining process, since a check may be dishonored if it is either **postdated** or **stale-dated**. Postdated checks bear a date in the future. The drawee has neither the authority nor a valid reason to honor this type of check. On the other hand, stale-dated checks were issued in the past; i.e., the item is not current. Under the Uniform Commercial Code, a bank is not obliged to pay a check presented 6 months or more after its issue date. Any such check *may* be returned unpaid.

Exceptions to this rule often occur. A corporation may issue dividend checks to its stockholders and find that many of them are not negotiated promptly, since some stockholders prefer to hold and accumulate them. In these cases, the drawee may assume in good faith that the checks are to be honored, or may have on file a specific authorization from the corporation, waiving the normal time frame for stale-dated items. U.S. government checks and travelers checks are other common exceptions to the general rule. It is also possible for the drawee to resolve any doubt by contacting the maker and obtaining permission to pay a stale-dated check.

Many checks bear a legend, "Not Good After ___ Days." This is an attempt by the maker to ensure that the items will be negotiated promptly. In examining checks, the drawee would be expected to identify any items presented after the stated time frame and to return them unpaid in accordance with the maker's wishes.

Endorsements. Examination of checks for proper endorsement is an integral part of the drawee's bank processing. When a drawer issues a check, the obvious intention is to make payment to a specific party, and the drawee is legally obliged to prove to its customer that the named payee endorsed the item. If anyone other than the named payee received the funds—for example, if the payee's endorsement were forged or if someone endorsed the check without proper authority— the drawee could be held liable to the drawer. The drawee could then try to recover payment from the party who took the check and obtained the funds through an unauthorized or forged endorsement.

Endorsement is the formal act that transfers rights to an instrument. An unqualified endorsement obligates the endorser to pay the item if it is dishonored for any reason. Without an endorsement, there is no similar legal liability. An effective endorsement must be on the instrument itself or on a paper so firmly affixed to the instrument that it becomes a part of it (Uniform Commercial Code, Art. 3-202(2)).

A depositor who determines that a check has been paid on the basis of an unauthorized or forged endorsement is legally allowed to enter a claim for reimbursement against the drawee, provided the claim is made within 3 years (1 year in California) after receipt of the item and the bank statement in which it was included.

Banks encounter many situations in which the endorsement on a particular check is vitally important. Many checks—for example, those issued by insurance companies or the trust departments of banks—specifically require the payee's written endorsement or mark. The endorsement serves as proof that the beneficiary of an insurance policy, the recipient of trust funds, or the party to whom an annuity payment is being made was alive when the check was received and negotiated and did, in fact, receive the stipulated amount. A drawee bank has every right to return unpaid any check that has not been properly endorsed.

Stop-Payment Orders. The first nonvisual test addresses the question of **stop-payment orders**. The drawer of a check has the legal right to countermand the original set of written instructions and to direct the drawee to dishonor the item. A dispute may have arisen between the drawer and payee; a projected business transaction may have fallen through; a check may have been issued in error; a customer's supply of blank checks may have been lost or stolen; or the drawer may, for any reason, simply wish to have the check returned unpaid.

The quickest means of notifying a drawee of a stop-payment order is by telephone. When a drawer contacts the bank by telephone and requests that payment on a check be stopped and the bank accepts this request, the depositor's verbal instructions are valid and binding for a period of 14 days under the provisions of the Uniform Commercial Code. The drawee, having accepted the telephoned request, should ask for a written confirmation for its files.

The UCC provides that stop-payment orders that have been confirmed in writing are valid and binding upon the drawee for 6 months. After that the check would become a stale-dated item and could be rejected for that reason. Written stop-payment orders can be renewed by the depositor as an additional form of protection.

The UCC also stipulates that the drawer's request to stop payment on a check must meet certain conditions. The drawee must be given a reasonable amount of time to act on the request; for example, if the stop-payment order is telephoned to the drawee and the check in question is paid at a teller's window within a few minutes thereafter, the bank clearly did not have an opportunity to comply with the order.

Through human error and oversight, a drawee may fail to observe a drawer's stop-payment order and may pay a specific check. When this happens, the depositor may bring suit against the bank for its alleged lack of care. In an effort to prevent this type of litigation, the stop-payment form provided by many banks to their customers contains a so-called escape clause. This clause states that the drawer will not sue the bank if the check in question is inadvertently paid.

However, the escape clause does *not* provide automatic protection for the drawee in every case. Some court decisions have been in favor of the depositor, whereas in other cases the ruling has favored the bank. Nevertheless, the burden of establishing the fact and amount of loss resulting from the payment of a check contrary to a binding stop-payment order is on the depositor (Uniform Commercial Code, Art. 4-403(3)). Article 4 of the Uniform Commercial Code addresses the matter of stop-payment orders and outlines the rights and protection afforded both to the depositor and to the drawee.

Holds. For a variety of reasons, a **hold** may be placed on an account to restrict part or all of the balance and thus to limit or prohibit payments against it. As part of the examining process, a drawee should determine whether a hold exists that would prevent the honoring of a particular check.

When a check has been converted into cash by a teller, its amount may be entered as a hold to protect the bank. Internal Revenue Service regulations provide that a tax levy can be issued against a delinquent taxpayer; under these circumstances, a drawee may be required to place a hold on the account. A bank may be served with a court order as a result of a judgment in favor of a plaintiff against the depositor and therefore may be directed to hold funds. The death of a depositor, certification of a check against an account, notice of the depositor's bankruptcy, or a legal declaration of the customer's incompetence also create the need for a hold.

When a customer deposits checks drawn on out-of-town banks, the bank may officially place a hold on the account to restrict payments against it for a period of time.

Sufficient and Available Funds. The two final nonvisual tests involve the balance in an account at the time checks are presented against it. These tests question, first, the amount of that balance and, second, whether that balance is available for the customer's use.

As mentioned earlier, fully automated bookkeeping systems post every check before it is examined. If this posting procedure creates a negative (minus) balance in an account, the bank must decide whether to allow that condition to stand. When it gives its approval, an **overdraft** is said to exist; that is, checks have been paid for an amount greater than the actual balance. Overdrafts exist *only* when the drawee permits them. If the bank decides not to allow an overdraft, the check or checks in question can be returned and the debit that was originally posted can be reversed.

As part of their relationship with customers, many banks extend overdraft privileges; that is, the depositor is allowed to issue checks even when no funds exist in an account to cover them. This pre-authorization is often referred to as a line of credit.

Banks that do not have fully automated bookkeeping systems can make decisions before the actual posting process, since bookkeepers can compare the dollar amount of checks presented with the balance shown on the ledger sheet. Any checks that would create an overdraft can be rejected at that time.

The most common single reason for returned checks in the United States is insufficient funds. Overdrafts actually represent a form of loan; in these cases the customers are using the bank's funds to make payments instead of using their own.

Checks are frequently presented against accounts in which the balance is sufficient but is not available. Under the concept of cash items, deposited checks increase the customer's book balance at once; however, each bank develops its own schedule of availability to indicate how soon those deposited checks may be drawn against. The drawee has the legal right to return unpaid any checks drawn against uncollected funds, since to honor them would create potential risk.

Returning checks drawn against insufficient or uncollected funds calls for a great deal of discretion and tact on the drawee's part. There are very few actions a bank can take that will antagonize customers as severely as a refusal to honor checks. The credit standing and reputation of an individual or business may be severely damaged in this manner. When a drawee returns checks unpaid, it must use all its knowledge of the size of the account relationship and its importance to the bank, the length of time during which the account has been maintained and the frequency of drawings against insufficient or uncollected funds, and the possible adverse consequences. On the other hand, the bank must be careful not to treat the matter casually and thus to create the impression that customers can issue checks without being concerned about the status of their account balances.

Statements

An inherent part of the bank's relationship with every checking account customer calls for the periodic issuing of statements, which furnish a record of all the transactions posted to accounts (see Figure 9-1). While this is a burdensome task for a bank with thousands of depositors, it is a necessary procedure that actually protects the interests of both parties. The customer who receives a bank statement is legally obliged to examine it and to notify the bank if any discrepancy is found.

Under the standard version of the Uniform Commercial Code (not entirely accepted by every state), a customer has 1 year from the time a statement and accompanying checks are made available to discover and report unauthorized signatures or alterations. Three years (except in California, which has a 1-year rule) are allowed for customers to discover and report any unauthorized endorsements. Other kinds of errors, such as those resulting from electronic transfers of funds, must be reported within shorter, specific time frames. Regardless of the care exercised, the customer who fails to act within these time limits is precluded from claims against the bank.

Cycle Statements. Depending on the number of statements that must be sent out and the preferences of customers, it may be convenient for the drawee to perform the entire statement task at one time. In the past, most bank statements were issued at month-end, principally because commercial customers maintained their own accounting records on a monthly basis.

However, banks with large numbers of customers find it impossible today to complete the statement work in a single day. They use the

Figure 9-1
Bank Statement

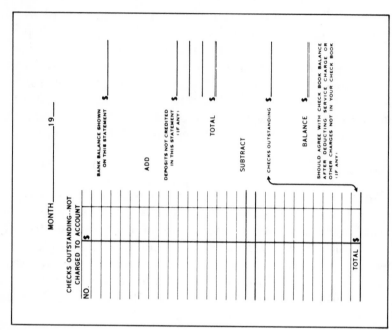

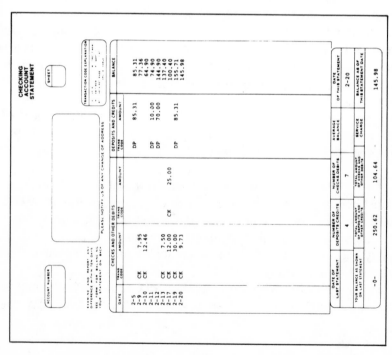

cycle statement system as a means of reducing the work load and overtime expense that would be required if all statements were to be sent out at once.

The cycle statement system divides all the bank's checking accounts into groups and designates the days of the month on which statements will be rendered to each group. The division into groups may be made by type of account (commercial, personal, etc.), alphabetically, or according to any other classification method the bank finds convenient. Ideally, as many as 20 categories of accounts would be created, so that one batch of statements would be mailed out on each of the 20 working days in a typical business month.

Under the cycle statement system, every customer receives the same *number* of statements per year; it is the timing that distinguishes this system from others. Telephone and utility companies, credit card issuers, and major businesses have used a similar method of rendering bills and statements for many years. An added benefit of the system is increased accuracy, since the employees who perform the work are under less pressure and are less likely to make errors.

Sorting and Returning Paid Checks. Closely associated with the rendering of bank statements is the task of sorting canceled checks and returning them to customers. Every paid check should be prominently canceled, by perforation or stamping, as a proof of payment and to prevent any possible reuse. Banks must use extreme care in matching checks with statements, so that all checks are properly listed and so that both checks and statements go to the appropriate customers.

Fully automated bookkeeping systems have made the preparation of bank statements quicker, simpler, and more efficient. The magnetic tape or discs that contain all the relevant information on each account can be coupled with high-speed printers to produce complete statements at any time during the month.

As an extra service to customers, many banks now encode the sequential number on each check in magnetic ink. By doing this, they are able to list paid items on the bank statement according to check number. This enables customers to prove and reconcile their statements far more easily and quickly.

Banks have always included in their marketing of checking accounts the argument that every canceled check would be returned to the drawer as proof of payment. As check volume has increased, however, and as the costs of mailing billions of paid checks have steadily grown, many banks have begun efforts to convince customers that paid checks need not necessarily be returned with statements. This is an example of **check truncation**.

Under this system, customers receive their regular statements, but the actual paid checks are microfilmed by the drawee and retained for a period of time. At the end of that period, they are destroyed. Should a customer require a copy of a paid check for any reason, the bank agrees to provide it.

Although thousands of customers at several major banks have agreed to accept truncation, a great deal of educational effort will be required if the system is to be more widely adopted.

Internal and External Reports

To meet the needs of various departments throughout the bank, the bookkeeping unit is in an ideal position to supply valuable information every day. The more extensive the bank's computer installation, the greater its ability to supply customized reports that can be used for a wide variety of purposes. Some banks have installed on-line computer systems that make information immediately available to tellers at their individual locations; for other banks, such extensive automation is not necessary or justified. The internal reports provided by the bookkeeping unit may include the following:

- Trial balance or daily journal reports, showing the debits and credits posted to each account on the previous day and the closing account balance for each customer.

- Reports of all drawings against insufficient or uncollected funds. These report forms can be designed to permit authorized bank personnel to enter their decisions on whether checks should be honored or returned.

- Reports on all opened and closed accounts and on all accounts that have shown large increases or decreases in balances.

- Stop-payment and hold reports.

- Listings of dormant accounts that have shown no activity for a period of time and have been placed under dual control.

In addition to the internal reports that the bookkeeping department can produce, there is a constant need to supply information to outside sources on the status of an account. Banks are logically called on to act as references for their customers; however, they must exercise a high degree of caution in answering inquiries and furnishing information. Every customer expects the account relationship to be treated confidentially; therefore, the bank must not only satisfy itself that an inquiry is legitimate but must also be extremely careful to give no information beyond what is absolutely necessary.

Inquiries regarding bank customers are often classified as "credit inquiries" and, depending on the individual bank's policy, may be handled directly by the **credit department** staff. At other banks, such inquiries are directed to the bookkeeping unit. In either case, certain basic principles must be carefully observed.

The identity of the inquirer and the purpose of the inquiry should be clearly established before any reply is made. A simple inquiry may be coming from a merchant who has been offered a check and contacts the drawee to ask if it is "good." In this case, the prudent answer simply states that the item is "good at present." This lets the merchant know that funds are on deposit to cover the check at that point in time. It provides no guarantee that the check will actually be honored when it is physically presented to the drawee.

An inquiry from another bank must be treated in a completely different fashion. It is a completely ethical and long-standing practice for banks to accept legitimate inquiries from other institutions and to exchange the appropriate amount of information. For example, suppose that two banks share a loan to the same corporate customer. Periodically, they will check with each other regarding approximate balance size, financial statement information, and general creditworthiness of the mutual customer.

In another common example, a merchant may contemplate doing business with a customer of whom she has no prior knowledge. She determines that the prospective customer maintains an account with Bank A, while the merchant herself banks with Bank B. It is perfectly proper for her to ask Bank B to obtain credit information on the customer from Bank A. Since it knows the reason for the inquiry, the size of the business transaction that is contemplated, and the right of the customer to give the bank as a reference, Bank A may respond by indicating how long the deposit relationship has existed, the level of balances, and whether Bank A feels the relationship has been satisfactory. Again, care and diligence must be exercised in handling such inquiries, and no information should be volunteered beyond that which is essential and relevant.

Dormant Accounts. The foregoing reference to internal reports from the bookkeepers included the term **dormant accounts**. Every bank, at one time or another, finds that some of its accounts have had no activity for a period of time, i.e., no deposits have been made and no checks have been issued. Once a stipulated period has elapsed, all such dormant accounts should be identified, segregated from all other accounts, and placed under dual control. There are several reasons for doing this.

In the first place, inactive accounts automatically constitute a source of temptation to any dishonest bank personnel who might be in a position to tamper with them. By placing the accounts under dual control, the bank ensures that any sudden activity will be noted and verified. Secondly, segregating dormant accounts removes them from the work that must be processed every day, so that bookkeepers' handling chores are reduced. Finally, state laws often stipulate that funds in dormant accounts must be turned over to state authorities after a specified amount of time has elapsed. Under the legal principle of **escheat**, a state has the right to claim all balances in dormant accounts. By segregating these accounts, the bank expedites this process, since it knows at all times exactly what funds have remained on an inactive basis throughout each calendar period.

Bookkeeping by Correspondent Banks. As a service to their smaller correspondents, many banks offer to perform the entire bookkeeping function on a direct-fee or compensating-balance basis. In this way a bank that cannot justify the expenses of automation can obtain all the benefits of the latest technology through the facilities of its larger, more active, more sophisticated correspondent. Obviously, this requires establishing complete schedules for delivery of all the necessary input and output. The smaller bank may have couriers deliver all the debits and credits for its customers' accounts to the larger bank at a certain time each business day. It must also arrange to have the messengers pick up all reports generated by the correspondent's bookkeeping system as soon as possible so that it will have updated information on the status of each account.

SUMMARY

The bookkeeping department of any bank, large or small, is one of the most sensitive of all the operating units. Regardless of which bookkeeping system a bank elects to use, its basic responsibility to exercise the highest degree of care in every phase of the process is inescapable. Accuracy is of paramount importance, and, although electronic data processing has revolutionized traditional bookkeeping methods, technology cannot reduce or eliminate the need for every drawee to protect itself and its depositors at all times.

The drawer of a check is issuing a set of detailed instructions to the drawee. The drawee, in turn, must be aware of its liability if it is negligent in any way in complying with those instructions. Similarly, a real risk exists if the drawee is negligent in applying to all orders for payment of funds those validity tests that are designed to ensure correct posting.

In addition to examining and posting checks and providing the input for many internal reports, a bank bookkeeping unit is also responsible for rendering periodic statements to customers and supplying information to legitimate inquirers. Here again, both accuracy and confidentiality enter into the picture.

QUESTIONS FOR DISCUSSION

1. What is the difference between a bank's bookkeeping department and its general ledger department?

2. From what sources does the bookkeeping department receive its daily work?

3. What is the advantage of a dual posting system? What is its disadvantage?

4. What information would usually be contained in the daily transaction tape? How is this tape used?

5. In fully automated bookkeeping, when are checks examined?

6. Identify five visual tests applied to checks during the examination process.

7. Distinguish between genuine signatures and authorized signatures. What is a facsimile signature?

8. Is a drawee legally liable if it pays a check that has been altered? Why?

9. List three reasons for placing a hold on an account.

10. What is the difference between an overdraft and a drawing against uncollected funds?

11. What is the advantage or benefit of the system of cycle statements?

12. What internal reports are usually generated each day through an automated bookkeeping system?

13. What precautions must bookkeepers take when answering credit inquiries from outside sources?

Suggested Readings

Bank Administration Institute. *General Ledger and Automated Financial Report.* Rolling Meadows, Illinois: Bank Administration Institute, 1976.

Bank Administration Institute. *Savings in Time Deposit Accounting.* Rolling Meadows, Illinois: Bank Administration Institute, 1975.

Davidson, Sidney, and Roman L. Weil. *Handbook of Modern Accounting.* 2nd ed. New York: McGraw-Hill, 1977.

Dwyer, John N. *Modern Bank Accounting and Auditing Forms.* Boston: Warren, Gorham & Lamont, 1970. Cumulative supplement, 1978.

Wendell, Paul J. *Modern Accounting and Auditing Checklists.* Boston: Warren, Gorham & Lamont, 1975. Cumulative supplement, 1978.

Chapter 10

Bank Loans and Investments: I

LEARNING OBJECTIVES

After completing this chapter, you will have an understanding of

- a bank's three basic objectives in its program of funds management;
- the consequences of a bank's overemphasis on any one of the three objectives;
- the process by which a bank calculates its liquidity needs;
- the four basic categories of bank loans;
- the factors intrinsic to participations;
- the distinction between time loans and demand loans; and
- the basis on which installment loans are granted.

C ommercial banks generate profits by rendering services, attracting and retaining deposits, processing payments in a prompt and efficient manner, and putting to profitable use those funds that, in management's judgment, are not immediately needed. One of the basic obligations perceived by every bank is the need to serve the credit requirements of customers and the community, and banks translate that credit function into a wide variety of loan and investment operations to meet that obligation.

In every manufacturing industry, profits result when a company obtains some form of raw material, processes it and converts it into saleable merchandise, and markets its product at a price above all the manufacturing, selling, and overhead costs. Banks operate in an identical way. Their raw material is their deposits, which they use to generate profits. When banks judiciously extend credit to meet the legitimate needs of their markets, they are doing nothing more than fulfilling their traditional role as the principal source of funds for every type of borrower.

Loans represent by far the largest source of bank income; typically, they provide 60 to 70 percent of total revenue. They have an equivalent importance on the bank's balance sheet, usually accounting for two-thirds of total assets.

As mentioned earlier, commercial banks in their credit function provide funds to governments, businesses, and consumers. As a group, they are by far the largest holders of U.S. government obligations, and their purchases of the debt issues of state, county, and city agencies and authorities of government enable those entities to continue to function. Out of every $100 borrowed by businesses of every size and type, commercial banks supply about $70. The installment loan, mortgage loan, and credit card facilities of commercial banks make money accessible to individuals. Truly, our society operates on credit, and the banks are the traditional and major suppliers of that credit.

COMPETITION FROM OTHER LENDERS

Despite their preeminent position as a source of credit, however, commercial banks face increasing and aggressive competition from many other types of lenders. Commercial financing firms are active lenders to businesses, and Merrill Lynch and General Electric Credit Company are among those firms that have entered that field. Organizations such as General Motors Acceptance Corporation are extremely active in the financing of automobiles. Small loan companies accommodate the borrowing needs of individuals. Savings banks and savings and loan associations have always been the principal lenders in the home mortgage field and were also active in home improvement loans and loans made against passbooks; legislation in 1980 and 1982 gave them additional lending powers, enabling them to compete more actively with commercial banks. Insurance companies are an important source of long-term credit for real estate financing; they also lend to policyholders against the cash surrender value of their policies. The nation's 22,000 credit unions are actively involved in lending to their members. Each of these lenders plays a part in America's overall borrowing picture and competes with commercial banks in the credit function.

However, banks differ from their competitors in one important sense: They are unique in their ability to meet every type of request for loans from businesses, agencies of government, individuals, other banks, churches, hospitals, and other borrowers. All the other lenders can extend *some* type, or *several* types, of credit; commercial banks are the only entities that can provide *all* types.

MANAGEMENT OF BANK FUNDS

It is a widely held misconception that commercial banks hold huge pools of money, belonging to the banks themselves, that they can use as they see fit. If this were true, a bank would be risking only its own capital when it approved a loan. However, the fact is that 9 of every 10 dollars loaned by commercial banks come from depositors' funds—*not* from the bank's. Each loan that a bank makes is an effort to put deposited funds to work for profit while simultaneously meeting a borrower's needs.

Because loans, generally speaking, are made not from the bank's own resources but from the funds entrusted to it by customers, commercial banks must constantly keep three objectives in mind in the daily management of funds. These objectives are *liquidity, safety,* and *income.* One of the highest skills required of bank management calls for the proper balancing of all three. Any overemphasis on one at the expense of the other two, or any neglect of them, will inevitably lead to very serious problems for a bank.

Liquidity

Every business, individual, agency of government, church, school, foundation, and educational institution continually faces the problem of everyday obligations and bills that must be paid. If this can be done with readily available cash or the equivalent of cash, a *liquid* financial position is said to exist. An individual who holds sufficient currency, demand deposits, or other assets that can be quickly converted into cash to cover debts, taxes, and other expenses, or a business that can pay its suppliers and creditors without difficulty, is considered to have a high degree of liquidity.

For a bank, the term **liquidity** has a somewhat different implication. No depositor ever leaves funds with a bank without expecting, at some future time, to recover the funds personally or to direct that they be paid to another party. Demand deposits can be withdrawn at any time simply by issuing a check. Unless a bank exercises its right to demand advance notice of intent to withdraw, a savings account customer can have access to all or part of the account's balance at any time. Time deposits mature at certain dates, and the bank must be prepared to pay back the principal plus accumulated interest. No bank can remain in business for any length of time if it finds it necessary to reject customers' requests for withdrawal or payment of funds on the grounds that it does not have the wherewithal to meet those requests. For a bank, then, liquidity is chiefly concerned with the ability to meet demands for payments of funds at any time.

However, the need for liquidity is not based entirely on the deposit function; it is also closely tied to the credit function. Every bank has customers who have dealt with it for many years and who, from time to time, have a legitimate need for credit. They expect their banks to meet that need and to make funds available to them. Liquidity enables a bank to provide for the loan demands of long-established customers who enjoy good credit standing.

The depositors' understanding of the principle of liquidity is inherent in their making deposits in the first place. Every deposit demonstrates a customer's confidence that the bank will be able to repay the funds when called on to do so. If that public confidence is lost, a run on the bank and a state of panic may result. When this happens, all usual patterns of inflows and outflows of funds change; new deposits no longer flow into a bank if there is any suspicion that it is illiquid, and depositors, at the same time, will withdraw funds in an effort to protect themselves. The wave of bank failures during the 1930s was caused, at least in part, by this type of panic reaction.

For the American public, which witnessed so many bank failures during that period, federal deposit insurance has brought a massive restoration of confidence. Today's customer feels far more secure because of the protection that the Federal Deposit Insurance Corporation and Federal Savings and Loan Insurance Corporation have afforded. The existence of these insurers, however, does nothing to diminish the banks' obligation to have sufficient liquidity to meet estimated outflows of funds.

Every commercial bank bases its daily operations on a variation of the fundamental law of averages. It is theoretically possible that every customer will want to withdraw funds at exactly the same time, but there is very little likelihood that this will ever actually take place. It is far more likely that new funds, in the form of deposits, will arrive at the bank every day while checks are being honored and orders for withdrawal are being accepted and paid. It is only when this law of averages is distorted that a problem occurs.

When a manufacturer encounters a sudden, unforeseen increase in demand for its product, it can usually cope with the situation by assuring customers that its assembly lines are doing everything possible to catch up with the demand and by promising delivery of the finished goods as soon as possible. Banks have no such option. Customers cannot be asked to wait patiently until the bank solves its liquidity problem and obtains the necessary funds. Every demand for payment or withdrawal of funds must be honored unless there is a compelling reason to refuse it (e.g., a time deposit that cannot be withdrawn before maturity). Liquidity is an absolute must, and for this reason it is always listed as the first of the three basic objectives in the management of bank funds.

The Deposit/Loan Relationship. The relationship between a bank's credit function and its daily liquidity position works in an additional direction. Typically, bank loans are made to existing customers and credited to accounts, or the proceeds of a loan are used to open an account. It is for this reason that commercial banks are said to have the ability to *create money.*

Suppose, for example, that a loan for $1,000 is approved and the proceeds are credited to an account. Two balance sheet items, loans (an asset) and deposits (a liability), are simultaneously increased. Assume that the bank is subject to a reserve requirement of 15 percent, meaning that $150 of the deposited funds must be placed in a reserve account. The remaining $850 can then be used for another loan to another customer, thus continuing the cycle. When the $850 is deposited, a reserve of $128 (15 percent) must be set aside, and the remaining $722 is available for further use. New loans generate additional deposits; after the bank makes provision for reserves, those deposits can be put to work in the form of additional loans.

If a bank chose to overemphasize liquidity at the expense of the other two objectives in the management of funds, it would keep large excess supplies of coin and currency in its vaults as a protection against possible increases in demands for withdrawals of funds. However, by doing so it would also reduce the percentage of its deposits available for loans, and its credit function would be impaired. It would, at the same time, be neglecting the requirement for safety, because those quantities of coin and currency on hand would make it more vulnerable to losses through holdups and possible internal thefts.

Thus, while recognizing the paramount importance of liquidity, a bank must always keep in mind that there are other basic considerations that cannot be neglected in its management of funds.

Calculating Liquidity Needs. To determine its liquidity needs, a bank usually tries to calculate its projected deposit floor and its projected loan ceiling. The deposit floor is the low point that deposits can reasonably be expected to reach. If current deposits are $50 million and all available information (data from past experience, seasonal factors, maturity dates for time deposits) indicates that they will drop to $40 million within a certain time frame, the bank needs $10 million of liquidity to meet the withdrawals. By the same line of reasoning, the loan ceiling is the maximum figure for outstanding loans that the bank expects to attain within the same time frame. If loans now total $29 million and all seasonal and money market conditions, coupled with information from customers as to their borrowing plans, indicate an increase to $33 million, the bank needs an additional $4 million of liquidity. The combination of the low point for deposits and the high point for loans yields the total estimated liquidity need: $14 million.

In times of extremely high demand for credit, the deposit/loan ratio changes greatly, and a credit crunch may occur. The banking system then finds itself hard-pressed to meet the legitimate credit needs of its markets. Conversely, when the demand for commercial bank credit decreases, the ratio moves in the other direction and liquidity projections change accordingly.

Table 10-1 shows the increase in the ratio of loans to deposits that has taken place since World War II.

Table 10-1
Ratio of Total Loans to Gross Deposits, All U.S. Commercial Banks, Selected Years

Year	Ratio
1950	33.7
1960	51.2
1970	65.2
1974	72.3
1980	82.6

SOURCE: *Federal Reserve Bulletin*, various issues.

Meeting Liquidity Needs. Liquidity needs at commercial banks are primarily met through a combination of various types of **reserves**. *Primary reserves* consist of cash on hand, demand deposit balances with correspondent banks, and reserves kept at the Fed. *Secondary reserves* consist of highest quality investments that the bank can convert into cash on very short notice. In the strict sense of the word, primary reserves offer more liquidity, since they are immediately available. On the other hand, they produce no income, whereas secondary reserves earn interest. For example, a demand deposit kept with another bank cannot produce interest income but is immediately available for use. A short-term U.S. government obligation, as a secondary reserve, provides interest income but must be sold in order to raise cash.

Safety

If it is essential that every bank be in a position to honor all anticipated demands for withdrawals of funds, it is equally essential that the bank take every possible measure to protect the funds entrusted to it. Every depositor must be made to feel that funds left with the bank are completely safe at all times. A loss of customer confidence that results in a run on the bank can be caused as easily by an indication of improper or imprudent loans and investments as by actual or rumored difficulty in meeting requests for withdrawals. Anything that a bank can do to bolster the confidence of its customers is to its advantage.

Again, however, the concept of balance in the management of funds enters the picture. If a bank were to try to provide the absolute maximum of safety, it could never assume any risk in putting depositors' funds to profitable use; therefore, it would make no loans or investments in which there was any potential for loss. By attempting to eliminate all risks, or as many as possible, a bank would become so overly protective of depositors' money that it would neglect the legitimate credit needs of its customers and community and would inevitably stagnate.

Income

There is a third objective that must always be part of a bank's program for management of funds. If liquidity and safety were the only factors it had to consider, a bank could build the largest and strongest vault imaginable, keep as much cash as possible under maximum security, and make only those loans and investments that carried an absolute minimum of risk. There would always be an adequate supply of currency on hand to meet demands for withdrawals and payments of funds, and losses that resulted from loans and investments would be held to an irreducible minimum. This course of action would completely neglect the third essential element, which is the need for *income.*

Unlike their counterparts in other countries, American banks are not nationalized and are not subsidized by the government. They are organized for profit, and their obligations to the shareholders who have invested in their future must be considered together with all other obligations to customers and communities. A bank that does not demonstrate adequate growth in its annual net income soon loses the confidence of its depositors, its stockholders, and the public.

Like the other two factors in the management of bank funds, however, income can never be considered alone. An overemphasis on profits, neglecting liquidity and safety, can be disastrous. It is unfortunately true that many banks in the nation's financial history elected to stress income at the expense of liquidity and safety and were forced out of business as a result.

Interest on loan accounts is by far the largest portion of a bank's annual income. Therefore, any bank that identifies improvement in earnings as its essential goal would have to expand its loan portfolio to build up interest income. This expansion would involve aggressive efforts to attract new borrowers. Experience shows that this course of action invariably leads to a lowering of the bank's normal credit standards, approving loans that the bank would not otherwise make, and assuming risks far beyond the norm.

Interest is simply money paid for the use of money. A borrower who is especially in need of funds will pay a higher interest rate. A bank that is anxious to improve its earnings, at the expense of safety considerations, will charge higher rates as a reflection of the increased risk it is assuming. Banks always seek to increase their profits, but they cannot do so if at the same time they ignore the basic need for liquidity and safety in the management of funds.

Priorities in Funds Management

A program for the management of bank funds must create a balance among all three objectives at all times. This requires establishing a schedule of actual priorities, and, since the most fundamental obligation is to meet all foreseeable demands for withdrawals of funds, the *primary* focus must be on liquidity. The deposit base is highly volatile—demand deposits more so than time and savings deposits—and a bank must be prepared for a shrinkage of that base at any time.

Because banks also have an obligation to try to satisfy the legitimate credit requirements of their depositors and the community, their estimate of liquidity needs also must include consideration of the demand for loans. A bank cannot remain in business if it neglects the credit function; the economy of the country relies on commercial banks to supply loans and make investments, and every discussion of liquidity must reflect that basic fact.

When, and *only* when, a bank has devoted sufficient attention to all its estimated liquidity needs, it can then concentrate on investments and nonloan products that will help it meet its profit objectives. Every commercial bank is under simultaneous pressures from its depositors and its stockholders. Customers deposit funds with those banks that have traditionally met their requests for credit; stockholders look for growth and profits. Reconciling these two essentials often calls for a high degree of management skill. Again, the demands placed on banks differentiate them from other lenders. If a small loan company or commercial financing firm rejects a request for credit, it loses only the interest income that it could have received. Conversely, a bank that refuses to lend to a long-standing depositor faces the potential loss of a valued account as well as the interest income.

BASIC TYPES OF BANK LOANS

For purposes of reporting to government agencies and for internal management information and planning, most commercial banks divide their loan portfolios into four basic categories:

- Real estate loans;

- Participations and interbank loans;

- Installment loans; and

- Commercial and industrial loans.

In those areas of our country where loans to farmers form a significant part of the credit function, a fifth category, agricultural loans, may be included.

The classifications often overlap. They are often subdivided according to the various lending activities that the bank engages in to accommodate customers.

Real Estate Loans

In many areas of the United States, banks in recent years have become increasingly involved in various types of real estate financing. They have provided the funds needed for new office buildings, shopping centers, condominiums and cooperatives, and other residential developments. Their involvement takes two forms, construction loans and mortgage loans.

Construction Loans. A real estate developer often requires funds at the very outset of a project to demolish and clear existing property and proceed with the erection of a new structure—for example, an office skyscraper or an apartment complex. A bank accommodates that developer by providing a **construction loan**.

Construction loans are usually unsecured and are short-term credits that will be repaid from the permanent mortgage financing arranged by the builder. The proceeds of the construction loan are used to pay architects and contractors for their services, to meet payrolls, and to purchase needed materials. It is a common practice for a commercial bank to extend the short-term construction loan and for another lender or combination of lenders (e.g., insurance companies, pension funds, institutions and foundations, and syndicates of foreign interests) to provide the long-term mortgage financing when the project is completed; however, the commercial bank may fill both of these lending roles if it so desires.

Mortgage Loans. Real estate **mortgage loans** are invariably long-term, and the property itself is the collateral for the loan. Commercial banks may extend mortgage loans on office buildings, apartment houses, and shopping centers if there is sufficient evidence that the regular income from rents in the project will be more than sufficient to meet a schedule of regular payments to the bank.

For many years, commercial banks were not active in the home mortgage field. People who sought funds to finance the purchases of homes obtained their mortgages from savings banks or savings and loan associations, and thrift institutions are still the primary lenders in that field. However, commercial banks in increasing numbers have recently turned their attention to home mortgage lending. The introduction of several types of variable- or adjustable-rate loans, in which the interest rate can be adjusted by the bank as money market rates change, has been a significant factor in this change in policy. In mid-1982, total mortgage debt in the United States on 1- to 4-family dwellings totaled $1 trillion, of which the commercial banks held $291 billion.

Residential mortgage loans are based on the value of the home itself and the borrower's income and creditworthiness. If the borrower defaults, the bank can foreclose on the home and sell it to recover the unpaid loan balance.

Since the end of World War II, home mortgage loans have consistently grown with the assistance of agencies of the federal government. The Veterans Administration and the Federal Housing Administration have been the leaders in providing loan guarantees to borrowers, thereby strengthening the credit of the applicant.

A fundamental principle in bank lending states that there should be a match between the loan itself and the type of deposit that is used to make it. Because time deposits are more stable than demand deposits and tend to remain with banks for longer periods of time, they are generally used to make mortgage loans. The traditional lead position of the thrift institutions in the home mortgage field reflects this principle.

In recent years, the problem of interest rates on home mortgages has received increased attention, and the activities both of commercial banks and of thrifts have undergone considerable revision. Traditionally, home mortgage loans were made at fixed rates; the borrower who obtained such a loan agreed to an interest rate that would remain constant for 20 or 30 years. Changes in the money markets have brought about a change in this traditional policy, and many mortgage loans are now made on a variable- (=adjustable) rate basis. The borrower understands that the lending institution may change the interest rate when credit conditions make this necessary.

Participations and Interbank Loans

Participations involve a sharing of a single loan by two or more banks. There are many reasons why participations exist. A single loan may legally be too large for one bank to assume. A corporation, for example, that maintains accounts with several banks and requires a large amount of credit may divide the loan among them. For practical policy reasons rather than legal ones, one bank may decide that a loan is too large for it to handle alone. Banks often refer loan proposals to their larger correspondents and invite the latter to participate with them.

Commercial banks today must often meet demands for substantial credit from a single customer. A foreign government, for example, borrows $250 million from a group of 40 American banks so that it can finance its internal economic development. A major domestic company enters into a $40 million loan agreement with five major banks to finance the construction of a new plant.

Interbank loans involve the direct extension of credit by one bank to another, often on the basis of a correspondent relationship. Included in this grouping would be loans made by commercial banks to their thrift institution customers, loans made by a large correspondent to assist a smaller bank, and **federal funds transactions**.

Not every federal funds transaction is a loan; a wire transfer of funds from one bank to another may use the reserve accounts each maintains with the Fed as the transfer vehicle so that there is immediate and unquestioned availability. However, Fed funds also move from one bank to another as direct borrowings. In these cases, the loans are made on an overnight basis by banks that have an excess amount in their reserve accounts at the Fed. Since the excess reserves produce no interest income, the banks that happen to have them can lend them to other banks and thus generate income.

Installment Loans

As was noted earlier, commercial banks in America, throughout most of their history, paid little or no attention to the credit needs of individuals and did not consider them appropriate candidates for credit. Banks were a source of funds for corporations, governments, and other banks, and not for the average working person. As a result, the consumer was forced to go to other lenders, such as the thrift institution for a mortgage, the small loan company for personal borrowings, or the automobile finance agency to obtain funds for the purchase of a car.

Today, this banking attitude no longer exists on its former widespread basis. Commercial banking, which traditionally was wholesale in nature, has shifted much of its emphasis to retail business, and the needs and wants of consumers have become extremely important in the overall banking picture.

Consumer credit today includes both the familiar installment loan and various types of **revolving credit** arrangements, in which the customer can have access to part or all of a predetermined amount at any time. Payments under a revolving credit decrease the borrower's outstanding debt; he or she can subsequently borrow again to bring the credit back to the original figure. Consumers who use their bank cards to obtain cash advances often operate under this type of consumer credit.

As the name implies, **installment loans** carry a schedule of fixed monthly payments. A form of coupon book is often given to the borrower for use in making each payment. Generally speaking, installment loans are made on an unsecured basis (the automobile loan, on which the financed auto is the collateral, is a major exception to this rule); that is, the bank relies on the signature of the borrower and his or her promise to repay. The applicant's job, annual income, length of employment, outstanding debts, and general credit history are evaluated by the lending bank.

Installment loans are made today to meet every type of personal need and want, including home appliances, automobiles, vacations, medical and dental bills, and educational expenses.

Government regulations require that the lending bank explain clearly to each borrower the *true* annual percentage rate (APR) charged on loans. In many cases installment loans are **discounted**; that is, the bank deducts the entire amount of interest for the life of the loan before giving the borrower the net proceeds. This, of course, is an advantage for the bank because it receives all the interest at once. On a 12-month installment loan, the true APR is approximately twice the discounted rate, and the lending bank must indicate clearly on all its notes and other loan forms the actual interest cost to the borrower.

As part of their installment loan operations, many banks work directly with automobile and appliance dealers and obtain loan applications from them. These dealers then become an important source of new installment loan business for the banks. In other cases, the banks enter into what is known as **floor plan financing**, in which they extend credit directly to the dealer. This financing allows the dealer to carry an adequate inventory of cars or appliances for display and sale.

Installment loans have proved extremely attractive to banks for many reasons. They enable the banks to compete on a broad scale with other types of financial institutions. The interest income is an important contributor to annual profits. Installment loans may be a source of new individual accounts for the lending bank. Finally, the mass of historical evidence indicates that most such loans are repaid as agreed. The loss experience of banks in the installment loan field shows that the average working individual can, in fact, be trusted to meet his or her obligations and repay his or her debts.

Bank Cards. At the time they were first introduced on a large scale, the pieces of plastic that are seen everywhere today were called credit cards; they were widely used for travel and entertainment purposes as well as for purchases of merchandise. Today, it is more appropriate to refer to them as bank cards rather than credit cards because of the far wider range of uses to which they can be put. In many cases, the card is used as a *debit* card through a point-of-sale terminal or other arrangement; that is, the card is used as the vehicle to transfer funds from the cardholder's bank account to that of the seller. The card creates a debit to the cardholder's account. The growth of bank cards is closely allied to the consumer credit concept. These cards often serve as substitutes for installment loans, because the cardholder uses his VISA, MasterCard, or other bank card to obtain goods and services without executing a loan application and promissory note. During 1982, the loans outstanding on bank cards consistently exceeded $23 billion.

Operational Considerations. Although the income from installment lending and bank cards remains attractive, other factors must be considered when a bank enters into these retail functions on a large scale. Specialized units are needed to establish and maintain monthly records and to implement all the required security procedures and controls over borrowings. There are relatively high handling costs in each extension of retail credit because of the quantity of internal paper (loan applications, notes, liability ledgers, and interest income reports) that is necessary.

Commercial and Industrial Loans

Table 10-2 shows that the fourth category of bank loans, commercial and industrial, is the largest. It is here that the widest variations in amounts and terms occur. Some commercial loans are made for relatively small dollar amounts; others may be for many millions of dol-

Table 10-2
Loan Portfolios, All Commercial Banks,
May 1982

Category	Amount Outstanding in Billions of Dollars
Commercial and industrial	378.9
Real estate	294.4
Individuals	186.2
Agricultue	34.3
Total	993.8

NOTE: Interbank loans are not included.
SOURCE: *Federal Reserve Bulletin*, July 1982, p. A 15.

lars. Some are made for intermediate or long terms (i.e., more than 1 year); most are made for shorter periods of time, and the most common single maturity period is 90 days. This reflects the fact that commercial loans are made largely on the basis of demand deposits, which are highly volatile. Quick turnover is desirable because it provides for liquidity and returns the borrowed funds to the bank so that they can be used again.

Many commercial loans are made on a **demand** basis; the bank can call for repayment at any time, or the borrower can repay the entire amount when convenient. Other commercial loans are made on a **time** basis, with a specific maturity date. Both types have advantages and disadvantages from the bank's standpoint. A demand loan, for example, requires more attention than its name might imply; the bank must make sure that interest is paid on a regular basis during the life of the loan and must also have some agreement with the borrower that the loan will not stay on the bank's books indefinitely. On the other hand, demand loans permit the bank to make any changes in interest rates that it believes are necessary during the life of the loan. Time loans traditionally have not allowed for any change in interest rates; like the original concept of the home mortgage loan, they keep the interest rate constant until the loan is repaid.

In addition to being short-term, most commercial loans are unsecured. The credit is extended on the basis of an analysis of all available information pertaining to the customer and the bank's confidence in that customer's ability and willingness to repay. However, it is a common practice for loans to business ventures to carry with them the personal guarantees of the principals in the business or some other creditworthy parties.

Agricultural Loans

As mentioned in Chapter 1, archaeological evidence testifies that agricultural lending is as old as civilization itself. The farmer in America today requires financing just as his predecessor in ancient Babylon did, and for many banks the four categories of loans that have been discussed are less important than a fifth one, which would show their farm credits. Farmers face the chronic problem of making investments in equipment and meeting operating expenses before their crops are harvested and sold, and banks provide the interim financing they need.

LOAN CLASSIFICATION

Although the four basic categories of loans offer a convenient method of classifying the components in a bank's portfolio, it must be noted that many loans can easily be placed under more than one heading. A major credit to a corporate borrower, shared by several banks, is both a participation and a commercial loan at the same time. A home mortgage loan is obviously a type of real estate credit, yet it is made to a consumer and is repaid on an installment basis. In classifying its loans, every bank must be careful to avoid any duplications so that the total picture is accurate.

For their internal information purposes, many banks classify loans on an industry basis in addition to the categories already discussed. In this way they are aware at all times of concentrations that may have built up in their loans to certain segments of the economy, such as the petroleum, aerospace, automobile, or tobacco industries. If a particular industry begins to display problems, having this information readily available enables the bank to take whatever action may be required.

SUMMARY

Despite the increasing competition they face from many other lenders, commercial banks remain the major source of credit for the American economy and provide every type of loan to every category of borrower. In doing so, they basically use depositors' funds rather than their own; therefore, their programs for the management of funds call for a delicate balance that must be maintained at all times among the three objectives of liquidity, safety, and income. None of the three can be neglected if the bank is to survive and remain profitable. Estimating liquidity needs is at best a highly educated guess; today's estimated figure may have to be revised drastically next week. The credit function is the major contributor to bank income, yet extending credit carries with it the assumption of risk. This risk is diversified among the four basic categories of loans that banks extend.

QUESTIONS FOR DISCUSSION

1. Why is liquidity so essential for a commercial bank?

2. What would be the consequences if a bank chose to overemphasize liquidity, safety, or income?

3. What two factors are considered when a bank tries to calculate its liquidity needs?

4. Distinguish between the two types of real estate loans that commercial banks extend.

5. Give two reasons why a participation might exist.

6. On what basis are installment loans generally made?

7. Why are most commercial and industrial loans made on a short-term basis?

8. From the information published by your bank, identify the amount of credit it has extended in each category of loans.

Suggested Readings

American Bankers Association. *A Banker's Guide to Commercial Loan Analysis.* Washington, D.C.: American Bankers Association, 1977.

American Bankers Association. *A Banker's Guide to Small-Business Loans.* Washington, D.C.: American Bankers Association, 1978.

American Bankers Association. *Bank Cards.* Washington, D.C.: American Bankers Association, 1983.

American Bankers Association. *Bank Investments.* Washington, D.C.: American Bankers Association, 1983.

Buchanan, Michael, and Ronald D. Johnson. *Real Estate Finance.* Washington, D.C.: American Bankers Association, 1983.

Freund, William C. *Investment Fundamentals.* Washington, D.C.: American Bankers Association, 1981.

Frey, Thomas L., and Robert H. Behrens. *Lending to Agricultural Enterprises.* Boston: Bankers Publishing Company, 1981.

Golembe (Carter H.) Associates. *Commercial Bank and Investment Banking.* Washington, D.C.: American Bankers Association, 1979.

McDonald, Jay M., and John E. McKinley. *Corporate Banking: A Practical Approach to Lending.* Washington, D.C.: American Bankers Association, 1981.

McKinney, Jr., George W., William J. Brown, and Paul M. Horvitz. *Management of Commercial Bank Funds.* Washington, D.C.: American Bankers Association, 1980.

O'Leary, Edward T., and Jane McNeil. *Introduction to Commercial Lending.* Washington, D.C.: American Bankers Association, 1983.

Roussakis, Emmanuel N. *Managing Commercial Bank Funds.* New York: Praeger, 1977.

Taylor, John Renford. *Consumer Lending.* Washington, D.C.: American Bankers Association, 1983.

Wills, Ronald K. *Consumer Credit Analysis.* Washington, D.C.: American Bankers Association, 1983.

Chapter 11

Bank Loans and Investments: II

LEARNING OBJECTIVES

After completing this chapter, you will have an understanding of

- the five restrictions that have been placed on bank loans;
- the distinction between asset management and liability management;
- the difference between the discount rate and the prime rate;
- such terms as amortization and balloon payments;
- the test that is applied to all collateral;
- a bank's system of priorities in making loans and investments;
- the difference between credit risk and market risk; and
- the advantages to a bank of investments in municipal bonds.

In Chapter 10, the basic categories and types of loans were discussed. However, every bank must make its own decisions as to the types of loans it will consider at any time and the degree of aggressiveness with which it will seek to increase its loan portfolio. At one time or another, a bank may elect not to make specific types of loans and to concentrate on others. State laws restricting the maximum interest rate that can be charged on certain loans, money market conditions, and other external factors may bring about a decision of this nature, as will management information systems that indicate an excessive concentration in one type or a failure of one category of loans to generate appropriate profits.

BANK LENDING POLICIES

Because the typical bank is a corporate entity, of which the board of directors is the active, governing body, the policy-making process begins at the board level. Directors of a bank are actively involved in the credit function. They must decide whether to enter new lending areas, such as leasing, credit cards, and installment loans. They must review the bank's portfolio of outstanding loans to ensure that the institution is truly meeting the credit needs of its customers and its community. They must assign credit authority in varying amounts to the bank's lending officers, so that each one knows the maximum loan amount he or she can individually approve and what combinations of additional authority are needed for larger amounts. Directors must conduct periodic audits of the bank's entire credit function to ensure that proper procedures are being followed in all cases. Finally, as a matter of policy, the directors have the ultimate lending authority on all loans above a certain stipulated amount.

The policies set by the directors and carried out by the lending officers must be reviewed regularly if they are to remain appropriate in a rapidly changing economy.

LEGAL RESTRICTIONS ON BANK LOANS

The importance of the credit function to the success or failure of a bank, the impact that bank loans have on the nation's economy, and the increased emphasis on consumerism in today's society have led to the placing of many federal and state restrictions on bank lending activities. Every lending officer must be thoroughly familiar with them. They include the following:

- The maximum dollar amount of a loan to any one borrower is restricted by federal and state laws. The general rule is that a national bank may lend no more than 15 percent of its capital and surplus to a single customer on an unsecured basis. If the loan is secured, the limit is increased to 25 percent. These laws compel banks to diversify their loans among a broader market base and prevent the problem of having "too many eggs in one basket." Many participations result from this restriction on a bank's legal lending limit.

- The sizes and maturities of real estate loans are restricted by the laws of various states and, in the case of national banks, by regulations issued by the Comptroller of the Currency.

- The laws of many individual states restrict the maximum interest rates that banks can charge on many types of loans, including home mortgage loans, installment loans, and loans resulting from the use of bank cards. **Usury** is the legal term for excessive and punitive interest, and any bank that is found guilty of usury faces heavy civil and criminal penalties. In an environment of high interest rates on deposits, many banks in various parts of the country have had to curtail portions of their lending activities because local usury laws made certain loans unprofitable; i.e., the maximum interest rate that could be charged on those loans was lower than the prevailing market rates that banks had to pay to attract and retain deposits.

- Various Federal Reserve regulations affect the lending activities of member banks:
  —Regulation B prohibits any discrimination by a lender on the basis of age, race, color, national origin, religion, sex, marital status, or receipt of income from public assistance programs.
  —Regulation O limits the amount that a member bank may lend to any of its own executive officers and requires that the borrowing officer report his or her loans to the board of directors.
  —Regulation U limits the amount of credit a member bank

may extend when (1) the loan is made for the purchase of listed securities or to enable the borrower to pay for listed securities already bought *and* (2) the loan is secured by stock market collateral. This regulation was designed to restrict stock market speculation by investors who borrow in order to buy stocks, use those stocks as collateral for further borrowing in order to buy more stocks, and so on.

—Regulation Z ("truth-in-lending") applies to all credit extended by member banks for personal, household, family, or agricultural purposes. It requires banks to meet certain standards in advertising credit services, to make full disclosure of actual loan costs, and to answer any complaints within a specified time period.

—Regulation BB implements the Community Reinvestment Act (CRA), which was passed by Congress in 1978. The CRA resulted from complaints that banks were guilty of a practice known as **redlining**. They were accused of attracting deposits from certain areas of their communities that were deteriorating but at the same time refusing to make loans in those same areas because they perceived the risks as being too great. It was alleged that in these cases the banks drew red lines around the borders of certain parts of their communities to indicate the areas where loans would not be considered. Federal examinations of banks must now include assessments of the extent to which the credit needs of the entire community have been met. Individuals who feel that a bank's record has not been satisfactory may register their complaints, and federal authorities may refuse to approve a bank's requests for additional branches or services if its constituents have criticized its credit policies.

Aside from these restrictions, the extending of credit is left largely to the judgment and prudence of each individual bank.

INTEREST RATES

Within the legal limits established from time to time by individual states or by federal regulations, the interest rates that banks charge reflect the fact that money is essentially nothing more than a supply-and-demand commodity. Its price fluctuates widely, according to factors that are often entirely beyond a bank's control. The interest rate charged on a specific loan may represent a combination of factors:

- The *availability* of money. If business activity increases, loan demand rises with it, and banks may be forced to revise their lending policies, possibly allocating loanable funds to those customers who appear to have the most valid claims.

- The degree of *risk* perceived by the bank. The creditworthiness of the borrower is considered when the interest rate on a loan is determined.

- The *time frame* during which the proposed loan will be outstanding. The longer the requested time for repayment, the greater the possibility that some unforeseen event will cause the creditworthiness of the borrower to deteriorate. A loan made for several years will necessarily carry a rate different from that applied to a short-term loan. To address this problem, a loan may be made with a provision that the rate will be adjusted as necessary during its life.

When the nation's economy is sluggish and business activity slackens, banks may find themselves with a larger supply of loanable funds because of the diminished demand for credit. In these cases, banks may become more aggressive and not only seek new customers but also enter into newer types of lending that will put available funds to work.

Obviously, the Federal Reserve plays a major role in controlling the supply of money and credit. By raising or lowering reserve requirements or the discount rate, and through the actions of the Open Market Committee, the Fed has always had a direct impact on the availability of credit at member banks and on the nation's money supply. The Monetary Control Act of 1980 broadened the ability of the Fed in this respect.

Historically, American commercial banks operated chiefly in the area of *asset management.* Demand deposits flowed in steadily on an interest-free basis, and the banker's task was simply to put those funds to profitable use in such assets as loans and investments. If a manufacturer functioned under these same conditions, one might say that he enjoyed the benefits of obtaining his raw material without costs and that therefore his profits were guaranteed.

Today, commercial banks enjoy no such luxury. Asset management, of course, still exists, but bankers today must also practice *liability management.* They must deal with customers who are well educated, more aware of the many opportunities that exist for high-yielding types of accounts and investments, and far more likely to move their funds to those areas where the rate of return will be greater. As was noted in Chapter 6, demand deposits no longer form the backbone of commercial banking; in mid-1982, savings and time deposits, representing purchased money on which banks pay interest, accounted for over 56 percent of total deposits in the banking system. Commercial banks must compete for funds today with other financial intermediaries. They must offer a variety of savings and time instruments, at competitive rates, to attract deposits and fund their daily operations. The interest rates that banks charge on loans are directly tied to the rates they must pay to attract and retain deposits. Interest expense today is by far the fastest growing, largest, and least controllable of all the factors on a bank's expense statement. If an institution is to operate at a profit, there must be an adequate spread between its cost of funds and the income it derives from putting those funds to work. Interest rates reflect this need for a profit margin as well as the risk involved, the term of the loan, and the costs incurred in making and servicing it.

A bank's ability to price its loans is conditioned in many cases by state laws. The maximum interest that can be charged on a specific type of loan is determined by the laws of the state where the loan originates, not by the laws of the borrower's state. It is for this reason that banks have established originating facilities in states whose usury laws are the most liberal.

In pricing loans, every effort should be made to match loans with the deposits that are used to make them. If, for example, a bank receives a loan request from a valued customer and must acquire funds in the CD market with which to accommodate that customer, there is an obvious, specific relationship between the interest rate to be charged on the loan and the interest rate paid to attract the funds. The concepts of pricing apply to each component of the loan portfolio.

THE DISCOUNT AND PRIME RATES

Two specific interest rates should be discussed here. The Fed's Regulation A allows each Federal Reserve bank to extend short-term seasonal and emergency credit to member banks under certain conditions if the borrowing bank supplies specified collateral. The Monetary Control Act extended these borrowing privileges to nonmember banks and financial institutions as well. In making loans, the Fed charges the **discount rate**. This rate reflects the local Federal Reserve bank's views of the money market conditions prevailing at the time.

The discount rate is logically lower than the rate of interest paid by a bank's own customers, since the credit rating of the bank is considered higher than that of depositors. Banks, in turn, classify their customers and typically charge a preferential rate to those whom they consider most creditworthy. This judgment is based on all available financial information concerning the customer, the length and size of his relationship with the bank, and the bank's past experience in dealing with him. The rate charged to the largest and most creditworthy customers is called the **prime rate**. It varies from one bank to another, depending on each institution's assessment of its costs of money and the risks it faces in dealing with its particular customer base. The prime rate also fluctuates in relationship to the overall economic climate (see Table 11-1).

Table 11-1
Prime Rate Changes
in Selected Years

Year	High Point	Low Point
1951	3.00	2.50
1959	4.50	5.00
1966	6.00	5.50
1969	8.50	7.00
1971	6.50	5.25
1975	9.50	7.00
1978	11.75	8.00
1979	15.75	11.50
1980	21.50	11.00
1981	20.50	15.75
1982	17.00	11.50

A study of the spread between the discount rate at the Fed and the average prime rate charged by banks over a 20-year period showed that the latter was usually 1 to 2 percent higher. Therefore, it was theoretically possible for a bank to borrow from the Fed, pay interest at the discount rate, and lend the same funds to a major customer with an immediate profit margin of 1 to 2 percent. In this connection, however, it must be noted that the Fed is under no obligation to extend credit to a bank. If it feels that the borrower is applying for credit simply to make its own loans and thus generate quick profits, the Fed can decline the application. It also has the legal right to impose a surcharge, over and above the discount rate, on any bank that attempts to borrow too frequently.

In establishing their prime-rate structure and modifying it as money market conditions change, many banks recognize that they have many smaller customers who enjoy good credit standing but whose financial condition does not warrant their being treated on the same basis as the largest borrowers who are prime-rate names. To treat these lesser customers more equitably, these banks have developed a two-tier system of prime rates, so that major corporations pay a higher rate. This system benefits the borrower of more modest size.

During recent years, highly volatile conditions in the money market have seen the Fed repeatedly change its discount rate (seven reductions took place from July 1982 to December 1982), while prime rates charged by major commercial banks fluctuated from a high point of 21½ percent in December 1980 to 11½ percent in December 1982. To reflect this volatility, banks have placed increasing emphasis on rate-sensitive loans; that is, they have restructured their pricing mechanisms in various areas of their portfolios and, wherever possible, have extended credit while retaining the option to change rates, within legal parameters, when money market factors and costs of funds make these changes advisable.

LOAN STRUCTURING

In addition to revising their pricing mechanisms, banks are also devoting more attention to the actual structuring of each loan as regards the time frame for repayment. Wherever possible, they seek a definite schedule of **amortization**, i.e., the reduction of the principal through periodic payments. Installment loans have always been made on this basis; the principle is equally applicable to other credits. In some cases, a loan may be made on the basis of a so-called **balloon** payment; the borrower makes a specified number of smaller regular reductions in the principal and then a final, large balloon payment.

BASIC CREDIT PRINCIPLES

The generic term *borrower* may refer to a consumer who has obtained a $200 installment loan or a nationally known corporation that has borrowed the bank's legal limit. In either case, the borrower should be subject to a standard set of guidelines and principles. Regardless of the size or type of credit involved, if these basic principles are followed in every case, they will definitely protect the bank against losses; if they are ignored, the bank's risk increases at once. These principles and guidelines *do not* create a perfect, foolproof guarantee that no losses will ever take place. No bank has ever been able to develop such an absolute formula or system. The principles are preventive; they do not, and cannot, give the lender total protection.

From time to time, a bank may lend against a savings account or a quantity of U.S. government obligations. In case of default in either of these cases, the bank can immediately charge the loan to the account balance or sell the securities to cover the loan balance. Thus, the risk involved is minimal. Loans of these two types, however, represent only a small fraction of the typical bank's portfolio. In the vast majority of bank loans, **credit risk** is present, and losses continue to take place even if all proper precautions are taken.

Within the last 15 years, commercial banks in the United States have suffered severe loan losses. Many nationally known companies have found it necessary to declare bankruptcy, leaving the banks with loans that had to be written off as uncollectable. In many cases, the losses suffered by individual banks were the largest since the years of the Great Depression. Losses might have been incurred even if every fundamental principle of credit had been applied; however, it is safe to say that even greater losses would have been experienced if those same principles had been ignored.

With the exception of loans that are completely secured by cash or its equivalent, each extension of bank credit carries a risk that unexpected events will occur that convert a "good" loan into a problem situation. An individual who has met all the criteria for some form of consumer credit may suddenly be forced out of work by the collapse of an employer's business. A corporation that previously displayed a strong financial condition may become the sudden victim of new competition or a change in consumer taste. Loans that seemed perfectly sound at the outset may have to be written off, not because the lending bank's credit judgment was poor but because the borrower has been hurt by conditions that cannot be controlled. In making its original credit decision, the bank may have considered all the traditional "C's" of credit: the *capacity* of the borrower to repay, the *character* of the borrower, the *creditworthiness* that exists, and the *capital* that the borrower possesses; yet unforeseen events always take place to create problems for the lenders.

Despite years of training and experience, loan officers never become infallible; losses are a necessary part of the business of lending. The best that can be hoped for, in the face of the many demands for credit that are made on banks each day, is that basic credit principles will always be observed.

Credit Analysis

The key to credit analysis is the decision as to where the bank can best pl. :e the funds it has available for loans so that there is a combination of maximum profits and minimum losses. The process of analysis involves the gathering of all the information that is available on the proposed borrower and using it to make a credit judgment. Analysis uses the past and present as reasons to explain what should happen in the future. It begins with certain fundamental questions, the answers to which should have been part of the initial interview with the borrower:

1. What is the requested amount?

2. What is the purpose of the loan? Is it legal and in conformity with bank policy?

3. For what length of time will the funds be needed?

4. What will be the source of repayment? From all available data, does the bank believe that the borrower will have the ability to repay?

5. Is any type of collateral available?

In extending credit to any borrower, the bank should be satisfied that the borrower's financial status is sound, that the purpose of the loan is legitimate and can be justified, that the specific source of repayment will materialize on time, and that there are reasonable alternate sources of repayment.

Source of Repayment

Regardless of the size or type of loan that is being discussed, a bank, in meeting with the prospective borrower, should make every effort to identify the funds from which its repayment will come. A farmer may need to borrow funds until harvest time. An applicant for a home mortgage loan or an installment loan should be able to show that his or her regular income will permit regular monthly payments to amortize the loan. A real estate developer must demonstrate that leases that have been signed for space in a new shopping center will generate a cash flow sufficient to meet the bank's repayment schedule. A toy manufacturer may need to borrow to obtain the raw materials he will process, display, and sell for the Christmas season; the bank's expectation is that the profits from those sales will be sufficient to repay the loan.

Collateral

Lenders have always sought to protect themselves by obtaining some form of security that they could attach and put to use in the event of default. Although most of the loans they make are unsecured, there are many situations in which commercial banks follow the same line of reasoning. The general term for all types of security on loans is **collateral**.

A farmer may assign the value of his land or equipment to a bank; the buyer of a new automobile may give the bank a security interest in the vehicle; home mortgage loans allow the lender to foreclose on the residence if payments are not made; and a business may offer the bank a **lien** (also known as a **chattel mortgage**) on some of its assets as security for a loan. The test of all collateral is its marketability. How easily could the collateral be sold? What will the yield be if it is sold?

Banks frequently accept as collateral government obligations, securities that are actively traded on a stock exchange, savings account passbooks, merchandise stored in a warehouse, and life insurance policies that have a cash surrender value. In every such case, the lending bank believes that the assigned property could be readily sold, if necessary, and that the proceeds of the sale would eliminate or reduce the loan. The bank must not only be convinced of the marketability of the collateral but must also provide for its safekeeping and control. Under the Uniform Commercial Code as it exists in many states, the lender is required to register its security interest in the collateral with appropriate authorities. If stocks and bonds have been assigned to the bank as collateral, vault facilities must be provided, dual control must be implemented whenever the securities are moved or any purchase or sale takes place, and accurate, detailed records must be kept at all times.

Collateral may strengthen a borrowing situation, but it should never represent the determining factor in the approval of a loan. Borrowers should be able to repay from income and profits, and the lending bank should not look to the collateral as the justification for extending credit. Banks are not in the business of repossessing cars, foreclosing on real estate, or seizing the assets of a borrower; they take these steps only when normal payment procedures have not been followed. If a bank is forced to exercise its rights to sell the collateral in order to liquidate the loan, there is some question as to whether the loan was sound in the first place.

In addition, there are usually additional costs associated with the foreclosure or repossession process, and a long period of time may elapse before that process is completed. During that time, the bank classifies the loan as nonperforming, and the loan is a nonearning asset.

In lending against collateral, a bank must also protect itself against any possible fluctuations in the value of the assigned property. For example, banks are generally willing to accept stocks and bonds as security for loans. The spread between the market value of the collateral and the amount the bank lends against it is known as **margin**; for example, the bank may calculate the market value and make a loan for 70 percent of that figure. The 30 percent differential is the margin, designed to protect the bank against decreases in market prices. If a bank accepts shares of stock as collateral and their market value at the time the loan is made is $100 per share, a drop in the market may reduce that figure to $85 per share; the borrower may then be asked either to reduce the amount outstanding or to furnish the bank with additional collateral.

Credit Investigation

There can be no excuse for a bank's negligence in obtaining all available information in order to make a credit judgment. Information on individuals and businesses is readily obtainable. Any failure to acquire it and to use it in the decision-making process increases the bank's risk and creates the potential for losses.

In the case of consumer credit, investigation usually consists of verifying the applicant's job, income, past credit history, and outstanding debts. In many cities, banks subscribe to credit bureaus, which are central information services that maintain records of consumer borrowings. Each subscribing bank provides the credit agency with daily input regarding new applications, approved loans, repayments, rejected requests, and delinquencies. The information supplied by an individual in applying for a loan or bank card can be checked against the central data file. Recent laws stipulate that if a bank declines a loan on the basis of unfavorable credit information, it must make that fact known to the applicant and furnish that information to him if asked to do so.

The investigative process for businesses is far more detailed, and the sources of information are far more numerous. The logical starting point is the bank's own credit department, in which a credit file is kept on each borrower. Credit files provide a complete history of the bank's relationship with its customers and contain reports of interviews, correspondence, data on average balances, overdrafts, previous loans, and internal memoranda.

Credit information is also obtainable from other banks, provided there is a specific and ethical reason for requesting it. It is entirely proper for banks to exchange appropriate credit information with one another.

Various credit agencies, the best known of which is Dun & Bradstreet, Inc., publish regular reports on business firms. Most commercial banks subscribe to these credit agency services and can obtain updated financial information regarding a business.

In lending to businesses, banks rely chiefly on the financial information—balance sheets, income statements, and supplementary schedules—supplied by the borrower. These figures should be thoroughly analyzed to detect trends in the business and to help assess the borrower's ability to repay the loan through the normal operations of the firm.

Trade references may also be made part of the investigation of a business borrower. In this case, the bank contacts a firm's suppliers and asks what their experience has been in selling to it on credit terms. Their responses indicate how well the firm has been able to meet its trade obligations.

Lines of Credit

There are many situations in which a bank uses its knowledge of a customer to make an advance judgment as to the amount of credit it feels can prudently be granted. This amount represents the customer's **line of credit** and is available in whole or part at any time. If the existence of the line of credit is confirmed in writing to the customer by the bank, it is called an **advised** line; if the line of credit is used only for internal purposes and the customer is not made aware of it, it is known as a *guidance* line. A major corporation of unquestioned credit standing that has done business with the bank for some time may be granted a line of credit as large as the bank's legal lending limit. A smaller business may have a more modest line of credit, and an individual may be granted overdraft privileges, or allowed to have bank card outstandings up to a certain dollar figure.

During the life cycle of a line of credit to a business, the signing of a promissory note converts the line into an actual loan. Similarly, an individual who has been granted a line of credit may take advantage of its existence merely by issuing checks or using his or her bank card to make purchases or receive cash advances. Each line of credit results from a bank's analysis of all available information and must be taken into consideration when the bank computes its liquidity needs.

Compensating Balances

A basic truth of banking states that customers deposit money with those banks that make credit available to them and that banks make loans to those customers who represent the major source of deposits. This is merely an example of the relationship between the deposit and credit functions. Traditionally, banks expect business borrowers to maintain balances in checking accounts or in other non-interest-bearing form that bear a direct proportion to the size of each line of credit or loan. Depending on money market conditions, a formula might require balances equal to 10 percent of the line of credit and 20 percent of the actual loan. A corporation with a $100,000 line of credit would therefore have to keep balances of $10,000 to support the line and would have to increase its balances to $20,000 when the line was used and the loan went on the bank's books. The cost of the compensating balances to the customer is over and above the direct interest expense.

Loan Review

The experiences of many banks indicate that loan losses are often the result of a lack of attention to information that develops during the life of the loan, such as a change in business circumstances. Loans that were considered of good quality when made can deteriorate. The loan review process in banking provides that a staff of specialists will examine the loans that have been made and will give an early warning of any potential problems.

Loan losses present a constant source of concern to banks. Loan review departments can prevent losses by taking timely action where it is warranted and, in some cases, by analyzing the loan to determine how partial repayment can be obtained.

The system of loan reviews gives management a form of assurance that loan officers have stayed within the bounds of their lending authorities, that policies have been adhered to, and that proper documentation has been obtained. If the bank's portfolio warrants it, the loan review process may include both secured and unsecured loans and existing loans as well as new ones. It may also include assigning a rating or grade—excellent risk, good or satisfactory risk, poor or unsatisfactory risk, or imminent workout situation—to every credit.

Whatever the size of a particular bank or the size and makeup of its loan portfolio, an impartial unit charged with the responsibility for scrutinizing each loan, identifying existing or possible problems, and recommending corrective action can make a real contribution to the bank's bottom-line profits.

BANK INVESTMENTS

The credit function of commercial banks is not confined purely to direct lending; it also includes the investments they make. Both loans and investments use the bank's available funds; however, there are two basic differences between them.

The first of these involves the bank's purposes and priorities. The basic business of banking is the lending of money to individuals, businesses, and units of government. It is expected that banks will help their communities prosper and grow by supplying the funds that customers in those communities legitimately wish to borrow. As mentioned earlier, the Community Reinvestment Act requires that banks work to meet the credit needs of the towns and cities they serve. There is, however, no comparable compulsion for banks to make investments. In allocating funds, they must give first priority to customers' credit needs; investments have lower priority and are usually made *only* after the demand for loans has been met.

The second difference reflects the relationships between the parties. When a bank makes a loan, it negotiates directly with the borrower regarding amount, purpose, maturity, rate, and all other factors; in most cases, it is dealing with a party known to it through a deposit relationship. Conversely, when a bank makes an investment, it does so through a dealer or underwriter. It relies on investment rating services to determine the quality of the investment and the credit risk involved. Local securities issues may not be rated by such agencies as Moody's or Standard & Poor's, and the bank may have to conduct its own investigation before investing in the securities. In many cases, the investing bank does not negotiate directly with the issuer, and that issuer may have no knowledge of who has purchased its securities.

Both interest on loans and income from investments obviously contribute to bank earnings, but the purpose is different in each case. Loans are not made primarily for the sake of the income they generate; they reflect the bank's basic obligation to meet the legitimate credit needs of its customers. On the other hand, investments are made chiefly for income purposes. The fact that a bank is contributing to the general well-being of its community by buying that community's notes or bonds is secondary to the income objective. Whenever loan demand increases, there will usually be a decrease in the bank's investment portfolio, because it will sell off part of its holdings to obtain the funds with which to make loans.

Risk enters into investments as it does in loans; however, there is more than one type of risk that banks face in each case. In loans, the primary concern is **credit risk**, which questions whether the borrower will be able to repay as scheduled. Investments carry not only the question of credit risk, i.e., whether the issuer will be able to raise the funds necessary to pay principal and interest; they also carry **market risk**. If the holder of an investment wishes to sell it at any time, money market conditions and the overall desirability of the security will determine the market value.

As interest rates, which are beyond the bank's control, fluctuate, the appeal of a bond issue paying a certain coupon interest rate may increase or decrease in the eyes of potential buyers. U.S. government bonds carry *no* credit risk whatever because there is no doubt as to the ability of the government to repay; however, they *do* carry market risk because interest rates on so many types of money market instruments change. A bank wishing to sell a government bond issued several years previously with a 5 percent coupon may find that it is unattractive to investors because new bonds, with higher coupon rates, are readily available. A sale of this type may create a direct loss for the bank.

In any given year, a bank may show profits or losses on sales of securities, depending on the market conditions that existed at various times during the 12 months. In some cases, a bank will deliberately sell some of its investment holdings at a loss to raise funds and then invest the proceeds in commercial loans that carry a far higher rate of return.

Diversification

For both legal and practical reasons, banks invest their funds in various types of issues. The legal reasons are twofold:

1. Banks are prohibited from investing in any common stock; and

2. With the exception of U.S. government obligations, a bank may not invest more than 10 percent of its capital and surplus in the securities of any one issuer.

The first of these legal restrictions traces back to the Great Depression and the wave of bank failures that accompanied it. Before 1933, banks actively invested in shares of stock issued by major corporations and were considered to have done so in many cases in the hope of making a quick profit. In this respect their optimism reflected that of the general public, which had displayed complete optimism in the future of the stock market. However, this type of investment was not and is not a legitimate use of depositors' funds, and the Glass-Steagall Act of 1933 restricted the ability of commercial banks to invest as well as to become involved in merchant banking and underwriting of debt issues.

The second legal restriction resembles the limit that is placed on bank lending to a single customer. It prevents banks from investing excessively large amounts of depositors' funds in the securities of a single issuer.

Each institution's practical investment policies will reflect its own changing priorities. A bank makes investments only after liquidity needs have been met and loan demand has been satisfied. If all available funds have been used for these two purposes, investment activity temporarily ceases.

Types of Bank Investments

A bank's investment portfolio consists of three types of holdings:

● Issues of the U.S. government: **bills** (short-term), **notes** (usually with 1- to 5-year maturities), and **bonds** (larger denomination, long-term obligations).

- Various **municipal** issues.

- Miscellaneous restricted investments, such as bankers' acceptances and certificates of deposit issued by other institutions. Highest quality **commercial paper** may also be used.

As mentioned earlier, Treasury bills offer the investing bank a dual advantage. Because they are immediately salable, they provide liquidity and are part of the bank's secondary reserves. At the same time, they form a source of investment income.

Municipals are bonds issued by any government or agency of government other than the federal. A state, county, city, town, turnpike authority, or other entity of local government raises the funds it needs for its operations over and above its other revenues by issuing bonds. These can either be backed by the full taxing power of the municipality (also known as "full faith and credit issues") or by the direct income that the issuer can generate. An example of the latter can be seen in the bond issues issued to build a new toll road; these are known as revenue bonds because the bondholder depends on the profits from the specific project to provide a source of repayment.

U.S. government obligations carry no credit risk but do contain an element of market risk. Municipals involve a greater degree of both types of risk. The credit risk reflects the fact that the credit rating of a municipal issuer cannot be as high as that of the federal government. The market risk on municipals is correspondingly greater. Investors at any time may find municipals unattractive, especially when news media publicize the debt problems of many major states and cities.

Banks invest in municipals for two basic reasons. The first of these is the tax advantage that municipal issues have always enjoyed— i.e., income from them is completely exempt from federal income tax and, in addition, *may* be exempt from local taxes. The federal income tax exemption on municipals makes them especially attractive to large commercial banks, which may be in a 40 percent range on federal taxes.

The second reason for bank investments in municipals lies in the commitment that banks make to their communities. They recognize today that their own well-being is tied closely to that of the communities in which they operate and from which they draw part or all of their profits. If a city or town is unable to raise the funds it needs and its economy begins to deteriorate, its banks will inevitably suffer along with it. Every investment in a municipal issue represents a vote of confidence in the ability of the municipality to maintain a healthy economy and to eventually repay its debts. By investing in municipals, banks display their understanding of the fact that as corporate citizens they must *give* to communities as well as *take* from them.

In mid-1982, total outstanding marketable securities of the U.S. government amounted to $738 billion, of which the commercial banks as a group held $78 billion. At the same time, the nation's largest commercial banks alone held $57 billion in various municipal issues.

SUMMARY

Based on the availability of funds and its own decisions as to the types of loans it wishes to make, each bank determines its loan policies and gives its loan officers stated amounts of credit authority with which to operate. They function, however, within the framework of an entire set of legal restrictions that have been imposed by federal and state governments. Banking today essentially consists of liability, rather than asset, management, and the pricing and structuring of loans to give the lending bank an adequate profit margin are essential. When a bank considers a loan, it should follow an established set of credit principles to ensure that all necessary information has been gathered and analyzed.

Bank investments are also part of the credit function, although they have a lower priority in the management of bank funds than loans. Commercial banks as a group are the largest holders of U.S. government obligations and have also made substantial investments in municipals, i.e., the debt issues of all other domestic governments, authorities, and agencies.

QUESTIONS FOR DISCUSSION

1. What role do the bank's directors play in the credit function?

2. Identify three Federal Reserve regulations that directly affect loans made by member banks.

3. What is usury?

4. Distinguish between the discount rate and the prime rate.

5. Why are banks today involved in liability management rather than asset management?

6. Distinguish between credit risk and market risk.

7. What test should be applied to all collateral to determine whether it meets the bank's standards?

8. Should a loan request be approved simply because the borrower offers collateral to the bank? Why?

9. Identify three commonly used sources of credit information regarding commercial borrowers.

10. Why must the total outstanding lines of credit in a bank be considered when that bank calculates its liquidity needs?

11. What risk does a bank assume, if any, when it invests in obligations of the U.S. government?

12. Identify the three common types of federal government obligations.

13. Define the term *municipals.* What advantages does a bank gain by investing in municipals?

Suggested Readings

American Bankers Association. *Bank Investments.* Washington, D.C.: American Bankers Association, 1983.

Cole, Robert H. *Consumer and Commercial Credit Management.* 6th edition. Homewood, Illinois: Dow Jones-Irwin, 1980.

Hayes, Douglas. *Bank Lending Policies, Domestic and International.* Ann Arbor: University of Michigan, 1977.

Hoffman, Margaret A., and Gerald C. Fischer. *Credit Department Management.* Philadelphia, Pennsylvania: Robert Morris Associates, 1980.

McKinney, Jr., George W., William J. Brown, and Paul M. Horvitz. *Management of Commercial Bank Funds.* Washington, D.C.: American Bankers Association, 1980.

O'Leary, Edward T., and Jane McNeil. *Introduction to Commercial Lending.* Washington, D.C.: American Bankers Association, 1983.

Prochnow, Herbert. *Bank Credit.* New York: Harper and Row, 1981.

Chapter 12

Bank Accounting, Pricing, and Profitability

LEARNING OBJECTIVES

After completion of this chapter, you will have an understanding of

- the reasons why detailed systems of bank accounting are necessary;

- the system of double-entry bookkeeping and the use of debits and credits in posting;

- the two basic reports that banks prepare to show the details of their financial condition;

- the distinction between the cash and accrual methods of accounting;

- the major asset and liability accounts that appear on a bank's balance sheet;

- the major income and expense accounts that appear on an income statement;

- the importance to banks of adequate systems of cost accounting and pricing;

- the four major ratios that are used to determine a bank's profitability; and

- the value to a bank and its customers of monthly account analysis.

Accounting has often been called "the language of business" because business facts and events are gathered, classified, and reported in accordance with accounting principles and procedures and in accounting terms. If a bank is considering a request for a commercial loan, it automatically expects the applicant to supply it with detailed financial statements prepared in conformity with general accounting standards. The absence of information concerning the firm's assets, liabilities, income, and expenses immediately tells the bank that the applicant simply does not know how the business is operating.

Commercial banks, in this respect, must be prepared to do even more than they expect from their borrowers. They are under even greater pressure than their customers to develop accounting systems that will record, present, and interpret the many transactions that occur each day, even in the smallest banks.

Every examination of a bank by state and federal authorities requires a determination of its true financial condition. Every federal and state regulatory authority requires the banks under its jurisdiction to file periodic **call reports**, which contain not only financial data but also a certification from management that the figures are accurate and up to date. National banks must file these call reports with the Comptroller of the Currency; state-chartered member banks, with the Federal Reserve; state-chartered insured nonmembers, with the FDIC; and all others with state banking authorities. For management's own purposes, each bank must systematically update all its asset, liability, income, expense, and capital accounts. Customers demand timely and accurate bank statements, showing all transactions and the current status of their accounts. Stockholders are clearly entitled to information regarding the bank's condition and profits. In summary, no bank can operate without an efficient system for recording all transactions and summarizing their effects on the bank's books.

TYPES OF ACCOUNTING RECORDS

Many bank transactions are entered on temporary records, such as adding machine tapes. These are used for daily proof purposes; they lose their value as the transactions are completed in other areas and the figures are posted to more permanent records.

Other bank records are more permanent. These may include summaries of temporary records or the originals or microfilm copies of documents.

A third category of records includes all those that must be kept for longer periods as required by law or bank policy.

A **journal** in bank accounting is a book of original entry. Each processing area in a bank will usually have some form of journal in which daily transactions are posted. Eventually, entries move from journals to the bank's **ledgers**, which are records of final entry. The typical bank will have both a **general ledger**, in which all financial information from each department and branch is consolidated, and **subsidiary ledgers**, in which those departments and branches have recorded their own data. Subsidiary ledgers usually are maintained for all demand deposit accounts, savings accounts, loans, fixed assets, and individual borrowers.

Double-Entry Bookkeeping

The fundamental technique used in bank accounting requires that every transaction affect two accounts and be recorded by a balanced set of entries. This is known as **double-entry bookkeeping**. Every **debit** must have an equal, offsetting **credit**, and total debits must equal total credits.

The posting of *debits* increases an asset or expense account, or decreases a liability, income, or capital account. The posting of *credits* accomplishes the reverse in each case; that is, credits increase a liability, income, or capital account and decrease an asset or expense account.

Suppose, for example, that a customer deposits $100 in a checking account. The transaction would be recorded by a debit, thereby increasing the cash account, and a credit, increasing the demand deposits account. The former is an **asset** of the bank because it represents something of value that the bank owns or that is owed to it. The demand deposit account is a **liability** of the bank because it represents money owed to a customer.

Unless a bank is insolvent, its total assets will be greater than its total liabilities. The excess of assets over liabilities is the **net worth** of the bank and is shown in its capital accounts. A fundamental equation in accounting states that total assets always equal total liabilities plus net worth.

Basic Reports

In bank accounting, two fundamental reports are produced to convey all the essential information regarding a bank's current condition and the results it has achieved. The **statement of condition**, also known as the **balance sheet**, is prepared as of a specific date, e.g., December 31. The **income statement**, also known as the **profit-and-loss statement**, covers a period of time, e.g., the year ended December 31. The former lists all the asset, liability, and capital accounts of the bank; the latter shows all revenues and expenses and the net profit or loss for the period.

The largest asset for a bank is invariably its total portfolio of loans; deposits are invariably the largest liability.

Table 12-1 lists the most common categories of asset, liability, income, and expense accounts.

Accrual Accounting

Many businesses operate on a basis of **cash accounting**; that is, entries to the firm's records are made only when cash is actually received as income or paid out as an expense. If banks were to follow this method, their income figures would be so severely distorted as to become meaningless.

Table 12-1
Account Categories

Category	Definition	Subdivisions
Asset Accounts	Items owned by or owed to the bank, having commercial or exchange value. May consist of specific property, claims against property, or items such as cash, drafts, and loans.	Loans and Securities Cash and Due from Banks Float Income Earned but Not Collected Fixed and Other Assets
Liability Accounts	Funds entrusted to the bank by depositors and/or obligations incurred through operations.	Demand and Time Deposits Loan Commitments Accrued and Other Liabilities
Income Accounts	Accounts that classify and segregate actual and accrued revenues.	Interest on Loans Interest on Investments
Expense Accounts	Accounts that classify and segregate actual and accrued expenses.	Interest Expense Salaries and Wages

As an example, consider the interest that must be paid to the holders of CDs at maturity and to savings account customers at the end of the quarter. Under the cash method, no entries would be made on the bank's books until the actual payouts to customers took place. This would ignore the fact that the interest expense was actually incurred earlier. By the same token, a customer who borrows $25,000 agrees to repay it, with interest, 90 days later. The cash method of accounting would give no recognition to the fact that the bank actually has been earning interest throughout the life of the loan.

Therefore, banks generally use the **accrual** method of accounting, which records expenses at the time they are incurred (regardless of when they are paid) and records income when it is earned (regardless of when it is actually received). Accrued Income Receivable is an asset account, as is Prepaid Expense; Accrued Liabilities and Unearned Income are liability accounts.

Statement-of-Condition Assets

The following items are listed as assets in the balance sheet:

- Cash on hand and due from banks: The currency and coin held in the bank's vaults, plus checks that are in the process of collection and balances maintained with correspondent banks.

- Investments: Direct obligations of the U.S. government, obligations of other agencies of the federal government, and municipals. Member banks would also list their Federal Reserve stock.

- Loans: All indebtedness to the bank, usually subdivided by category and/or by domestic and global credits.

- Fixed assets: Real estate owned by the bank, furniture, fixtures, and equipment.

Statement-of-Condition Liabilities

The following items are listed as liabilities in the statement of condition:

- Deposits: All moneys owed to depositors, subdivided as to demand deposits, savings deposits, and time deposits. Correspondent bank balances would be included here. If the scope of the bank's overseas operations warrants it, deposits might also be broken down between those held in the United States and those domiciled at foreign branches.

- Taxes payable: All federal, state, and local taxes that must be paid.

- Dividends payable: If the bank's directors have approved payment of a quarterly dividend to stockholders but the actual disbursement has not yet been made, this entry will show the bank's liability.

Income-Statement Entries

Typically, the sources of bank income, in the order of their size and importance, are

1. interest on loans;

2. interest and dividends on investments; and

3. fees, commissions, and service charges.

Expenses, again in the order of their size and importance, would include

1. interest paid;

2. salaries, wages, and benefits; and

3. taxes.

The bank's income statement produces a net income (i.e., revenues less expenses) figure that is usually translated into earnings per share, so that stockholders know how much each share of outstanding stock earned during the period.

Tables 12-2 and 12-3 are specimens of a major commercial bank's statement of condition and income statement. The tables include additional categories of data that have not been mentioned in this dis-

Table 12-2
Consolidated Statement of Condition
Assets

	December 31		
(In Thousands)	19XX	19XX	Change
Cash and Due from Banks	$ 1,649,334	$ 1,332,586	$ 316,748
Overseas Deposits	458,313	460,396	(2,083)
Investment Securities:			
U.S. Treasury Securities	881,081	982,654	(101,573)
Securities of Other U.S. Government Agencies and Corporations	199,318	243,420	(44,102)
Obligations of States and Political Subdivisions	738,813	396,948	341,865
Other Securities	88,278	92,032	(3,754)
Total Investment Securities	1,907,490	1,715,054	192,436
Trading Account Securities	14,846	66,140	(51,294)
Funds Sold	168,600	108,450	60,150
Loans (Net of Reserve for Loan Losses and Unearned Discount)	9,715,728	8,074,132	1,641,596
Direct Lease Financing	147,860	134,472	13,388
Premises and Equipment, Net	133,506	132,320	1,186
Customers' Acceptance Liability	372,835	248,271	124,564
Accrued Interest Receivable	133,840	123,719	10,121
Other Real Estate Owned	34,332	13,668	20,664
Other Assets	103,939	131,711	(27,772)
Total Assets	$14,840,623	$12,540,919	$2,299,704

Table 12-2
Consolidated Statement of Condition (continued)
Liabilities and Stockholders' Equity

| | December 31 | | |
(In Thousands)	19XX	19XX	Change
Demand Deposits	$ 3,543,141	$ 2,937,065	$ 606,076
Savings Deposits	3,585,808	3,485,886	99,922
Savings Certificates	1,635,215	1,391,107	244,108
Certificates of Deposit	1,827,420	1,601,707	225,713
Other Time Deposits	424,592	313,811	110,781
Deposits in Overseas Offices	1,468,003	722,950	745,053
Total Deposits	12,484,179	10,452,526	2,031,653
Funds Borrowed	897,189	924,501	(27,312)
Long-Term Debt	44,556	43,766	790
Acceptances Outstanding	373,022	249,088	123,934
Accrued Taxes and Other Expenses	142,756	122,064	20,692
Other Liabilities	171,904	122,890	49,014
Total Liabilities (Excluding Subordinated Notes)	14,113,606	11,914,835	2,198,771
Subordinated Notes: 8 ¼ % Capital Note to Wells Fargo & Company, due 1998	25,000	25,000	—
4 ½ % Capital Notes due 1989	50,000	50,000	—
Total Subordinated Notes	75,000	75,000	—
Stockholders' Equity: Capital Stock	94,461	94,461	—
Surplus	300,036	251,512	48,524
Surplus Representing Convertible Capital Note Obligation Assumed by Parent Corporation	10,065	14,589	(4,524)
Undivided Profits	247,455	190,522	56,933
Total Stockholders' Equity	652,017	551,084	100,933
Total Liabilities and Stockholders' Equity	$14,840,623	$12,540,919	$2,299,704

Table 12-3
Consolidated Statement of Income

(In Thousands Except Per Share Data)	Year Ended December 31	
	19XX	19XX
Interest Income:		
Interest and Fees on Loans	$ 823,415	$693,463
Interest on Funds Sold	6,429	3,496
Interest and Dividends on Investment Securities:		
U.S. Treasury Securities	69,938	59,883
Securities of Other U.S. Government Agencies and Corporations	16,520	25,228
Obligations of States and Political Subdivisions	22,504	15,846
Other Securities	7,067	7,268
Interest on Overseas Deposits	24,394	37,658
Interest on Trading Account Securities	4,419	3,478
Direct Lease Financing Income	33,371	32,560
Total Interest Income	1,008,057	878,880
Interest Expense:		
Interest on Deposits	463,733	414,832
Interest on Federal Funds Borrowed and Repurchase Agreements	35,193	33,019
Interest on Other Borrowed Money	17,751	12,882
Interest on Long-Term Debt	21,232	19,079
Total Interest Expense	537,909	479,812
Net Interest Income	470,148	399,068
Provision for Loan Losses	41,028	46,379
Net Interest Income after Provision for Loan Losses	429,120	352,689
Other Operating Income:		
Trust Income	21,635	19,649
Service Charges on Deposit Accounts	25,511	24,254
Trading Account Profits and Commissions	(268)	1,690
Other Income	43,797	23,324
Total Other Operating Income	90,675	68,917

Table 12-3
Consolidated Statement of Income (continued)

	Year Ended December 31	
(In Thousands Except Per Share Data)	19XX	19XX
Other Operating Expense:		
Salaries	168,085	145,746
Employee Benefits	41,028	32,126
Net Occupancy Expense	34,919	31,636
Equipment Expense	20,648	19,234
Other Expense	94,331	68,317
Total Other Operating Expense	359,011	297,059
Income before Income Taxes and Securities Transactions	160,784	124,547
Less Applicable Income Taxes	73,484	61,076
Income before Securities Transactions	87,300	63,471
Securities Gains (Losses), Net of Income Tax Effect of $(1,233) in 1977 and $48 in 1976	(1,020)	40
Net Income	$ 86,280	$ 63,511
Income Per Share (based on average number of common shares outstanding):		
Income before Securities Transactions	$4.03	$3.16
Securities Transactions, Net of Income Tax Effect	(.05)	—
Net Income	$3.98	$3.16

cussion of basic concepts. It is not the purpose of this text to attempt to present a comprehensive study of the principles and techniques of bank accounting, since that subject warrants a separate and lengthy course of study. The American Institute of Banking and many other educational institutions offer courses devoted entirely to the field of bank accounting.

It should be noted that the scope of each financial report can be varied according to the needs of its audience. The exception to this rule is found in the call reports; their format is dictated by the regulatory authorities to which they must be submitted. For management purposes within the bank, computerized reports that focus on any individual component of the balance sheet can be prepared as an internal control. Statistical tables can also be prepared to show changes in assets, liabilities, income, expenses, and capital over a period of time. Those furnish an easily read basis for comparison, showing the bank's progress.

Pricing

In recent years, banks have placed increased emphasis on specialized accounting to arrive at a better understanding of what the true expenses are in each day's operations. This new emphasis reflects the basic change that has taken place in the overall deposit structure and the efforts that banks have made to meet increased competition.

When commercial banks enjoyed the benefits of large, relatively inactive demand deposit balances, the need for detailed cost accounting was not as readily perceived. The prevalence of substantial interest-free deposits virtually guaranteed profits, and as asset managers the bankers simply concentrated on putting those deposits to profitable use. The general philosophy held that companies that maintained large checking accounts with banks were entitled to services, without concern on either side as to what those services cost.

Considerations of true costs and adequate pricing are an essential part of banking today. The excess demand deposits that bankers formerly depended on have been replaced by expensive forms of time and savings deposits. New services have been introduced in large numbers in an effort to compete with other financial intermediaries. Labor costs in an inflationary economy have escalated steadily. *Knowing* the costs of each service or product and *recovering* those costs through pricing mechanisms are vital to banks today, not merely for their profitability but, in many cases, for their actual survival in the competitive marketplace.

The Monetary Control Act of 1980 directed the Federal Reserve to implement a system of explicit pricing for its services. In this respect, the Fed's position was like that of the commercial banks; since 1913, it had been providing services free to member banks (with the exception of loans) because of the reserve balances they maintained with it. The new price schedules called for by this legislation created a further need for banks to be aware of their operating costs and to recover those costs, *plus* a profit margin, from those who use their services.

If justification existed in the past for banks to give away their services, it has disappeared in the face of increased labor costs, interest expense, and externally imposed cost factors. Today's banking requires implementing an integrated system that will analyze job functions to determine exactly what expenses are incurred in each task, recognize all the indirect costs (overhead and administrative expenses) that must be added on, compute a price for the complete service, add on the appropriate profit margin, present the final price figure to the customer, and recover it through compensating balances or fees. This methodology has been practiced by major corporations for many years.

Consider an operation in the bank as basic as the acceptance of a customer's deposit by a teller. The first step in a complete system of cost accounting and pricing analyzes the components of the task and the time needed for each. The teller's hourly salary then forms a base for determining the actual expense generated by the work performed. Appropriate branch and administrative overhead can then be added as a percentage, and a profit margin is superimposed to arrive at the final price.

In the credit function, functional cost analysis gives recognition to the cost of the funds that were used for a loan or investment and thus tells the bank what rate of return should be sought.

For comparison purposes, banks can obtain from the Federal Reserve detailed studies of various services, showing the competitive prices for those services as averaged throughout the commercial banking system.

After prices have been determined for each service and product, the bank can turn its attention to the means of recovering costs and generating profits. There are two traditional methods of compensation to banks: fees and compensating balances. The latter has traditionally been favored by corporate customers and accepted by the banks; more recently, however, there is a definite trend toward payment of fees.

In the discussion of bank loans earlier in this text, it was mentioned that banks traditionally have expected borrowing customers to maintain adequate compensating balances to support their loans. Today, however, many corporate customers request that an "all-in-the-rate" system be used and that balances be ignored in the negotiations. Thus, the interest rate that the bank quotes will be all-inclusive, reflecting its cost of funds and all other expense and profit factors. In the case of other services—lockbox, payroll preparation, check collection, and wire transfers, for example—many customers expect to be given specific price schedules and intend to pay the bank through direct fees, rather than through balances.

There are several reasons for this trend. Fees constitute a direct business expense and, as such, can be deducted when the corporation's tax return is being prepared. If balances need not be maintained with the banks to pay for services rendered, those funds can be freed up and put to work by the corporate treasurer, using any investment media that are available. Finally, many corporate officials feel that the earnings allowances that banks have extended on compensating balances as a means of offsetting the expenses of an account have been too low. The use of fees as a payment vehicle makes it easier for the financial officer to compare one bank's prices with those quoted by others.

The questions of pricing and recovery of costs have received additional emphasis because of the widespread offering of NOW accounts. Banks that suddenly find that a substantial portion of their total deposit base is in the form of these new interest-bearing relationships must determine how to price them. Typically, this process results in establishing a minimum balance that the depositor must keep; should the balance fall below that minimum level, a schedule of service charges goes into effect.

Profitability

Any discussion of commercial banking in the United States must recognize the fact that banks here are organized for profit; they are not nationalized or subsidized, as are their counterparts in many other countries. Therefore, their measures of profitability are important to their stockholders, their depositors, the government agencies that regulate them, their managers, and the public in general. The concept of profitability determines the effectiveness of a bank in its performance and indicates how well the bank has managed the resources under its control. High or increasing profitability constitutes the only way that a bank can expand its operations on a long-term basis and lead investors to purchase new offerings of its stock or debt issues.

For internal management purposes and for use by investors, stock market analysts, and state and federal government agencies, various ratios have been developed to determine how profitably a bank is operating. The measures most widely used in this regard are

- Return on assets (ROA);

- Return on equity (ROE);

- Capital ratio; and

- Earnings per share (EPS).

Return on assets is obtained by dividing the bank's average total assets during a period by its earnings before securities transactions. Table 12-4 shows the relative ROA ratios for two major commercial banks in selected years from 1968 through 1976. An analysis of these ratios shows that the ROA for Bank A steadily declined; even in years when its earnings grew, its ROA decreased because its assets grew at a far faster rate and evidently were not being put to the most profitable use. If one looked only at the growth in assets that Bank A displayed, one would conclude that its performance was excellent, since its assets increased 113 percent from 1968 to 1976. However, when its ROA is analyzed, a different conclusion is reached.

The performance of Bank B during the same years is far more impressive. Its earnings increased 176 percent from 1968 to 1976, while its assets increased 90 percent. The conclusion is obvious that Bank B not only grew in terms of total assets, but employed those assets in such a way that the return on them grew more rapidly and far more meaningfully.

Table 12-4
Return on Assets

Year	Earnings Before Securities Transactions (million dollars)	Average Total Assets (million dollars)	Return on Assets (percent)
		Bank "A"	
1974	35.0	3,580	0.98
1976	41.6	4,411	0.94
1978	42.1	5,341	0.79
1980	55.5	8,577	0.65
1982	42.9	8,332	0.51
		Bank "B"	
1974	10.7	1,566	0.68
1976	12.7	1,668	0.76
1978	16.7	2,018	0.83
1980	23.3	2,573	0.91
1982	29.5	2,978	0.99

The second measure of profitability is **return on equity**. This is calculated by dividing a bank's earnings before securities transactions by the dollar amount of stockholders' equity. ROE, then, measures the rate of return a bank has achieved on the funds that have been directly invested in it. Table 12-5 uses the same two commercial banks that formed the basis for the ROA table and shows their ROE figures for the same period. Table 12-6 gives recent ROA and ROE data for the 15 largest bank holding companies.

Whenever a charter application is submitted for a new bank, regulatory authorities question the dollar amount of capital that has been contributed by the incorporators. The bank's capital base subsequently grows as additional investments in it are made by the stockholders. Every examination of a bank by federal or state authorities tries to determine whether its capital is adequate to support its operations. Thus, the third ratio of profitability is known as the **capital ratio.** It is calculated by dividing stockholders' equity by total assets. The stronger the bank's capital position (and, therefore, its capital ratio), the greater the appearance of solidity it projects. Capital serves as a cushion against temporary losses and a protection to uninsured depositors and holders of liabilities in the event the bank is liquidated. Capital ratios of 4, 5, or 6 percent are common in commercial banks today.

The final ratio, **earnings per share,** simply divides the bank's bottom-line income figure by the average number of shares of stock outstanding. Growth in EPS is commonly regarded as a key indicator in the performance of a bank. EPS figures also provide a means of determining how highly the bank's stock is regarded in the market-place. If its earnings per share are $5 for a given year and a share of its stock is selling at $25, the price/earnings ratio is 5, and this can be compared with the ratios for other banks and corporations.

A complete analysis of a bank's profitability requires detailed attention to each of these ratios over a period of several years, rather than a focus on one ratio for a single year. For example, a bank's board of

Table 12-5
Return on Equity

Year	Earnings Before Securities Transactions (million dollars)	Average Shareholders' Equity (million dollars)	Return on Equity (percent)
	Bank "A"		
1974	35.0	316	11.1
1976	41.6	347	12.0
1978	42.1	398	10.6
1980	55.5	467	11.9
1982	42.9	513	8.4
	Bank "B"		
1974	10.7	100	9.4
1976	12.7	111	11.4
1978	16.7	128	13.1
1980	23.3	153	15.2
1982	29.5	187	15.8

Table 12-6
Comparative ROA and ROE Data for the 15 Largest Bank Holding Companies

BHC	ROE		ROA	
	2nd Qtr., 1982	1981	2nd Qtr., 1982	1981
Bankamerica Corp.	11.7	13.1	0.41	0.47
Citicorp	13.1	10.6	0.50	0.37
Chase Manhattan Corp.	(4.0)	15.8	(0.08)	0.54
Manufacturers Hanover Corp.	12.6	12.5	0.44	0.41
J. P. Morgan & Co., Inc.	15.4	17.2	0.71	0.75
Chemical New York Corp.	14.0	15.0	0.53	0.50
Continental Illinois Corp.	(13.9)	14.7	(0.51)	0.54
First Interstate Bancorp.	14.1	17.0	0.63	0.75
Bankers Trust New York Corp.	14.1	14.0	0.55	0.51
Security Pacific Corp.	14.4	16.7	0.57	0.68
First Chicago Corp.	9.8	9.4	0.37	0.38
Wells Fargo & Co.	10.7	10.0	0.45	0.39
Crocker National Corp.	5.0	11.1	0.26	0.45
Marine Midland Banks	8.3	10.8	0.37	0.46
Mellon National Corp.	12.8	12.2	0.69	0.69

SOURCE: *American Banker*, July 27, 1982, p. 3

directors and senior management may have made a heavy commitment of resources in one particular year in order to enter a new service area or expand the bank's network of branches. The results of that policy significantly affect the performance ratios for the year in question, but they must also be measured over the course of time.

Information for Customers

The information systems that have been designed to give bank management information on the profitability of account relationships are also of importance and value to customers, especially in the case of major corporations that maintain accounts with several banks. **Account analysis** is the generic term used to describe the information systems that give specific details on the elements involved in servicing an account and the profit or loss that the account creates for the bank. Customers use account analysis to monitor their bank balances and to compare the earnings allowances and schedules of service charges supplied by their various banks.

The following elements would enter into a full account analysis:

1. Calculation of the average daily book balance for a month, *less* the average daily float. This yields the average daily collected balance.

2. Deduction of the required reserves that the bank must maintain against collected balances. This yields the average daily loanable or investable balance; i.e., the net amount that the bank can put to use in making loans and investments. This figure is important because the float and reserves represent book balance figures that have no earnings value to the bank.

3. Application of earnings credit to the average daily loanable balance. The earnings credit is stated in terms of an annual percentage and represents an allowance to customers in exchange for the value of their balances. It must be noted that this cannot be construed as interest, since that would be a violation of federal regulations regarding demand deposits. Rather, the earnings credit is an offset for the customer against the expenses the bank has incurred in rendering services on the account for a month.

245

Suppose, for example, that an account has had an average daily investable balance of $100,000 for the month and that the bank feels an earnings credit allowance of 6 percent is appropriate for that month. The actual credit would be shown as $500 for the month ($100,000×0.06, divided by 12).

The account analysis would then list all the service and activity charges for the month—e.g., 15 deposits @ $.__ per deposit; 463 deposited checks @ $.__ per check; monthly maintenance charges of $____; 3297 checks paid @ $.__ per check; 6 wire transfers @ $__ per transfer. The total for all activity charges would then be compared with the earnings credit and a net profit or loss shown for the month.

If the earnings credit exceeds the total charges, the account is profitable to the bank. If the opposite is true, the relationship operated at a loss and the bank officer handling the account would be expected to approach the customer to ask for increased balances.

It should be noted that the system of detailed account analysis shown here should not and cannot be applied to every checking account. It is used for the large, active business accounts in the bank rather than for smaller personal accounts.

The Income Statement

In analyzing the factors affecting a bank's profitability, one must pay as much attention to the components of the income statement as to the ratios that measure performance. The **spread**, or profit margin, between interest income and expense, for example, is critical to a bank today because its costs of funds are its largest, fastest growing, and least controllable expense factor. Analysis of the income statement also provides information as to how well the bank is keeping its direct operating costs, such as salaries and wages, under control; annual increases can be expected in an inflationary economy, but the percentage of such increases must be related to productivity and the actual growth in the institution's volume of business.

A bank's income statement, when subdivided in detail to show all the components of both revenue and expenses, is an important management tool that can be used in the decision-making process. If the bank has incurred major losses through its international loans, that fact will clearly appear and corrective measures can be taken. If the network of branches is not meeting management's profit objectives, a detailed analysis of the income statement will disclose this, and the bank's senior management can be guided accordingly.

SUMMARY

Bank accounting systems are designed to record, present, and interpret information concerning all the transactions that take place every day. The figures are vital for the bank's own management, are required by federal and state regulatory authorities, and are expected by stockholders and customers. The public cannot place faith and confidence in banks that lack information as to the profitability of their operations and the factors that contribute to that profitability.

Bank accounting systems generally employ double-entry bookkeeping and always develop two basic reports, known as the statement of condition and the income statement. Through application of cost accounting techniques, these systems enable a bank to know its costs for every service and product; thereafter, the bank must develop its own methodology for recovering its costs and generating profits.

Through several critical ratios, the degree of success a bank has achieved in putting its assets to profitable use and generating an adequate rate of return on its stockholders' equity can be measured. These ratios enable one to assess the bank's profitability over a period of time. In an age of consumerism, there can be no justification for a bank's failure to disclose all the relevant facts concerning its financial condition at any time. Similarly, at a time when the basic deposit structure of commercial banking has changed and the costs of doing business have increased so dramatically, there can be no excuse for a bank's ignorance of the factors that create its revenues and expenses or for its lack of expertise in knowing and recovering its costs.

QUESTIONS FOR DISCUSSION

1. What is the difference between a journal and a ledger in bank accounting? Is a general ledger necessary? Why?

2. What effect would the posting of a debit have on an asset or expense account? How would credits affect a liability account?

3. If the assets of a bank exceed its liabilities, what term is given to the difference? If the liabilities are greater than the assets, what does this indicate?

4. Identify the two basic reports that are produced through bank accounting.

5. Explain the difference between the cash and accrual methods of accounting.

6. What is a bank's largest asset item? What is its largest liability? What are the largest income and expense factors?

7. How does the Monetary Control Act of 1980 affect the need for banks to price their services and recover their costs?

8. Why might a corporate customer prefer to compensate the bank with fees rather than balances?

9. Identify the four major ratios that are used to determine a bank's profitability.

10. From your bank's published figures, calculate its most recent ROA and ROE.

Suggested Readings

Brock, Horace R., and Charles E. Palmer. *Accounting Principles and Applications.* 4th edition. New York: McGraw-Hill Book Company, 1981.

Brown, Howard. *Modern Bank Accounting and Auditing Forms With Commentary.* Boston, Massachusetts: Warren, Gorham & Lamont, updated regularly.

Chapter 13

Regulation and Examination of Banks

LEARNING OBJECTIVES

At the completion of this chapter, you will have an understanding of

- the reasons for state and federal supervision and regulation of commercial banks;

- the four tests applied to requests for charters;

- the agencies involved with each type of commercial bank;

- the purposes of bank examinations;

- the American emphasis on unit banking;

- auditing and the three elements it must contain;

- the basic operating safeguards that are part of a bank's system of internal controls; and

- the distinction between positive and negative systems of verification.

T he evolution of commercial banking in America has been repeatedly marked by confrontations and compromises between two groups whose viewpoints on government regulation of the banking system are directly opposed to each other. The early colonists strongly opposed any form of nationalized banking and vehemently resisted the idea of centralized control. The so-called Free Banking laws, passed by the legislature in Michigan in 1837 and subsequently adopted in other states, gave legal sanction to this laissez-faire philosophy and made it possible for virtually anyone to open a bank and to operate it with an absolute minimum of government supervision. Unfortunately, widespread bank failures, counterfeiting of bank notes, and wildcat banking resulted, so that public confidence in the banking system became virtually nonexistent.

The doctrine of free-enterprise banking, however, was not without its prominent opponents. For example, Alexander Hamilton favored a strong central bank and the imposition of federal controls over the banking system, on the grounds that, when human beings failed to do what was just and reasonable, it was the basic function of government to take action. Although Hamilton did not succeed in his attempts to persuade Congress to charter a federal institution modeled on the Bank of England, his influence led to establishing the First and Second Banks of the United States.

The confrontation between those who were in favor of federal intervention in the banking industry and those who opposed it resulted in a compromise. The National Bank Act contained elements of both viewpoints. A new institution, the national bank, was created and placed under the supervision of a newly created federal official, and national bank notes came into existence. However, no bank was forced to seek a national charter; then and now, freedom of choice operates, and banks could and can operate under state charters if they wish.

Similarly, the Federal Reserve Act of 1913 represents a compromise, in that state-chartered banks were allowed to remain outside the Federal Reserve System if they chose to do so. In addition to that basic option, the Act permitted state-chartered banks that joined the Fed to resign from it at any time, and national banks, which were legally required to become members, could convert to state charters and then withdraw from the system.

The Banking Act (i.e., the Glass-Steagall Act) of 1933 also contains an element of compromise, since it did not force every commercial bank to become a member of the newly formed Federal Deposit Insurance Corporation. In this case, the confrontation was not as great, since the wave of bank failures during the early 1930s made the need for banking reform evident to all. Nevertheless, instead of compelling all banks to join the FDIC, the Act did provide the banking industry with options.

As these three historical situations show, federal regulation of banking developed largely in response to basic weaknesses, problems, and money crises. The Acts of 1863, 1913, and 1933 all came into being because it was felt that *only* in this way could improvements be made in the banking system.

Today many observers, both within and outside the banking industry, have characterized it as the most rigidly, frequently, and thoroughly regulated and examined of all the industries in our country. The external controls imposed by government agencies do not apply only while a bank is in existence. Before it can open its doors and accept its first deposit, it must pass a series of qualifying tests to determine whether its application for a charter should be approved. Throughout its life cycle it can expect to be continually subjected to a host of controls that place it in the harsh spotlight of detailed examinations and restrict the scope of its operations. Even after the bank has officially gone out of business, external controls apply until the last depositor has been repaid and the final claim settled. Few, if any, nonbank businesses have so many regulatory agencies and statutory restrictions with which to cope.

BANK CHARTERING

When Salmon P. Chase and his colleagues drafted the text of the National Banking and Currency Acts, one of the issues they specifically addressed was chartering. It had become apparent that the new system of national banks could not be allowed to follow the Free Banking concept; the political abuses and uncontrolled activities that had occurred under that concept had created so many problems that a new method of regulating the opening of banks was absolutely necessary. Therefore, the acts specified that those wishing to establish a new national bank had to submit a charter application to the Office of the Comptroller of the Currency. The application would be subjected to four basic qualifying tests:

- Is the new bank actually needed in the community?

- Is it backed by a sufficient amount of capital?

- Are the incorporators and proposed senior officers experienced, capable, and of impeccable character?

- Is the new bank likely to grow, serve the community well, and be profitable?

These four basic questions are as valid today as they were in 1863, and they remain as the fundamental considerations in the appraisal of every charter request. In addition to the approval of the Comptroller of the Currency, an application for a new national bank charter must also be approved by the Federal Reserve and the FDIC, since national banks must belong to both.

An application for a state charter is submitted to the state banking authorities, who basically apply the same four qualifying tests. If the proposed new bank desired membership in the Federal Reserve and/or the FDIC, its application would also be reviewed by those agencies.

REASONS FOR BANK REGULATION

There has been a great deal of criticism of the existing system of bank regulation and examination, both from those who consider it excessive and from those who propose that the regulatory agencies be consolidated and placed under a single supervisory head. Any such criticisms, however, must be tempered by the realization that the basic nature of the banking industry justifies governmental controls. The early colonists in America did not accept this premise; chaotic conditions resulted. Those who resent the fact that banking is subjected to more extensive restraints and controls than any other industry must recognize the uniqueness of banking and must appreciate the fact that many of those controls came about because the banks themselves created the need for them.

What unique factors in banking justify the number and the scope of the restrictions that have been placed on it?

The first of these relates to the impact of banking on the nation's money supply. Not only do commercial banks, as the holders of the largest amount of demand deposits, control a large part of that supply; aside from the federal government itself, they are the only institutions (except for those thrift institutions given expanded lending powers under 1980 and 1982 legislation) that have the ability to create money through their credit function. It is entirely proper that agencies of government should have a strong interest in the soundness of the one industry whose operations are so closely tied to the money supply.

The second reason for the existence of so many and such rigorous government controls over banking was stated by Alexander Hamilton almost 200 years ago. He pointed out that governments must intervene for the general good of the public when the private sector has not carried out its tasks and met its obligations properly. In the case of banking, it is essential to the country's well-being that public confidence in the system be built up and preserved. Government regulation and examination of commercial banks (and thrift institutions) helps to assure the public that deposits are secure and that the banks are well managed.

There is no industry, through its daily actions, that affects as many others as banking does. The services to individuals, businesses, and governments that flow from the deposit, payment, and credit functions of banks are indispensable to the nation's total economy. It is logical that federal and state agencies should be deeply concerned about the soundness of the single American industry on which so many others depend.

Finally, government agencies recognize today that there is a high degree of interdependence between the well-being of the banks and that of the communities in which they function. The concept of social responsibility requires banks to render a service to the community by becoming involved in local problems. Regulation of the banking industry in some cases has taken the form of legislation, such as the Community Reinvestment Act, requiring banks to take positive steps to improve their communities. In other cases, laws directly affect the relationships between banks and the individuals who live in their communities (e.g., legislation prohibiting any form of discrimination in lending). Each state is the sum total of its communities and municipal entities, and the nation is the sum total of the 50 states; therefore, there is a rationale for federal laws that require banks to help improve the quality of life in their geographic localities.

The criticism of the present system of federal and state regulation of banking mentioned earlier becomes louder and more numerous whenever there is news of a bank failure. Questions are then posed as to why the problem areas at such banks were not identified earlier, how the failures were allowed to take place, and whether the existing system really works. It is then suggested that additional new controls over the industry be instituted or that new supervisory agencies be created.

Such criticisms, questions, and corrective measures may have some validity, but only if they lead to improvements in the present system, and not if they call for its abolition. Even the most outspoken advocate of the free-enterprise concept would find it impossible today to support the removal of all forms of government controls over banking. Banking is indeed different from all other industries, and realization of this fact brings with it recognition of the need for external controls that will protect the interests of the nation as a whole.

REGULATORY AGENCIES

The compromises in the 1863, 1913, and 1933 acts created different categories of banks; therefore, various agencies of government were assigned *primary* responsibility for supervising each category. Four such agencies, each having regulatory authority over certain segments of the banking industry, can be listed.

The Comptroller of the Currency has jurisdiction over the 4,500 national banks, which operate some 22,000 branches. The Office of the Comptroller is responsible for chartering, examining, and supervising all national banks. All requests by any of these banks for the opening of new domestic or foreign branches or for the offering of new services (e.g., in the fiduciary area), and all merger or acquisitions involving national banks must have the Comptroller's approval. The many functions of this agency are carried out through regional administrative offices throughout the country. The Comptroller, ex officio, is also a member of the Board of Governors of the Federal

Deposit Insurance Corporation and the Depository Institutions Deregulation Committee.

The seven-member Board of Governors of the Federal Reserve System consists of individuals who are appointed by the President of the United States, subject to confirmation by the Senate. The seven members must come from seven different Fed districts. In addition to its basic tasks in the area of national monetary policy, the Fed is responsible for regulating all members, examining those members that are state-chartered, supervising all bank holding companies and considering requests from those companies for acquisitions or for expansion of services, and overseeing the international operations of member banks.

The Federal Deposit Insurance Corporation insures some 98 percent of all commercial and savings banks in the United States. It sets standards to which its members must conform, assesses them according to the size of their average annual deposits, and can examine a member bank at any time.

Each of the 50 states has its own banking authority, which can regulate branch banking within the state's borders, approve charter requests, set maximum interest rates on certain loans, and otherwise supervise the banks' actions.

All national banks *must* be members of the Federal Reserve System; all Fed members must also belong to FDIC. Therefore, every national bank is technically subject to three different regulatory agencies of the federal government. To ensure a sound, well-run banking system, each agency, together with the banking departments of each state, has the right to conduct an examination of the banks that fall under its jurisdiction.

OTHER REGULATORY BODIES

In addition to those state and federal agencies named, there are many other nonbank agencies that exercise some degree of control over the operations of commercial banks. For example, the Department of Justice has the right of approval on any bank merger that, in its judgment, may create a trend toward monopoly. The Securities and Exchange Commission requires banks and all other corporations that issue and sell stock to the public to file regular, detailed reports with it. The Treasury Department's Office of Law Enforcement has implemented the Bank Secrecy Act through extensive record-retention and reporting requirements.

Banks that lend under programs administered by the Veterans Administration or the Departments of Labor, Interior, Housing and Urban Development, and Health and Human Services are to some degree regulated by those agencies. Banks are also directly affected by all federal, state, and local legislation regarding equal employment opportunity, discrimination in lending, fair credit reporting, truth in lending, and collection practices on delinquent debts.

BANK EXAMINATIONS

The process of periodic examinations has become an accepted part of the U.S. banking system. Every commercial bank in the country receives at least one such examination each year, and the frequency may be increased if conditions in a particular bank seem to warrant it. However, it would clearly be impossible for every regulatory agency to examine every bank under its jurisdiction. Even if this were physically feasible, it would involve much unnecessary duplication of effort, with a consequent increase in expense to the taxpayers. For example, if a national bank were to undergo separate examinations in one year by the Office of the Comptroller of the Currency, the Fed, and FDIC, its operations would be disrupted on each occasion and three examinations would have been conducted when a single thorough one would probably have sufficed.

Therefore, to avoid duplication and waste, the federal regulatory agencies have agreed on an examination format acceptable to all of them. The results of any one examination are transmitted to all other interested agencies *and* to the bank's board of directors. Table 13-1 shows how the primary responsibility for bank examinations has been allocated to various agencies. It must be noted, however, that this system in no way inhibits the right of any agency to conduct its own examination of a particular bank. If, for example, the Comptroller of the Currency uncovers information showing that a problem exists at a national bank, both the FDIC and the Federal Reserve, on the basis of the Comptroller's report, could immediately conduct their own independent examinations if they felt this was appropriate.

Table 13-1
Bank Regulatory Authorities

Type of Bank	Regulatory Authority	Annual Examination Conducted By
National Bank	Comptroller of the Currency Federal Reserve FDIC	Comptroller of the Currency
State Member Bank	Federal Reserve FDIC State Banking Department	Federal Reserve*
State Nonmember Insured Bank	FDIC State Banking Department	FDIC
State Nonmember Noninsured Bank	State Banking Department	State Banking Department

*Examinations of state-chartered member banks are often conducted jointly by state banking department examiners working closely with Federal Reserve examiners.

Purposes of Bank Examinations

The basic purpose of every bank examination is to determine certain facts about that bank. The examiners representing a federal or state agency *do not* specifically try to locate fraud or embezzlement. Rather, they perform an evaluation of the bank's reporting systems for all its assets, liabilities, income, and expenses. They determine the bank's degree of compliance with all the laws and regulations that affect it. They assess the quality and effectiveness of the bank's management, as judged by the policies and procedures that can be noted. They determine the adequacy of the bank's capital, since the size of a bank's capital and surplus protects the stockholders and depositors by ensuring that it could withstand losses and adverse conditions.

In summary, every external examination of a bank must answer the following questions:

1. What is the bank's true financial condition? Every commercial bank is required to submit detailed balance sheet and income statement data to regulatory authorities. The examiners verify these to ensure that all assets, liabilities, income, and expenses have been accurately recorded.

2. Are all appropriate laws and regulations being observed?

3. Are capital funds sufficient to support the bank's operations?

4. What improvements can be made?

The fourth question indicates that one purpose of a bank examination is to identify ways in which the institution could operate more profitably, correct any weaknesses that exist in it, and serve the needs of its customers and community more effectively.

In addition to submitting a copy of their report to the bank's board of directors, which presumably will take whatever corrective action is needed, the examiners representing state and federal agencies have the right to call a meeting of the directors to discuss specific problems.

Those same federal agencies periodically prepare a "warning list" of banks at which weaknesses and problems have been found. Any bank that has been placed on this list can expect to receive much closer scrutiny from government regulators. In addition to more frequent and/or more detailed examinations, a bank in this category may also be required to accept certain actions taken by the regulators in an attempt to keep it from failing. For example, FDIC may make a direct loan to the bank, purchase some of its assets, deposit funds with it to ensure that it will have adequate liquidity, or—as happened frequently in 1981 and 1982—bring about a merger of the troubled bank with a stronger insured bank.

BRANCH AND UNIT BANKING

The reader who has lived or worked in California, New Jersey, Arizona, or New York and has observed the proliferation of bank branches in those states may have been led to believe that they are typical and that branch banking exists throughout the country. This is not the case. Branch banks actually are in the minority; *unit* banks, which have no branches, predominate, and this is the result of a consistent upholding of the principle of states' rights by the highest courts in our country.

The National Bank Act of 1863 contained no mention of branch banking, but was amended in 1865 to permit a state-chartered bank that converted to a national charter to retain any branches it already had. National banks had no branching powers until 1927, when an important piece of federal legislation known as the McFadden Act was passed.

The McFadden Act permitted national banks to open branches, but *only* to the extent that state-chartered banks could do so under the laws of their respective states. Illinois, for example, is a unit banking state, as is Texas; therefore, each commercial bank in either of those states must be a unit bank and is not allowed to establish branches. The McFadden Act applies this state restriction to national, as well as state, banks. The right of each of the 50 states to regulate branching within its borders has been repeatedly preserved by the courts, and *all* banks, regardless of their type of charter, that operate in any state must be governed by that state's laws on branching.

There are more unit banks than branch banks in the United States, partly because of the restrictive laws that exist but also because many banks do not find it necessary to open branches, even where they could legally do so. Many unit banks adequately serve the needs of their communities through a single location and see no need to incur the expenses of operating branches.

259

The number of actual brick-and-mortar branches in the United States will undoubtedly be reduced still further through the adoption by the public of **electronic funds transfer systems** (EFTS). The most modern and sophisticated automated facilities, activated by bank cards, will accept deposits, handle requests for withdrawals of funds, initiate transfers between accounts, and provide cash advances. While the initial costs of these new installations are high and the technology to support them is expensive, they offer significant advantages over the long run and can be expected to replace many existing branches.

Interstate Branching

The point that the U.S. banking system is quite different from those in other countries has repeatedly been made, and one striking example of that difference can be seen in the fact that nationwide branch banking does *not* exist in the United States. In Great Britain, Canada, and France, for example, banks operate branch systems in every part of the country. In America, federal laws effectively prohibit commercial banks from operating full-scale branches outside their own states.

If an American commercial bank wishes to open a branch office in a foreign country thousands of miles away, it can do so with relative ease simply by gaining the approval of the federal regulatory agency to which it is subject. Obviously, the foreign country would also have to approve this request. However, that same American bank cannot open a full-scale branch across a state line, even when that boundary is 1 mile away.

In 1919, federal legislation known as the Edge Act was passed to enable banks to establish offices in other states to assist customers in international trade transactions. Many American banks have done so in such cities as Houston, San Francisco, and Miami. In other cases, banks have opened loan production offices and representative offices outside the borders of their own states. Because these facilities, and Edge Act offices, do not accept deposits and qualify as full-scale branches, they are legally permitted.

Electronic Terminals

The question of whether point-of-sale terminals and automated teller machines are to be considered as branches of banks, and therefore subject to federal and state restrictions on branching, is one that has caused controversy and created litigation in recent years. The 50 state banking departments are not unanimous in their thinking on this basic question. As of March 1983, 26 states had enacted laws stating that remote terminals were not branches and 9 states held that such facilities were. Six states have EFT statutes that are silent on the branch status of an EFT facility. Of the remaining states, 6 are without comprehensive EFT statutes but do have either Attorney General or State Regulator's opinions stating that EFT facilities do constitute branches, and 3 states have neither statutes nor opinions on the issue.

In this area, as in many other aspects of the financial marketplace, the nation's commercial banks see themselves as having been placed at a major competitive disadvantage. For example, according to a 1981 ruling of the Federal Home Loan Bank Board, which supervises the nation's federally chartered savings and loan associations, any such S&L is permitted to establish 24-hour automated teller machines *anywhere* in the United States. Similarly, all the nonbank competitors of commercial banks have complete freedom to operate across state lines. Sears Roebuck has accounts receivable of over $7 billion, generated in every part of the country; American Express Company's dispensing machines sell travelers checks nationwide; and General Motors Acceptance Corporation's accounts receivable, created by financing automobiles in every one of the 50 states, averaged $45.5 billion during the second quarter of 1982. Commercial banks enjoy no such latitude in their operations.

INTERNAL CONTROLS

All the arguments that have been used to justify the need for systems of external controls over banking apply with at least equal validity to the need for a thorough and ongoing program of internal controls within each bank. The owner of an automobile may have complied with all state regulations regarding inspection and may have obtained adequate insurance coverage, but he or she is still responsible for the day-to-day operation of the vehicle. A corporation may have satisfactorily met all federal and state requirements pertaining to its business, but its management must still do all that is necessary to run the firm properly. By the same token, it is the clear and inescapable duty of bank management to take any and all steps that are necessary to protect the assets of both the bank and its depositors and to see to it that all operating procedures are efficient and safe.

The typical U.S. commercial bank is corporate in its structure; like all corporations, its active governing body is its board of directors. They are elected by the stockholders and are responsible for the proper conduct of all the bank's affairs. Members of the board can be held personally liable for what they do or what they fail to do. If their actions or their failure to act should result in the bank's liquidation, they may be subject not only to civil suits brought by stockholders who claim that their interests were not properly protected, but also to criminal prosecution. Directors must ensure that a system of efficient internal controls is established and must take steps to ensure that the system is meticulously followed. They cannot adopt a passive attitude and wait for federal or state examiners to identify problems for them, nor can they point to the existence of insurance as a protection for the bank.

Generally speaking, it is physically impossible for directors to spend their time visiting every branch and department of the bank, and looking at every phase of its daily operations, to satisfy themselves that everything is as it should be. The board delegates this responsibility, most commonly by naming one officer who will have primary responsibility for checking on the observance and effectiveness of every aspect of the internal controls program. For purposes of uniformity and as a functional description of the job, that officer will be referred to throughout this discussion as the bank's **auditor**. As a matter of policy, most banks require not only that the auditor be appointed directly by the board but also that he or she report to them, bypassing other levels and members of management.

At smaller banks it may not be possible to justify the appointment of a full-time auditor, and the position may be filled by an officer who has other responsibilities. In all such cases, there must be a clear and complete separation of duties. Auditors cannot become involved in banking transactions, such as the originating of debit and credit entries, which they subsequently must examine and approve.

A distinction must be made here between auditing in a bank and examinations of the bank that federal and state examiners conduct. The objectives of the examinations were stated earlier in this chapter, and the point was made that external examinations do not specifically try to locate instances of embezzlement or fraud. Conversely, auditing does so. The auditing function aims at identifying and correcting weaknesses and problems *before* federal and state examiners visit the bank.

The difference between the terms "auditing" and "controls" must also be noted. Controls are established first; auditing is the process through which the existence and effectiveness of the controls are verified. For example, a bank establishes a control over one aspect of its safe deposit operation by requiring every person who wishes to gain access to a box to sign a signature slip. This control is designed to prevent unauthorized persons from gaining entry to safe deposit boxes. In an audit, the auditors would determine whether this control procedure was being followed on every occasion. Similarly, a teller's proof is a control device; it establishes the fact that certain procedures were followed; during an audit, the auditors would check to see whether the proof sheets had actually been prepared and verified each day. Bank policy may state that all debit and credit tickets must bear evidence of dual control, so that two staff members indicate that they have knowledge of a transaction and assume responsibility for its correctness. Audits will determine whether this policy has actually been followed. The examination of a bank by federal or state examiners would not focus on these points; it is the auditor's duty to do so.

Auditing

As a function, auditing embraces a great many duties, including the design and implementation of the bank's internal controls system. The auditor is the individual responsible for determining the accuracy of all the bank's accounting records, specifically those that affect asset, liability, income, expense, and capital accounts.

Because the auditor must certify that all figures for these accounts have been properly stated and that all entries affecting them are correct, he or she has full authority to examine any and all departments and branches of the bank through which those entries originate. The auditor, in reporting directly to the board of directors, identifies the degree of care and skill with which the internal controls program is being put into daily practice and suggests changes and new procedures as necessary.

Every commercial bank expects to be examined at regular intervals by representatives of the government agencies that have jurisdiction over it. However, the most thorough and demanding check on all procedures is invariably the one conducted by the bank's own auditing staff. This is exactly as it should be. No bank can neglect the task of keeping its own house in order. Systematic and thorough auditing guarantees that all financial information is accurate and that all appropriate internal controls are in place and are functioning.

Elements of Successful Auditing. If an audit program is to be successful, it must contain three basic elements: *independence, control,* and *surprise.* The auditor's independence makes it possible to examine part or all of the operations of any unit, branch, or department of the bank at any time. No member of bank management should have the authority to limit this independence. The auditor alone has the right to decide which areas should be visited and which phases of the operations in those areas should be audited.

Similarly, the auditing staff must have full control over each audit. The validity of the entire process would be negated if the officer in charge of a branch or department were to be allowed to tell the auditors which records would be made available to them and which would be kept private.

The third element, surprise, is indispensable in any successful auditing program. One of the best-kept secrets in the bank must be the schedule that shows when and to what extent certain units will be examined. There should be no set routine for this, nor any predictable timetable. The most efficient units in any bank are those in which the staff has performed every task and maintained every record as if everyone knew that an audit would be performed on the next day.

Verification With Customers. As part of the auditing process, it may be appropriate to send verification letters to the bank's customers, asking them to confirm the accuracy of the figures shown on the bank's books. Using a system of random sampling, the auditors may select certain customers and ask them to verify the balance in a checking or savings account, the outstanding amount of a loan, or the securities that the bank is holding as collateral or in a fiduciary capacity. Verification may be either positive or negative.

Positive verification requires that every customer who is contacted during an audit must sign and return a form letter, agreeing or disagreeing with the figures as shown. This is the more expensive and time-consuming of the two methods, since follow-up letters are frequently necessary and the audit is incomplete until each customer has replied.

Negative verification is the more widely used method. It calls for a reply from the customer *only* when there is disagreement with the figures as shown. The typical checking account statement is the most common example of negative verification, since the depositor is expected to contact the bank only if he or she finds a discrepancy between the bank's figures and his or her own records. If the customer does not do so, the bank is allowed to assume that its figures are correct.

Verification involving thousands of customers is obviously impractical; however, when a percentage of the total customer base is contacted, verification serves an extremely useful purpose. If a bank employee has somehow been able to destroy or manipulate transaction entries or records, an audit might not disclose the irregularity; verification would do so at once.

Control Systems

To protect its own assets and those entrusted to it by its customers, the typical commercial bank has designed and implemented a set of internal controls. Because these help to provide the security that is so essential to banking, they will be discussed in the next chapter, which specifically deals with the related questions of security and personnel.

SUMMARY

Commercial banking in the United States is the most thoroughly regulated, frequently examined, tightly restricted, and closely supervised of all industries. There are valid reasons for this degree of regulation and examination. In the earliest days of U.S. banking, government controls were kept to an absolute minimum because the colonists did not see the need for systems comparable to those in the countries they had left. Charters for new banks were easy to obtain, and the day-to-day operations of each institution went almost completely without local or federal supervision. It became apparent that legislative action was needed for the common welfare.

The banking acts of 1863–1864, 1913, and 1933 were passed because uncontrolled banking had been so detrimental to many segments of our economy and society. Today, all commercial banks are subject to chartering requirements, regular examinations, and operating constraints designed to ensure that each institution is operating in both a legal and a sound manner. A single bank may be subject to the requirements of many different federal and state regulatory authorities.

Internal controls and auditing are justified on the same grounds as are external controls. The directors and officers of banks are directly responsible for seeing to it that the institution operates as efficiently and safely as possible. Each bank must police itself and do whatever is necessary to protect its own assets and those that have been entrusted to it.

QUESTIONS FOR DISCUSSION

1. List the four qualifying tests that are applied to requests for new bank charters.

2. Which agency of the federal government would have primary responsibility for examining a national bank? Which other agencies might also examine the same bank?

3. What four questions does every examination of a bank by a government agency attempt to answer?

4. Who appoints a bank's chief auditor? To whom does the auditor report?

5. Identify the difference between controls and auditing.

6. What are the three essential elements in every auditing program?

7. What two forms of verification are used in bank auditing? Explain the difference between the two.

Suggested Readings

American Bankers Association. *Bank Control and Audit.* Washington, D.C.: American Bankers Association, 1983.

American Bankers Association. *Guide to General Examinations for National Banks.* Washington, D.C.: American Bankers Association, 1977.

Federal Deposit Insurance Corporation. *Manual of Examination Policies.* Washington, D.C.: U.S. GPO, 1973. Updated with loose-leaf supplements.

Federal Reserve Bank of New York. *A Guide to Federal Reserve Regulations.* Washington, D.C.: Board of Governors of the Federal Reserve System, 1977.

Golembe, Carter H., and David S. Holland. *Federal Regulation of Banking.* Washington, D.C.: Golembe Associates, Inc., 1981.

U.S. Comptroller of the Currency. *Comptroller's Manual for National Banks.* Washington, D.C.: U.S. GPO, 1977. Updated with loose-leaf supplements.

U.S. Comptroller of the Currency. *The NBSS Bank Performance Report, A User's Guide for Bankers and Examiners.* Washington, D.C.: U.S. GPO, 1977.

Chapter 14

Personnel and Security

LEARNING OBJECTIVES

After completion of this chapter, you will have an understanding of

- the importance of staff members as the bank's human resources;
- the selection process in bank hiring;
- the importance of personnel policies and procedures;
- the need for personnel training and development;
- the role of job descriptions;
- the emphasis on internal security in banking;
- the measures commonly taken by banks to create security; and
- the physical and psychological factors that influence bank personnel.

T he recent emphasis on automation in many aspects of banking and the steady increase in customer acceptance of such electronic funds transfer systems as direct deposit and ATMs sometimes give rise to a question as to the future of people in the industry. That question need never be posed. Banking always has been, is now, and will continue to be a people-based industry. Regardless of the extent to which modern technology is introduced, banking will always depend on the interpersonal relationships of staff members with the public and with each other. It is a service industry that, like all service industries, will grow in importance in years to come.

Automation has not eliminated jobs in banking; it has created new ones and has provided opportunities for many employees to move from monotonous, assembly-line work to more interesting and challenging tasks. There is no reason whatever to fear that the importance of skilled and dedicated staff members will decrease in the future. Many banks no longer have "personnel" units; the term "human resources department" now identifies the area in which all the functions that are connected with selecting and hiring, training and developing, evaluating, and retaining employees are performed. The new name given to this department reflects the fact that individuals are a real resource of the bank, just as any of its other productive assets can be considered on that basis.

Customers may increasingly use ATMs to handle banking transactions instead of doing business with tellers, and they may take advantage of new capabilities that electronic technology creates, but there will always be situations and tasks requiring the direct involvement of bank personnel. Even though various forms of automation have been in existence in banks for many years, banking still employs over 1 million workers, and its future is limited only by the imagination of those people and their commitment to the professionalism that is needed. New services are continually being introduced. They will demand the productive efforts of personnel who are trained and ready to help their banks prosper and grow. The challenges are great, but so are the opportunities. The importance of qualified, productive employees will increase, rather than decline, and the future belongs to those who believe in it, recognize their own role in it, and are prepared to cope with its problems and take advantage of the opportunities for personal growth that it presents.

OBJECTIVES OF PERSONNEL MANAGEMENT

Commercial banking is designed to render services and to manage the assets of the institution in such a way that the best interests of all parties will be satisfied. This includes the generating of adequate profits. To achieve these objectives, people who differ from each other in skills and backgrounds must work productively together under effective leadership. The management of a bank's human resources embraces all the functions that will lead to accomplishment of the institution's stated objectives.

Personnel policies form the foundation of this area of management, and it must be recognized at the outset that the workers are the instruments of policy and not its object. The long-range objectives of policies are the desired results. Those results will be produced *by* people and *through* people, and in no other way.

To be effective, personnel policies must have certain characteristics and must be implemented in a certain way:

- They must be based on the goals of the organization;

- They must originate with senior levels of management;

- They must establish ground rules that support the effective operation of the bank;

- They must be clearly written, definite in content, and widely disseminated to the staff;

- They must indicate *what* officers and supervisors will do and *why* they will act in a certain way.

The following are some brief examples:

Wherever possible, vacancies on the staff will be filled by promotions or transfers from within.

The bank will provide equal employment opportunities to every worker without regard to race, creed, color, sex, age, or national origin.

All new employees serve a probationary period. This period normally lasts 90 days but may be extended if doubt exists as to the individual's capability.

PROCEDURES AND PROGRAMS

After policies have been approved by senior management, often with the concurrence of the bank's board of directors, they are usually disseminated in the form of detailed manuals. These must be updated promptly to reflect changes in policy. Staff meetings may be necessary for officers and supervisors to make employees aware of changes that affect them and to ensure that policies are clearly understood.

Policies are translated into daily procedures and programs. For example, to implement the policy that staff vacancies would be filled from within the organization wherever possible, the bank would institute a system of job posting so that existing staff members are made aware of opportunities elsewhere in the organization. Job posting systems describe the nature and location of the work, the salary range, and the basic qualifications and encourage interested employees to apply for the vacant position.

SELECTION AND HIRING PROCESSES

The standards a bank sets when it first chooses its employees may well be the most important factor in determining its future success. The salary expenses incurred in hiring the right individuals for the right positions can easily be justified if the candidates bring to the bank the qualities and skills it needs. No individual can be expected to prove reliable, loyal, and dedicated if he or she has been made to feel underpaid.

Recruiting at the management trainee level is conducted by many banks at colleges and universities, and individuals who seem to have the potential for future positions of responsibility may be interviewed on the campus and then brought to the bank for further screening. Recruiting programs may also be conducted at local high schools to attract other candidates. In addition, public advertising is used extensively, and current employees are encouraged to refer friends or acquaintances when openings occur.

The selection and hiring process is fruitless if the bank does not make a specific correlation between the individual's experience, education, aptitudes, and interests on the one hand and the position for which he or she is being considered on the other. The skilled member of the bank's human resources staff not only must select the best candidate in each case but also must match that candidate against the institution's specific need.

Selection and hiring processes must be geared to the future as well as the present. The need for a stated number of clerks and tellers to fill current vacancies is obvious; what may be less obvious is the problem of management succession. How many of the existing number of officers and supervisors can be expected to leave the bank within a certain time frame? How many lending officers must be trained and developed to meet the bank's projected staffing needs 2, 5, or 10 years hence?

As an essential part of the hiring process, it is incumbent on the bank to verify all the information the candidate for employment has supplied. There can be no excuse for failure to check on credentials, whether in education or employment. Did the individual actually attend the schools as claimed? What was his or her academic record? Are the time frames regarding previous employment correct? What impression did the person make on previous employers?

Personal references are less valuable in hiring. Obviously the candidate will supply only the names of those individuals who are most likely to give a favorable report, and in most cases the parties who are given as references will be only those who will recommend him or her.

For certain sensitive areas of banking, the hiring process may involve administration of a lie detector (polygraph) test; however, the officials of the human resources department who decide that such testing is advisable should familiarize themselves thoroughly with local laws on the subject and should be completely satisfied that the operators of the polygraph equipment can interpret the results accurately.

JOB DESCRIPTION AND EVALUATION

No employee of a bank at any level should be at a loss to know how well or how poorly he or she is doing. Similarly, no employee at any level should be unsure about the tasks that his or her job requires, the lines of reporting, and the results that are expected. The first step in ensuring that employees are informed about their own positions calls for preparing job descriptions. In addition to their direct effect on the incumbents in each position, job descriptions also enable the bank to develop equitable programs of salary compensation and to assist personnel officers in filling vacancies as they occur. Federal, state, and local laws regarding affirmative action and equality of opportunity demand that each bank's hiring be based on completely objective criteria and not on any type of subjective discriminatory judgment.

The job descriptions for every level of staff member in a bank also provide a tool for periodic evaluation and for personal interaction with the person who is being reviewed. The reviewer is able to match the employee's level of performance with the requirements and objectives of the position. This periodic review process should not be a one-way street. The individual who is evaluated should have every opportunity to agree or disagree with the review. A common policy among banks calls for the staff member to sign the position evaluation as a permanent record of the fact that he or she has seen it and has discussed it with the reviewer. The signature does not necessarily indicate agreement with the contents of the evaluation.

SALARY ADMINISTRATION

If banks are to overcome the stigma sometimes attached to the industry regarding its compensation programs, they can do so only by making sure that they pay competitive salaries for similar work and that they meet the prevailing wage scales offered for comparable positions in the community. One test of the effectiveness of a bank's compensation program is the frequency with which its staff members resign in order to join other banks or accept nonbank positions.

It is an unavoidable and obvious cliché to say that programs for salary administration in banking must reward those who are productive and penalize those whose performance does not meet standards. Experience, however, indicates that this truth has not always been accepted by banks. If an employee has displayed outstanding performance and an unusually large salary increase appears warranted, there should be no reluctance to grant it. The converse of this statement is equally important. No bank can afford the luxury of a salary program that automatically rewards employees simply for having completed another year of service without giving due consideration to the results that the individual has achieved and the contribution he or she has made.

Enlightened personnel management today reviews the demands of each department and branch and measures the tasks performed in it. If this process identifies areas that appear to be overstaffed, the bank is paying for poor productivity, and employees are not earning their pay.

The area of compensation for bank employees is not confined to actual salary and wage payments; it also includes the fringe benefits that are common throughout industry today. Medical and surgical insurance, noncontributory pension plans, deferred compensation based on profit sharing, and other indirect expenses for the bank must be considered as parts of an overall package that the candidate for employment will match against those offered elsewhere.

CAREER PATHS

In bygone years, progression through the banking ranks was slow and often painful. Individuals accepted the fact that they would remain in the same job for long periods of time and that promotion would come only after a senior employee retired or died. In today's work environment, this policy has largely disappeared, and the employee's aspirations often create an immediate rejection of it. Individuals not only want to know how well they are doing in their current positions; they are also anxious to learn whether they will be considered for advancement and, if so, how long the waiting period may be.

The program of periodic evaluation carried out by many banks today includes a specific mention of career paths. For what positions, in what areas of the organization, can this individual be considered? Within what time frame is promotion a possibility, assuming continued qualifying performance? Is the employee a square peg in a round hole, and would the best interests of both the bank and the employee be served through a transfer to another area?

A basic function of personnel administration is to attune the objectives of the individual with those of the institution. It is both helpful to the employee and conducive to the basic objective of human resources management if workers who have the potential for promotion can be identified *and* can be told of the organization's future plans for them. The fact that a teller, clerk, or junior officer may not have become familiar with all the textbooks and theories of industrial psychology does not mean that he or she does not seek the self-actualization and the assumption of added responsibility that leading researchers have identified. A frank discussion, as part of the regular performance review, spelling out management's projected career path for the staff member is a valuable adjunct to the overall process.

Again, a two-way street exists in this regard. Employees must be told what they are expected to do for themselves in order to become promotable. It is not simply a matter of having a member of management indicate what plans the bank has for the individual; the opportunity to move ahead carries with it an obligation for the employee to demonstrate efforts toward self-improvement.

TRAINING AND DEVELOPMENT

Within the bank itself, the need for improved productivity and quality in individual performance is at least as great today as the need for mere increases in the size of the staff. Banking is steadily becoming more and more complex. Skills that were never required in the past are now essential if the institution is to meet its performance objectives and satisfy its customers. The changes in the basic deposit structure, the corresponding emphasis on liability management, the increasing importance of electronic funds transfer systems, and the new stress on many aspects of global banking are but a few of the examples that support this viewpoint. In the personnel area itself, a far more enlightened approach exists today; the autocratic methods of the past, in which banks were often criticized for their lack of a people-oriented attitude, are disappearing.

Many commercial banks have instituted systems of employee profile forms; these are detailed documents, often generated and updated through the computer, that give a complete picture of an individual's educational background, job experience, special aptitudes, hobbies, and interests, and performance ratings to date. Through the use of these profiles, management can determine what training and development programs are advisable if the individual is to progress to the desired level. The profiles likewise indicate areas of deficiency that must be remedied to make the employee more productive and better prepared to meet the needs of the bank for the future.

The management of a bank's human resources must include an identification of employee needs so that proper programs can be developed to meet those needs. Again, the process of performance evaluation can be tailored to include a specific mention of problem areas that can be resolved through training. Perhaps a manager is not displaying the required sensitivity to his or her subordinate's attitudes. Perhaps the review will mention the fact that an individual is not entirely comfortable in customer situations or is not aware of the cross-selling opportunities inherent in his or her present position. Perhaps the employee can be taught new techniques directly related to the job. Most basic of all, it may be that the individual simply does not feel a part of the overall institution and cannot relate to its objectives.

Banking today includes an almost infinite number of internal training programs designed to enhance the skills of employees, prepare them for additional future responsibilities, and give them the knowledge they need in a rapidly changing industry. Teller training, credit training, communications training, and marketing training are but a few of these. The number and content of the programs must be revised continually to meet additional organizational and individual needs.

The difference between training and development can be highlighted here. Training is intended to increase the knowledge and skills of a person. It may help him or her to make better decisions, but it will seldom result in his or her wanting to do so. On the other hand, development describes personal growth and motivation. Development may be said to come from within, because the individual has been conditioned to want to change. For example, a bank's program designed to provide the nucleus of its future officer cadre will include both credit *training*, which teaches the candidate the necessary judgmental skills and shows the steps in evaluating a loan request, and management *development*, which gives the candidate the needed encouragement to assume responsibility and to use his or her talents.

External programs for the training and development of bank personnel are at least as numerous and comprehensive as those provided internally. At the forefront of these must be listed the curricula of the American Institute of Banking. No industry-sponsored adult-educational institution anywhere in the world can equal AIB in the breadth of job-oriented programs that are offered each year through hundreds of local chapters in every part of the country. There are also a host of other graduate and undergraduate schools of banking that offer both basic and advanced banking-related education. Few, if any, industries offer employees the opportunities for improving their job-related knowledge that exist in banking. Tuition refund plans at many banks enable employees to obtain an education and be reimbursed for their expenses. After-hours education is widely supported and encouraged by banks because it provides a means of supplementing internal programs and helps to prepare workers for new opportunities that exist.

SECURITY

From their very earliest days, banks have been the natural, prime targets for every type of fraud, embezzlement, and robbery. In their unceasing effort to create and tighten internal security, banks have unfortunately found that each procedure and system they introduce has brought corresponding new attempts to find loopholes in those procedures and to frustrate those systems.

A bank may implement a set of special codes to prevent unauthorized money transfers; an individual finds a method of penetrating those codes and initiates a transfer of funds to a foreign bank for his own benefit. Another bank assigns a staff member to audit its dormant accounts; that person identifies a weakness in the system of controls and embezzles a seven-figure sum by manipulating those accounts. Banks consistently update their vault facilities and alarm systems in an effort to provide maximum security; robbers turn to new laser technology and employ electronic equipment to bypass the alarms, gain entry to the vault, and steal the contents of customers' safe deposit boxes as well as the banks' supplies of cash. In other instances, thieves have studied the daily opening procedures used by banks and have taken advantage of a moment's negligence or inattention to enter the premises and stage a robbery. Many banks have installed protective shields of heavy plastic in front of tellers' windows; robbers ignore these and gain their objective by threatening platform personnel with purported dynamite or bombs. A bank places cameras in its branches to record transactions; a holdup team enters a branch and immediately covers the camera lenses with black paint to frustrate the system. The list is endless. The cost of insurance protecting banks against losses from holdups and defalcations has become so prohibitively high that many banks have dropped this coverage and canceled their policies, thereby assuming the risks and losses themselves.

Discouraging though the preceding paragraph may be, none of it should be construed to mean that the number of robberies and embezzlements makes security programs useless. It is the exception that creates the headlines and draws attention to the banks; the millions of transactions that are handled efficiently every day are ignored. Security must always be a prime concern, and the controls designed to protect the bank's assets and those of its customers can never be ignored or neglected. Bank management personnel must remain aware at all times that it is far better to prevent a loss than to recover one. The principle that underlies all systems of internal controls is that temptation can be reduced among weak people, opportunities for theft can be minimized among strong people, and innocent people can be protected from temptation.

It is unfortunately true that one significant responsibility of a bank's directors and officers must focus on the possibility of losses through employee dishonesty. The very nature of the business makes large quantities of money accessible to staff members every day, and in an inflationary era, when society stresses creature comforts and the importance of keeping up with the Joneses, pressures and temptations may prove overpowering to an employee. Banks recognize the need for external controls imposed by federal and state agencies, but by the same token every employee should accept the systems of internal controls and auditing as a form of protection rather than as an indication of management's lack of faith in their honesty. Indeed, the measures that banks take in the area of security often provide employees with both physical and psychological support.

Internal Controls

The primary responsibility for providing security in the bank rests with the board of directors, who elect officers and delegate to them the day-to-day management of the bank's affairs. Internal controls, however, cannot be considered as the responsibility of one or two groups alone; rather, they are the concern of every staff member and the responsibility for implementing them is shared throughout the entire institution. These controls involve every conceivable method of protecting the bank against losses caused by robbery, fraud, or larceny perpetrated by outsiders or caused by internal embezzlement, inefficiencies in management, or negligence and carelessness. Therefore, they affect every area of daily operations.

Many banks have found it necessary to appoint one or more individuals as internal security officers, who are responsible for deriving maximum benefits from the various controls. In addition, the bank may designate a compliance officer, who is in charge of filing all the necessary reports to federal and state regulatory authorities regarding the bank's conformity to legal requirements.

The following paragraphs illustrate some of the internal controls that banks generally install. The listing is by no means all-inclusive but is intended merely to identify some of the standard safeguards and practices that banks employ.

As mentioned earlier, *personnel policies and procedures* are an integral part of banking security systems. Financial institutions are always targets for individuals who seek employment there for some illicit purpose, and the entire concept of internal controls can be negated if these individuals are allowed to join the staff. Every prospective employee should be thoroughly investigated and any doubt resolved in favor of the bank. Many banks now require fingerprinting as part of the hiring process, while giving job applicants the right to refuse to be fingerprinted if they feel this is appropriate. The policies and procedures that are part of the selection process for bank employees often exist in order to conform to the requirements of insurers, who issue some form of bonding covering the operations of the institution.

There are many cases on record in which bank employees have used their own low salaries as the rationale for having embezzled. To protect against this possibility, each bank should assure itself that it is paying employees a fair and equitable salary. Policies regarding annual increases, evaluations of performance, merit raises, and promotions should be established and clearly understood. Employees who have financial, family, or emotional problems should be made to feel that the bank is ready and willing to provide counseling, monetary help, or some other form of direct assistance. By measuring its salary and benefit program against others in its community, a bank's management can take a positive step toward improving employee morale. Personal job satisfactions are an intangible but important part of the total system of internal controls, and an employee who has been made to feel that he or she is truly a part of the organization is less likely to succumb to any temptation that is presented.

Every bank should follow a policy of *mandatory vacations* for all employees, specifically including members of the official staff. Business pressures should not be accepted as an excuse for ignoring this requirement. The reason for this rule is that those individuals who refuse to take vacations each year may have something to hide and are afraid that a replacement might uncover evidence of this during their absence. In the case of national banks, the Comptroller of the Currency requires a special report each year listing the names of officers who have not taken 2 consecutive weeks of vacation.

The value of *dual control* as an aid to security in daily bank operations was also mentioned earlier. It requires that two staff members be involved in a transaction. Wherever possible, work is divided between two parties, and the person who originates an entry affecting the bank's books should not be the same individual who posts or approves it.

Rotation of duties among personnel can be another effective method of internal control. A clerk who has become familiar with one aspect of the stock transfer or letter of credit operation may be rotated to another part of the department. A teller who has been assigned to savings accounts for a period of time may be moved to paying and receiving duties involving checking accounts. This type of rotation of duties offers additional advantages to the bank, over and above the concept of security, because it provides management with flexibility in filling vacancies and contributes to the overall training of the individual.

Unannounced cash counts are an integral part of internal control programs. Without any predictable timetable, supervisory personnel should conduct cash counts to ensure the accuracy of tellers' proofs. The bank's auditors usually make a cash count the first item on their agenda when an audit is being conducted.

Prenumbered forms are commonly used in banking. These provide an operating safeguard because every form must be accounted for, whether used or voided. The ledgers in which prenumbered forms are recorded can be made part of the system of dual control; i.e., those who use the forms must account for their use to a supervisor, who maintains a record in the ledger. The forms may be designed with an additional copy for auditing use.

Cameras and alarm systems are required under the terms of the Bank Protection Act passed by Congress in 1968. The act specifies that one officer or other individual in each bank must be designated as the security officer and that each bank must install devices that will discourage robberies and assist in the identification and apprehension of persons who commit such acts. The Bank Protection Act also sets specific requirements for internal control procedures, including control of coin and currency.

The multiplicity of forms used in today's complex world of banking, the number of work-flow systems that are in effect, and the annual increases in labor costs are among the factors that contribute to the need for *efficiency controls* in each institution. It has been claimed that banks lose more money through simple inefficiencies than through all forms of embezzlement. Simply redesigning a form or rearranging the flow of work in a department can reduce operating costs and improve accuracy. Systems reviews should be conducted periodically to ensure that the most modern equipment and techniques are being employed and that management is obtaining all the information it needs on each day's operations. Work measurement and establishing standards of productivity make it possible for bank management to establish reasonable goals. Many banks publicize the successes they have had in improving a particular operation or reorganizing a department; their counterparts should review their own procedures to determine if they can learn from those successes. Banks can also exchange information regarding work measurement, performance standards, and operating costs so that each institution has a basis for comparison.

SUMMARY

Despite the increased emphasis on automation in banking and the introduction of electronic funds transfer systems, the importance of having dedicated and skilled staff members on hand has not decreased. If a bank is to achieve its objective of rendering services while generating profits, there can be no substitute for effective personnel management so that the right individuals are hired, retained, and rewarded for their contributions. Policy manuals represent one standard method of making employees feel that they are a part of the organization and giving them information regarding the personnel policies that affect them.

In an ideally integrated program of human resources management, recruiting and hiring practices are established, job descriptions are prepared, an equitable program of salary administration is designed, and a system of periodic evaluations and reviews of performance is implemented. Because career development is so important today, programs to assist employees in their personal growth are established both within the bank and through external sources, such as the American Institute of Banking.

The directors and officers of each bank have a direct responsibility to see to it that the institution operates as safely and efficiently as possible. No bank can neglect internal security at any time for any reason. Each institution must police itself and do whatever is necessary to protect its own assets and those entrusted to it.

QUESTIONS FOR DISCUSSION

1. Identify three characteristics that effective personnel policies should have.

2. What is the difference between policies and procedures?

3. What purposes do job descriptions serve?

4. List four operating safeguards or procedures that a bank might include in its program of internal controls.

5. List three examples of efficiency controls that could be helpful to a bank.

Suggested Readings

Dessler, Gary. *Management Fundamentals: A Framework.* 2nd edition. Reston, Virginia: Reston Publishing Company, 1979.
Summers, Donald B. *Personnel Management in Banking.* New York: McGraw-Hill Book Company, 1981.

Chapter 15

Trust Department Services

LEARNING OBJECTIVES

After completion of this chapter, you will have an understanding of

- the most important terms used in reference to trust operations;

- the steps involved in settling estates;

- the distinction between the functions of a trustee and those of an agent;

- the duties and responsibilities of a bank acting as transfer agent, registrar, paying agent, or trustee under indenture; and

- the major legal restrictions affecting banks in their trust operations.

Over and above their basic services in the areas of accepting deposits, processing payments, and extending credit, full-service banks provide other ways of serving the financial needs of every category of customer while generating profits. One of these areas of specialized services is the trust department, or, as it is called at some of the larger institutions, the fiduciary division.

The basic concept of a trust can be traced back to Roman history, when citizens bequeathed property in their wills to fraternities or trade unions, and through the Middle Ages, when representatives of the church were authorized to safeguard the wills of deceased persons. A **trust** may be defined as a relationship in which one party holds property belonging to another, with some particular benefit in mind. A **trustee**, therefore, whether bank, individual, or corporate, has assumed the responsibility and the problems of holding and administering some form of assets for the benefit of another, who is known as the **beneficiary**. In the United States, many financial institutions were organized specifically to act as trust companies; they operated under state charters and were chiefly involved in the handling of investment funds. During the last decade of the nineteenth century, more trust companies than national banks were operating in New York City[1]; over the course of time they gradually assumed some of the basic functions of commercial banks, accepting demand and time deposits and extending short-term loans. In 1913, national banks were authorized to begin offering trust services for the first time through the Federal Reserve Act.

Major commercial banks today offer a broad range of trust services for individuals, businesses, units of government, and educational institutions. The 1981 figures for the 10 largest banks in the trust field are shown in Table 15-1. It should be noted that these 10 banks alone handle trust assets having a market value of over $700 billion and their activities in various areas of trust operations generated income of over $873 million.

Banks that offer trust services, and other financial institutions competing with them in this field, are said to enjoy a **fiduciary** relationship with their clients. To justify the faith and confidence implied by the Latin meaning of that term, they must act in the clients' best interest. The function of a trust department is to hold secure and administer the clients' assets in such a way as to protect those interests while generating profits for the bank.

TYPES OF TRUST SERVICES

Depending on the needs of its market and the volume of business it is able to produce, a modern commercial bank may offer any of the following fiduciary services:

Table 15-1
1981 Trust Data

Rank in Trust Income	Bank Name	Trust Income (millions of dollars)	Trust Assets (billions of dollars)
1	Morgan Guaranty Trust (New York)	164	35.2
2	Citibank, N.A. (New York)	126	33.6
3	Bank of New York	94	101.1
4	Chase Manhattan (New York)	89	181.7
5	Bankers Trust Company (New York)	75	50.5
6	Manufacturers Hanover Trust (New York)	73	119.2
7	Bankamerica Corp. (San Francisco)	68	36.6
8	Chemical (New York)	65	109.4
9	United States Trust Company (New York)	61	21.9
10	Northern Trust (Chicago)	58	32.9

SOURCE: *American Banker*, June 30, 1982, p. 24

- Settling estates;

- Administering trusts and guardianships;

- Providing agency services;

- Acting as trustee under indenture;

- Administering employee benefit and individual retirement plans;

- Assisting in estate planning and tax counseling.

In each of these cases, the technicalities of trust operations and the legal background of fiduciary services depend largely on a specialized vocabulary. Trust department personnel must be familiar with a terminology that is not used elsewhere in the bank.

Settling Estates

The legal term for anyone who has died is a **decedent**. When an owner of property dies, the sum total of that person's assets is known as the **estate**. If the person left a valid will, according to state laws, he or she is said to have died **testate**; if no will exists, or the will is invalid for any reason, the person is said to have died **intestate**.

In the decedent's **will**, he or she leaves specific instructions as to how the estate is to be distributed. The will designates a bank, law firm, or other party as the **executor** who is to carry out these instructions. Each will must be admitted to **probate**; that is, a special court must examine and approve it, confirm that the executor is qualified to perform the duties of settling the estate, and confirm the process by which assets will be transferred to the heirs and beneficiaries.

If the decedent died intestate, if the will is invalid, or if the executor cannot or will not serve, the court appoints an **administrator**. The duties of an executor and an administrator are essentially the same; they must take the following steps, in sequence:

1. An inventory must be taken to determine the exact value of the estate. All of the assets of the decedent must be listed and a specific dollar value shown for each.

2. All necessary federal and state tax returns must be filed, and appropriate taxes, based on the value of the estate, must be

paid. All debts and claims against the estate must be settled.

3. The remaining assets are then distributed, either according to the terms of the will or as directed by state laws.

Whenever a bank acts as executor or administrator, it is legally liable for maintaining detailed records of all its actions and rendering an accounting to the court and to the beneficiaries.

Administering Trusts and Guardianships

Trust funds administered by banks are again subdivided as to specific type. The most common are testamentary trusts, living trusts, and institutional trusts.

Testamentary Trusts. A **testamentary trust** is created by a decedent's will. In this case the decedent is also known as a **testator** because he or she directed that a trust fund be established with the proceeds of the estate, for the benefit of named beneficiaries. As a testamentary trustee, the bank's duties include managing the assets turned over to it by the executor or administrator and paying the income to the designated beneficiaries.

Living Trusts. As the name implies, **living trusts** do not involve decedents; they are created by the voluntary act of an individual who has executed a trust agreement and has transferred certain property to the bank. One who establishes a trust fund in this fashion is called a **trustor** or **settlor**. Every living trust carries with it specific terms and conditions that the trustor includes in the written trust agreement.

Institutional Trusts. **Institutional trust** funds are established when a college, university, hospital, or charitable organization turns over cash and securities to a bank. The bank's duties then involve active management of the investments that have been and will continue to be made. None of the net earnings of an institutional trust may go to an individual or private shareholder.

Guardianships. **Guardianships** (also called **conservatorships** in some states) are established by order of a court for the benefit of a minor or an incapacitated person. A minor is defined by the laws of the state as one who is not of legal age, while the category of incapacitated persons includes those who are declared incompetent because of illness or senility. A guardianship may also be established voluntarily by an individual who asks a court for assistance.

Guardianships may be "of the person" or "of the estate or property." A guardian "of the person" acts in place of a parent and provides for the necessities of life for the ward, including food, clothing, shelter, and schooling. Banks generally prefer not to act in this capacity. They do, however, act as guardians or conservators of the estate or property, in which case they receive, hold, and manage certain assets for the benefit of the ward.

Agency Services

The third category of trust services includes all cases in which a bank acts as **agent** for an individual, a business, or any other customer who wishes to take advantage of the capabilities of the trust department. There is a significant legal difference between the role of agent and that of trustee. Trustees assume legal title to property that is turned over to them; agents are given specific authority by the **principals**, who retain legal title to the assets.

The most common **agency** services for individuals include safekeeping, custody, managing agent, and escrow. For corporations, banks provide transfer agent, registrar, and paying agent or dividend disbursing agent services. At large banks, the areas of agency services are often subdivided between the personal and corporate services.

Safekeeping. The simplest and least expensive agency service for individuals requires no more than the protection of certain property that the principal turns over to the bank. This service is known as **safekeeping**. The bank has no active duties; it merely accepts, holds, and returns upon request the stocks, bonds, or other assets that the principal has delivered to it.

There is a major difference between safekeeping service and the role of a bank in the safe deposit relationship. In providing safekeeping, the bank must maintain an itemized record of all property turned over to it and must issue a specific receipt for that property. In the safe deposit area, no such requirement exists.

Custody. **Custody** services include the basic safekeeping of assets *plus* the collection of income for the principal and crediting that income to an account, buying and selling securities when the bank is specifically told to do so by the principal, and furnishing timely information to the principal on all matters affecting his or her interest, such as stock splits, notification of annual meetings, bond maturities, and special stockholder votes.

Banks also provide custody for correspondent banks and for agencies of government.

Managing Agent. As **managing agent**, the bank performs all the duties of a custodian *plus* those responsibilities and powers that are specifically granted to it by the principal. In handling securities for the principal, the bank's duties generally include reviewing his or her investment portfolio periodically and recommending retention, sale, exchange, or conversion, in addition to purchases of new securities. The managing agent may be given discretionary power; that is, may be granted authority by the principal to buy, exchange, or sell securities within the portfolio without prior approval from the principal in each case. As custodian, the bank could not act without the principal's written instructions to do so. Discretionary accounts exist only when the bank has held a series of meetings with the principal to determine his or her objectives.

As managing agent, banks frequently handle real estate instead of securities. In these cases, they collect rental income, pay the taxes on the real estate, provide for the maintenance of the property, and credit any net income to the clients' accounts.

Escrow Services. Business transactions, particularly those that involve real estate, often require that an impartial, trusted third party be appointed as agent for the two principals. This third party, approved by both of the principals, becomes the **escrow agent**. The escrow agent takes possession of deeds to property or other assets and documents and safeguards them until the business transaction is completed.

Because all parties to an escrow arrangement must be in complete agreement as to the responsibility and duty of the agent, specific, signed agreements are always part of the escrow service. These agreements are often prepared by the bank itself, since as agent it is legally liable for exact compliance with all the instructions given to it.

Corporate Agency Services

To assist their corporate customers in handling the tremendous volume of detailed work that results from securities transactions, commercial banks are the leaders in providing corporate agency services under several headings.

Transfer Agent. As **transfer agent**, a bank acts on behalf of a corporation and is responsible for changing the title to ownership of that corporation's shares of stock or registered bonds. It acts as agent *only* for its corporate customer, and its appointment as transfer agent must be confirmed by the corporate directors. Purchases and sales of corporate securities may require issuing new stock certificates showing the name of the new owner.

Registrar. As **registrar**, a bank acts on behalf of *both* a corporate customer and that customer's stockholders. Every corporation is legally authorized to have a certain number of shares of stock outstanding. The registrar's task is to maintain records of the number of shares canceled and reissued so that no overissue can take place. In this sense, the registrar monitors the activities of the transfer agent to ensure that the legal limit on outstanding shares is not exceeded. As registrar, the bank protects the interests of the stockholders of the corporation while rendering a service to the corporation itself. This work readily lends itself to computerized processing.

Paying Agent. As **paying agent**, a bank may act on behalf of an agency or unit of government, in which case it is often referred to as fiscal agent. In this capacity, the bank is responsible for making all periodic payments of interest or dividends to the holders of the debt issues of that government and also for redeeming all those debt issues as they mature.

Banks also recognize the wide diversification of stock ownership that exists today. Major corporations may have hundreds of thousands of individual owners of their stock. When a corporate board of directors has reviewed the corporate earnings statement and has voted a quarterly dividend, there can be a huge amount of work involved in computing the amount of the dividend check that each stockholder is to receive, in mailing these checks to the stockholders, and in posting the paid checks to an account and reconciling the balance. As paying agent (dividend disbursing agent), a bank can assume this entire burden and, in addition, provide ancillary services such as reinvestment of dividends.

Trustee Under Indenture. When a corporation issues bonds as a means of raising funds from investors, it must execute a legal agreement called an **indenture**. A bank or trust company must be appointed as trustee under this agreement. The trustee is responsible for seeing to it that all the terms of the agreement are met, for the protection of the bondholders. The trustee guarantees that the issued bonds are authentic, makes all payments on them, and ensures that each bond is destroyed after redemption so that it can never be presented for payment again.

Employee Trusts. One of the fastest growing and most competitive areas of trust services is that of employee benefit trusts. In increasing numbers, corporations and banks have established various types of trust funds for the benefit of their employees. This is sometimes the result of union negotiations, sometimes a competitive means of attracting and retaining employees, and in other cases results from an increased emphasis on the social responsibility of an employer in providing for the well-being of its workers.

A bank or business may establish a **pension** or **profit-sharing** (deferred compensation) trust fund and make regular contributions to it. If the employees also invest their own funds in the plan, it is called **contributory**; if the employer alone makes payments into the fund, it is known as a noncontributory trust.

The bank's duties involve accepting the payments, investing them, maintaining detailed records to show the accrued value of the trust to each employee, making all payments to employees, and providing accounting data on every transaction.

All employer contributions to qualified pension and profit-sharing plans are business expenses and therefore deductible for tax purposes. Earnings and gains on the funds are likewise exempt from taxes.

Once a bank or corporation has established a pension fund to provide retirees with a regular source of income, it is required to make fixed, regular contributions into the fund. On the other hand, the employer's contributions to a profit-sharing fund fluctuate according to each year's net profits.

Individual Retirement Plans

As mentioned earlier, Congress has repeatedly broadened the areas of individual retirement funds, i.e., Keogh (HR-10) and IRA (Individual Retirement Account) relationships. Keogh plans are available for all self-employed individuals. IRA relationships were originally authorized only for those individuals whose income was not covered under a qualified pension plan. However, Congress abolished that restriction in 1981 and made IRAs available even to those workers who were already covered by pension or retirement plans. This change expanded the already large pool of money represented by Keogh plans and IRAs and therefore intensified the existing aggressive competition among banks, brokerage firms, and insurance companies for these funds. To illustrate this point, a news article in 1982 indicated that Merrill Lynch had received $700 million from 160,000 IRA relationships established with it during the first 4 months of that year and that the Prudential Insurance Company was opening IRAs at the rate of 10,000 per week.[2]

Through their trust departments, banks now offer a wide variety of investment vehicles into which funds for Keogh and IRA participants can be placed. These instruments generally earn interest at rates tied to those paid on U.S. Treasury bills or money market certificates. Deposit instruments for Keogh plans and IRA relationships may carry a fixed or floating rate of interest without a rate ceiling.

Sweep Accounts

Through their trust departments, or through other internal capabilities developed in recent years, many banks now offer a type of account relationship that gives the customer an attractive option and may prevent that customer from transferring funds to some other higher yielding area. This new product is commonly known as a **sweep account** because all balances in an interest-free checking or a NOW account above a stated figure are "swept" into money market funds each day. This type of relationship allows the customer to keep his or her deposit balance (*and* the federal insurance that covers it) while simultaneously earning the high rates of interest that money market funds offer. Federal deposit insurance does not apply to the invested portion of the total relationship. If the customer's checking or NOW account balance falls below the predetermined figure, shares of the fund will be automatically redeemed and the proceeds of the sale credited to the account.

New technology has made the sweep product possible; high interest rates in the money markets, and the products that nonbank competitors are offering, have made it necessary.

Repurchase Agreements

For many years, commercial banks, through their trust or treasury departments, have accommodated their major corporate and institutional customers by providing them with investment opportunities in the form of **repurchase agreements**, commonly called **repos**. For competitive reasons, many institutions have now extended this concept to individual accounts and have widely advertised it as a new type of relationship with the consumer. It should be noted that a repo is *not* a deposit, and the funds that are turned over to the bank are *not* covered by any type of federal insurance. In a repo the customer is actually making an investment by giving the bank funds for a stated period of time. These funds are used by the bank to purchase federal government obligations, and under the terms of the agreement the bank agrees to "buy" the securities back from the customer at a specified time. The advantage of the retail repo to the individual customer lies in the interest rates that can be earned. The customer, however, does not actually *own* the securities; he or she has an interest in them if the bank does not fulfill its agreement.

Retail repos are not exclusively the function of the bank's trust department; depending on each bank's policy, they may be handled through the branches along with other personal account activity, even though they are not deposit relationships.

Financial Planning and Counseling

The structure of federal and local taxation is such that America's growing number of affluent individuals must give increased consideration to all the problems of estate planning. Many banks have provided a valuable service to their clients in this regard by working with them to design and implement plans that will reduce the tax burden on an estate, ensure that assets go to the survivors as desired, and thus provide maximum benefits to the client's heirs and beneficiaries.

Counseling with clients involves first gathering information about their current financial situations and their needs and goals. This information is evaluated and a plan of action is proposed so that the bank can provide the services necessary for the client to achieve his or her goals.

Competition in this field is both widespread and intense. Insurance companies and brokerage firms vie aggressively with the banks, often by capitalizing on existing relationships with their policyholders and customers.

The skills required to provide these services illustrate a problem that all banks face in the trust field. Trust departments must be staffed by personnel who have a wide range of specialized skills. Attorneys, investment analysts, and tax experts are usually necessary members of the department's staff so that the best interests and individual objectives of each client can be served.

The basic purpose in appointing any fiduciary is to obtain the benefits of expertise, group judgment, maximum safety, long experience, financial strength, and continuous accessibility; in other words, the agent or trustee must always be available to answer questions, give advice, and solve problems for the principals and beneficiaries. In meeting their competitors in the trust areas, commercial banks have or can obtain all the skills required to provide those benefits. Their remaining task is to make that fact known. Although they have always prided themselves on their professionalism and their ability to provide quality services, they have not always resorted to marketing as a means of attracting new business.

TRUST MARKETING

Marketing in the trust area today must involve the same considerations that apply to other units in the bank. The trust department should be considered as a profit center that contributes directly to the bank's earnings, and as such it must price its services in a realistic way and ensure that the right services are sold to the right customers in the right way. This effort requires detailed planning and market research to identify market opportunities, proper systems of cost accounting to determine pricing strategies (to the extent this is permissible under various state laws that may restrict the fees that can be charged), new product development to meet the changing needs of customers and prospects, and actual marketing of the various services.

Earlier in this text, the many different products and services offered in the trust area were described. However, in marketing these the bank must be aware of the fact that customers and prospects are not concerned with product names. Rather, the effort must focus on individual needs, wants, and goals, and the product must frequently be tailored to meet the client's particular situation and objectives. An unsophisticated prospect can be—and often is—lost to the bank because the marketing does not address this point.

In past years, trust units in banks catered only to the very wealthy. Today, the market has expanded tremendously, and those banks that do not design and market trust services must face the loss of a significant amount of potential business to the many competitors who are aggressively seeking it. They should capitalize on the inherent advantages they possess, including the following:

- **Convenience**: A full-scale trust department can serve the same client as banker, administrator, advisor, accountant, and investment and tax consultant, all under one roof. There is no need for the customer to go to various different sources.

- **Accessibility**: The bank is always available; individuals outside banking may not be. Trusts are often handled on a team basis, so that at least one individual on the bank's staff is always familiar with each situation and can be called on at any time.

- **Expertise**: An integrated trust department has full-time, skilled money managers, access to the various markets to secure the best investment media, and legal, tax, and accounting knowledge. On a highly personalized basis, its staff can demonstrate a sensitivity to client needs and objectives, drawing up detailed proposals and implementing them to suit the particular situation.

- **Complete Service**: Trust departments can provide safekeeping in their vaults, can collect income and pay bills, can manage property, can file tax returns, can prepare complete financial reports, and can meet all legal requirements.

LEGAL RESTRICTIONS

The management of all forms of wealth has become an increasingly complex problem because of constantly changing laws and tax requirements imposed by federal and local governments. Whenever a bank acts as trustee or agent, it becomes involved in this process of money management and incurs a serious responsibility. Many trust services are specifically intended for the protection and benefit of dependents, minors, heirs, beneficiaries of estates, and retired individuals whose entire standard of living may be determined by the pensions or other payments they receive. The general legal principle that courts apply in such cases states that a bank, in its fiduciary capacity, is subject to heavy penalties if its actions, or its failure to act, should cause any harm to a principal or beneficiary.

A number of specific legal restrictions apply to the trust operations of commercial banks. The first of these provides that no bank may begin offering trust services without first obtaining approval to do so from the proper authorities. For example, a national bank that wished to establish a trust department would have to apply for permission to the Comptroller of the Currency; its request would also require the approval of the Federal Reserve and FDIC, since as a national bank it must be a member of both.

A second legal requirement, which varies among the individual states, is designed to give additional protection to all principals and beneficiaries. This requirement compels the bank to set aside securities of unquestioned value, such as U.S. government debt issues, as a form of pledge for the proper performance of trust duties. A bank's balance sheet will show the dollar value of the government obligations that have been segregated for this purpose.

The third legal restriction on the operations of bank trust departments is found in the laws of those states that establish the maximum fees that banks can charge for certain trust services.

PRINCIPLES OF TRUST INSTITUTIONS

To suggest standards of operation for fiduciaries over and above all legal requirements, the American Bankers Association has published a list of the basic principles that banks should follow. The list includes the following:

1. **The "Prudent Man" Principle.** In a court opinion issued in 1830, it was held that a trustee must act faithfully and with sound discretion, acting as a prudent, intelligent person would. This principle requires that a bank act with the skill, care, diligence, and prudence that such a person would display under the same circumstances. As part of this principle, it should be noted that a prudent person would exercise *more* care and skill in handling someone else's property than in handling his or her own. When one is dealing only with one's own property, certain risks may be willingly assumed on the grounds that any profit or loss affects no other party. On the other hand, prudent persons would logically be expected to display more care in dealing with any assets entrusted to them in faith and confidence.

2. **Segregation of Trust Assets.** Under this principle, the property of each individual trust must be kept separate from that of all other trusts and from the bank's other assets. The trust departments of many banks are physically removed from the rest of the institution and domiciled in separate buildings, with their own vaults, data processing equipment, and other facilities. An imaginary wall must exist between the trust officers and their counterparts in other areas of the bank; they should never exchange information on, or participate jointly in meetings with, accounts that both may share.

3. **Separate Policy-Making and Audit.** A special committee of the bank's board of directors must conduct an annual audit, separate and distinct from that provided for other areas of the bank. This trust committee also sets the policies that will be followed concerning the size and type of trust relationships to be accepted and the investment policies that are to be followed.

4. **Specialized Skills.** A bank is expected to use all the expertise in trust operations that it now has, *plus* all the skill that it can reasonably acquire. Banks should continually seek to improve their present degree of skill so as to render even better service to clients, and each institution should regularly review all its trust operations in an effort to identify possible improvements.

5. **Conflict of Interest.** The final ABA principle of trust operations is specifically designed to prevent any accusation of a con-

flict of interests. It is aimed at the practice of self-dealing and states that a bank should have no personal interest whatever in any investments bought or sold for its trust funds and should not purchase for itself any property from any of its trusts. All dealings between the bank's directors, officers, and staff members are prohibited under this principle.

SUMMARY

Through their trust departments, America's banks manage hundreds of billions of dollars of property and generate significant income, in addition to providing a wide range of services to a growing clientele. Trust activities entail a high degree of responsibility, and in settling estates, administering trusts, and providing agency services, banks must exercise the highest possible skill and care so that the interests of all parties are protected at all times. Trust operations are generally labor-intensive and require the specialized knowledge of large numbers of personnel. They also create large amounts of paperwork because of the meticulous records that must be kept. The legal technicalities of trust work are covered in detail through courses offered by the American Institute of Banking and other educational organizations.

QUESTIONS FOR DISCUSSION

1. Define each of the following terms:

   a. executor　　　　　d. guardianship
   b. settlor　　　　　　e. administrator
   c. testamentary trust　f. indenture

2. What legal difference exists between the role of a bank as trustee and its role as agent?

3. List, in order, the steps that must be followed in settling an estate.

4. Describe the duties a bank would be required to perform in the following roles:

a. custodian   d. trustee under indenture
b. escrow agent   e. registrar
c. managing agent

5. Distinguish between Keogh plans and IRAs.

NOTES

1. Margaret G. Myers, *A Financial History of the United States,* New York, Columbia University Press, 1970, pp. 249–250.
2. David O. Tyson, "Prudential Sees 250,000 IRAs by June," *American Banker,* May 13, 1982, p. 1.

Suggested Readings

American Bankers Association. *Trust Fact Book.* 2nd edition. Washington, D.C.: American Bankers Association, 1980.
American Bankers Association. *Trust Management.* Washington, D.C.: American Bankers Association, 1979.
Bank Administration Institute. *Trust Account Administration.* Rolling Meadows, Illinois: Bank Administration Institute, 1976.
Blevins, Ronald L., John M. Clarke, James Mitchell, Jack W. Zalaha, and August Zinsser, III. *The Trust Business.* Washington, D.C.: American Bankers Association, 1982.

Chapter 16

Other Bank Services

LEARNING OBJECTIVES

After completion of this chapter, you will have an understanding of

- The importance of global banking today;
- Such key terms as banker's acceptance, irrevocable, commercial and consular invoice, and bill of lading;
- The benefits gained by each of the parties in a letter of credit transaction;
- The steps in a typical letter of credit transaction;
- The operation of trust receipt financing;

- The operation and benefits of such cash management services as lockbox, depository transfer checks, and account reconciliation; and

- The basic safeguards employed by banks in their safe deposit operations.

T he success or failure of a commercial bank results directly from its ability to provide those services that its market segments require. In meeting the needs of every category of customer, today's full-service banks offer many specialized services that go beyond the basic and traditional deposit, payment, and credit functions. This chapter addresses three of the most important of these service areas: the international department, the cash management unit, and the safe deposit department.

GLOBAL BANKING

One of the most dramatic increases in any phase of commercial banking since the end of World War II has taken place in the international field. "Global" banking has become a critical factor in the profitability of many major American banks, and even in those institutions whose global business does not require the facilities of a complete, independent department, the demand for many specialized services relating to foreign trade increases each year. Table 16-1 shows the tremendous growth in overseas operations of U.S. banks over a 15-year period.

In expanding their global operations, America's major commercial banks followed the example of their corporate customers, who identified the potential for sales and profits in foreign countries and began to market their products on a worldwide basis. For the year 1981, U.S. companies exported merchandise with a total value of $234 billion. At the same time, major foreign corporations have devoted much greater attention to American markets for their automobiles, apparel, television sets, and other merchandise, and the dollar value of their exports to the United States for the same year was $261 billion. The resulting deficit in the balance of payments, $27 billion, is a problem that has repeatedly been addressed by the President, Congress, and business associations.

Table 16-1
Foreign Activities of U.S. Banks

Year	U.S. Banks Operating Foreign Branches	Number of Foreign Branches	Assets of Foreign Branches (billions of U.S. dollars)
1965	13	211	8.9
1967	15	295	15.3
1969	53	460	35.3
1971	91	577	59.8
1973	125	699	121.9
1975	126	762	176.5
1977	130	738	258.9
1979	139	779	364.2

SOURCE: *ABA Banking Journal*, August 1981, p. 80.
NOTE: At year-end 1981, 156 Fed member banks operated 800 overseas branches. In mid-1982, total assets of foreign branches of U.S. banks were $458.6 billion. Sources: Board of Governors of the Federal Reserve System, *68th Annual Report: 1981*, and *Federal Reserve Bulletin*, September 1982, p. A56.

The steady increase in foreign trade during the past 20 years has created the need for a host of customized products and services. Commercial banks have been in the forefront as providers of these, and the result has been a steady and remarkable growth in the importance of their international departments. In 1980, foreign earnings represented 47.3 percent of the total consolidated earnings for the 10 largest commercial banks in the United States.

SERVICES TO IMPORTERS

Although many U.S. banks do not maintain their own international departments, depending instead on their larger correspondents to provide any needed services, many others have found it both necessary and highly profitable to create a specialized unit, often called "a bank within a bank." In those units the technicalities of foreign trade, the problems of each country's regulations and customs, the differences in languages, and the customized processing of transactions that foreign trade requires can best be handled.

Figure 16-1
Commercial Letter of Credit

Irving Trust Company

⑦

One Wall Street
New York, New York 10015

CREDIT NUMBER OF ISSUING BANK 12345   DATE March 14, 19xx   OF ADVISING BANK _____

IRREVOCABLE DOCUMENTARY CREDIT

ADVISING BANK

Kensington Bank Ltd
153 Parliamentary Rd.
Glasgow, Scotland

APPLICANT

Scotch Import Company
14 Westlane Road
Bronx, New York 10791

BENEFICIARY

Joe Yorke & Sons
146 Dundas St.
Glasgow, Scotland

AMOUNT $10,000.00
EXPIRY July 19, 19xx
IN Glasgow, Scotland _____ FOR NEGOTIATION
NEGOTIATION CHARGES ARE FOR YOUR ACCOUNT

GENTLEMEN:
WE HEREBY ISSUE IN YOUR FAVOR THIS DOCUMENTARY CREDIT WHICH IS AVAILABLE BY NEGOTIATION OF YOUR DRAFT AT sight

DRAWN ON US

ALL DRAFTS MUST BE MARKED: "DRAWN UNDER IRVING TRUST COMPANY NEW YORK CREDIT   (INDICATING THE NUMBER AND DATE OF THIS CREDIT)   " YOUR DRAFTS MUST BE ACCOMPANIED BY THE FOLLOWING DOCUMENTS (COMPLETE SETS UNLESS OTHERWISE STATED; ALTERNATIVELY, IF ANY DOCUMENT IS ISSUED AS A SINGLE ORIGINAL ONLY, SUCH ORIGINAL SHALL BE DEEMED A COMPLETE SET)

Invoice in triplicate.

Special U.S. Customs Invoice.

Insurance certificate/policy in negotiable form

Packing list in triplicate.

Original inspection certificate issued by Genera _____ Company.

SPECIMEN

Clean onboard ocean bills of lading issued to order of shipper and endorsed in blank, marked "Notify Scotch Import Company" and "Freight Prepaid".

COVERING Two Blending Machines, C.I.F. New York.

SHIPMENT FROM Glasgow, Scotland TO New York	LATEST July 14, 19xx	PARTIAL SHIPMENTS permitted.

SPECIAL CONDITIONS

EXCEPT SO FAR AS OTHERWISE EXPRESSLY STATED, THIS DOCUMENTARY CREDIT IS SUBJECT TO THE "UNIFORM CUSTOMS AND PRACTICE FOR DOCUMENTARY CREDITS" (1974 REVISION) INTERNATIONAL CHAMBER OF COMMERCE PUBLICATION NO 290.

WE HEREBY ENGAGE WITH DRAWERS AND/OR BONA FIDE HOLDERS THAT DRAFTS DRAWN UNDER AND NEGOTIATED IN CONFORMITY WITH THE TERMS OF THIS CREDIT WILL BE DULY HONORED ON PRESENTATION.

THE AMOUNT OF EACH DRAFT MUST BE ENDORSED ON THE REVERSE OF THIS CREDIT BY THE NEGOTIATING BANK

ADVISING BANK'S NOTIFICATION

YOURS VERY TRULY,

756/00M (12-76) REV. 12-76 AUTHORIZED SIGNATURE

Place, date, name and signature of the advising bank.

Letters of Credit

Of all the international services that commercial banks offer today to customers who are involved in foreign trade, the best known and most frequently used is the **commercial letter of credit.** Whenever a buyer of goods requires assurance that the merchandise being bought will conform exactly to specifications, and/or whenever the seller of goods requires an assurance of payment after the shipment of goods has taken place, a letter of credit can be used to minimize the risks to both parties.

Letters of credit can be used in many domestic business transactions, or simply as a guarantee of performance. However, this discussion of their use is confined to the area of foreign trade.

A **letter of credit** (L/C) is an instrument issued by a bank, substituting the credit standing of that bank for the credit standing of the buyer (importer) of goods. It guarantees that the seller (exporter) will be paid *if* all the terms of the contract are met. At the same time, it protects the buyer by guaranteeing that no payment will be made unless and until that contract is fulfilled (see Figure 16-1).

Letters of credit can be issued either in **revocable** or **irrevocable** form. The revocable L/C is rare, since its terms allow it to be canceled or amended by either party without the approval of the other. The irrevocable L/C, conversely, stipulates that no changes can be made without the full consent of the buyer and seller.

Letters of credit may also be issued on either a *sight* or *time* basis. The sight L/C calls for immediate payment against the documents evidencing a shipment of goods; the time L/C specifies a later date by which payment must be made.

Assume, for example, that a company in San Francisco has negotiated with a firm in the Federal Republic of Germany for the purchase of a quantity of machine tools. The price of the total order has been agreed upon; however, the American firm wants assurance that the terms of the purchase contract will be met and the German company requires some form of guarantee of payment. The San Francisco buyer therefore approaches a local bank and completes an application for an irrevocable sight letter of credit in favor of the exporter. If the California bank is convinced of the buyer's financial responsibility and integrity, it will agree to the application and will usually stipulate certain conditions:

- It (i.e., the issuing bank) maintains a security interest in all property covered by the credit.

- It is not responsible for physically counting or otherwise examining the goods being ordered, nor is it responsible for the genuineness of any documents submitted to it.

The application submitted by the California firm for a letter of credit will specify the documents that are required. It is understood and agreed that the bank will rely on those documents as proof that the specified shipment has been made. Among the commonly used documents required in connection with letters of credit, the following may be mentioned:

- **Commercial invoices** list the goods that have been ordered and shipped and usually specify the price and terms of the sale.

- **Insurance certificates** provide that the merchandise will be safeguarded during transit.

- **Bills of lading** are issued by the carrier (steamship company, airline, trucking firm, or other transporter) that is handling the shipment of goods.

- **Consular (customs) invoices** are issued by representatives of the country to which the goods are being shipped. In the example, these invoices would be issued by U.S. customs officials to verify the quantity, value, and nature of the shipment and to ensure that import laws are not being violated. Consular invoices also provide a basis for statistical reports on imports.

- **Certificates of origin** specify the source of the material or labor used in producing the merchandise.

- **Certificates of quality** are issued by recognized appraisers, i.e., individuals who have specialized knowledge regarding particular commodities. Certificates of quality provide assurance that the goods being shipped conform to the buyer's orders.

The bill of lading is among the most important of these because it serves three simultaneous purposes. It is a receipt issued by the carrier for a specific shipment of goods; it is a title document, proving that the carrier has legal possession of the goods; and it is a contract, by which the carrier agrees to transport the merchandise from and to specific locations.

The importer's bank in California reviews the application and approves it on a liability basis; that is, the bank is willing to accept the applicant's guarantee that he will provide funds to cover drafts drawn in accordance with the terms of the credit. The California bank then becomes known as the **issuing** or **opening** bank. It forwards notification to a bank in the Federal Republic of Germany, showing that the L/C has been opened; the German bank, in turn, contacts the exporter and therefore becomes known as the **advising** bank. The advising bank is usually a correspondent in the seller's country.

The seller is now the **beneficiary** of the letter of credit, provided that all the terms and conditions of the contract are met. The seller arranges for the completion of all the required documents and has now been given a guarantee of payment, assuming those terms and conditions have been fulfilled.

In order to obtain payment, the beneficiary draws a draft on the California bank and presents it, with all accompanying documents, to his own bank, which may or may not be the advising bank. The bank used by the beneficiary may act merely as a collection agent and send the letter of credit and all documents to the issuing bank in San Francisco; in this case, the latter will examine them carefully and make payment to the German bank.

Frequently, however, the exporter will present the letter of credit, draft, and documents to his bank and request immediate payment. That bank may then examine the documents and, finding them in order, honor the draft at once. It can do so with confidence, since it knows that the opening bank must make payment if all documents are in order.

Regardless of which method of payment is used, funds will flow from the California (issuing) bank to the German (paying) bank, and the former must then recover those funds from the buyer's account with it.

Banker's Acceptances

If the L/C had been established on a time basis, the exporter's draft would be forwarded to the issuing bank with all documents so that they could be examined and payment approved. If the seller requested immediate payment and all documents were in order, the issuing bank could, at its option, stamp the draft with the word *accepted,* have it officially signed and dated, and remit the funds. A draft that has been accepted by a drawee bank in this manner is known as a **banker's acceptance.** The original order to pay is converted into the bank's unconditional promise to pay. Every banker's acceptance is a direct, irrevocable obligation of the accepting bank. There is a ready market for these instruments; that is, they are bought and sold in large quantities every day. The purchaser or holder of a banker's acceptance realizes that the full faith and credit of the accepting bank supports it. That bank *must* make payment at maturity, whether or not it has been reimbursed by its customer.

Trust Receipts

The California company that is importing the merchandise from Germany may need to take possession of it, process it, display it to potential customers, and sell it in order to generate income. At the same time, it may not have sufficient funds to permit its account to be charged for payments under the terms of the letter of credit. This is a chronic problem faced by importers and solved by their banks through the issuing of trust receipts.

Under a **trust receipt** agreement, the importer is allowed by the bank to take possession of merchandise, process and sell it, and repay the bank from the proceeds of its sale. Trust receipt financing represents a specialized type of secured lending, because the bank holds full legal title to the merchandise until the loan is paid. Under the terms of the Uniform Commercial Code, a bank extending this type of financing should record its security interest with state authorities to protect itself should the importer default.

The borrower under a trust receipt agrees to keep the merchandise, and any funds received from its sale, separate and distinct from his own property and agrees that it is subject to repossession by the bank if the borrower fails to make the specified repayment.

Warehouse Receipts

Under certain conditions, merchandise that has been imported and stored in a bonded warehouse may be acceptable to a bank as collateral for a loan. Because a **warehouse receipt** is a legal document of title, the importer may endorse it and transfer his rights to the merchandise to the lending bank. The bank verifies the existence and value of the stored goods and extends a loan on that basis. The warehouse receipt, presented to the bank by the importer, must be in negotiable form. As his loan is reduced or paid, the importer can obtain release of part or all of the stored merchandise from the bank.

Negotiable warehouse receipts are also issued in purely domestic transactions, not involving imported goods. Commodities such as soybeans, cotton, and grain are often placed in bonded warehouses as soon as produced. Properly executed warehouse receipts for these commodities may be used as collateral for any domestic bank loan that might be needed until such time as they are processed and sold.

Other Services to Importers

Aside from letters of credit, banker's acceptances, trust receipts, and warehouse receipts, there are other specialized services that banks offer to importers. If credit information regarding a foreign firm is needed, the importer's bank can readily obtain it, either through its own foreign branches or through correspondents. Banks also make direct loans to importers, following the same credit procedures used in domestic lending.

Another important bank service to importers involves the use of foreign exchange contracts. Suppose, for example, that an importer has agreed to make payment, in yen, to a Japanese exporter 90 days after agreeing to buy certain merchandise. The importer calculates the cost of the shipment in dollars at the prevailing rate for foreign exchange but is anxious to pay no more than that amount, regardless of any fluctuations in the rate of exchange for yen versus the dollar. The importer's bank can enter into a contract by which it commits itself to make payment for the stated number of yen, and therefore becomes responsible for any changes in exchange rates that may take place during the 90-day time frame.

For the convenience of their customers who are engaged in importing and are required to make payments directly in foreign currency, many major banks maintain holdings of the major currencies and make these available as necessary.

SERVICES TO EXPORTERS

Major banks offer a wide range of services to American exporters of merchandise. They will accept drafts drawn in foreign currencies, treat these as noncash (foreign collection) items, collect them through overseas branches or correspondents, and credit the net proceeds to the exporter's account. They can provide the exporter with credit information regarding a firm to which he is considering selling his products; this information will help the exporter decide whether, and on what terms, to do business with that firm. Many banks publish periodic economic reports on individual foreign countries; these reports contain information on customs restrictions, currency regulations, the stability of the government, and the like. If his credit standing justifies it, a bank may provide the exporter with letters of introduction that can be used to assist him in his dealings with foreign banks or businesses.

SERVICES TO INDIVIDUALS

To assist individual customers who are visiting foreign countries, banks may make supplies of various local currencies available. When larger amounts are involved, a bank may issue a **traveler's letter of credit**, guaranteeing payments of funds up to a stated limit. All payments against this L/C are made in local currency by branches of the issuing bank or through its correspondents abroad. The paying bank reduces the unused portion by the appropriate amount.

For the traveler's greater convenience, the L/C has largely been replaced by **travelers checks**, issued both by banks and by such nonbanks as American Express Company. These have the advantage of easy negotiability throughout the world. Each check is signed at the time it is purchased and must be countersigned as it is used. Hotels, restaurants, airlines, or other parties that accept travelers checks are guaranteed repayment by the issuer (see Figure 16-2).

Individuals may also ask their banks to give them letters of introduction, which can be used to establish their identity with foreign banks and provide proof of the traveler's creditworthiness and integrity.

GLOBAL CREDIT OPERATIONS

The activities of U.S. banks in countries throughout the world can be grouped under two major headings. The first of these includes such basic services as accepting deposits, processing payments in local currencies, and extending credit. In this case the customer base consists of individuals and smaller businesses.

The second category is far more important and is a source of real concern in today's economic environment. It includes the broad spectrum of loans, often made as participations with local banks, to foreign governments and corporations. The exposure of U.S. banks in such countries as Mexico, Poland, Zaire, and Argentina accounts for a significant portion of their overseas activities and creates a corresponding need for timely information on the status of each loan so that bank management can take appropriate measures to assess the risk and protect the bank's interests. From 1973 to 1981, the long-term debt of less-developed countries (LDCs) to all lenders grew from $97 billion to $425 billion, and as of March 1982 the total claims of U.S. banks on the governments of foreign countries were $409 billion. With increasing frequency, questions have been raised as to whether economic conditions in many of these countries will ever permit full repayment of the loans. **Global** (or **country**) **risk analysis** is the

Figure 16-2
Traveler's Check

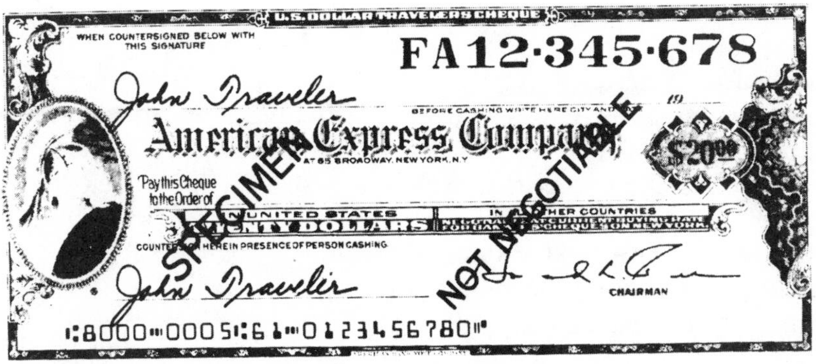

Reproduced by permission of American Express Company.

term used to describe the management information system that reports on and classifies the bank's outstanding loans in each part of the world. In analyzing the figures and assessing the loss potential, the lending bank must also consider all the local factors—stability of government, new economic conditions, political climate, and the like—in addition to normal credit criteria. Loans that are made directly to a foreign government may simply be repudiated; i.e., the authorities refuse to honor the obligations at all.

Despite these problems, international lending has proved to be profitable and has served as the means for developing many worthwhile relationships.

The Edge Act

In 1919, Congress passed legislation intended to help commercial banks serve those customers who were actively involved in foreign trade. This legislation is known as the **Edge Act**, and the facilities that banks have established as a result of it are known as Edge Act offices. It is important to note that these offices *can* be established across state lines and that they are *not* permitted to offer complete banking services. The bank that opens an Edge Act office in San Francisco, Houston, or Miami does so to assist certain customers with services that will aid them in their foreign trade operations; it cannot use that office for normal deposit, payment, or credit functions.

CASH MANAGEMENT SERVICES

The history of commercial banking in the United States is one in which the "wholesale" aspect was emphasized. The deposit, payment, and credit functions were used as the basis for services to businesses, governments, and correspondent banks. Bank of America grew to become one of the world's largest banks by developing its "retail" business and stressing services to consumers, in addition to serving corporate and institutional customers, but in doing so it was a notable exception to the general rule.

In the years immediately following the end of World War II, a tremendous expansion of the American economy took place. Those corporations that had prepared themselves to meet the demands of millions of returning veterans and supply all the consumer goods that a peace-time economy demanded were able to increase their sales volume throughout the country, and along with their growth there was a need for specialized banking services. Commercial banks, particularly those in the money market centers and those that handled the accounts of the largest corporate customers, identified that need and developed a response that not only would benefit the users of services but also would generate the new deposits that could be used as a base for loans and investments.

Starting in the 1950s, banks began offering new services to corporations to help them

- Collect incoming payments more quickly;

- Manage and reconcile outgoing payments more efficiently; and

- Obtain timely and complete information on the status of their bank accounts.

The generic term for this entire product line is **cash management**. As the foregoing indicates, the cash management capabilities of major banks provide deposit, payment, and information services that have been widely accepted by corporate, government, and correspondent bank customers and have become extremely important to the banks as a source of both balances and fees.

Lockbox Service

Earlier in this text, the discussion of *float* mentioned the life cycle of a check and pointed out that uncollected funds had no real value to the depositor *or* to the bank that gave immediate provisional credit for deposited checks. The corporation or unit of government that receives large quantities of checks each day has a strong interest in any procedure that will reduce the number of days otherwise required to receive checks through the post office, examine those checks and deposit them with banks, and convert the checks into available funds. **Lockbox** service, the first cash management service directly addressing this problem, has provided a solution.

Acting as agent for its customer, a bank will establish a post office box in that customer's name and will use its messenger service to make frequent pickups from the box of all incoming mail. The service operates on an around-the-clock basis throughout the year. Bank messengers deliver all mail to a central processing unit where clerks open the envelopes, examine incoming checks for negotiability, and endorse and deposit them. Information from each check is recorded for the customer's purpose. In many cases, the unit of government, corporation, or correspondent bank that is the user of this service requires a photocopy of each deposited check for its posting purposes; in others, all check information is entered on magnetic tape and transmitted from the bank's computer to the customer's.

Because the bank has access to the post office box around the clock, the actual receipt of payments is expedited. Because the bank, as agent, is making regular deposits to an account and is sending deposited checks to drawees by the quickest possible means, float is reduced and availability increased. Finally, because the bank assumes all the work of receiving, examining, endorsing, and depositing checks and supplying some type of daily information, the customer's clerical costs are reduced and an audit trail is provided on every payment.

The first users of lockbox service were large corporations. Banks in many parts of the country then began offering it to units of government as a means of collecting property, sales, and income tax payments, automobile registration fees, and tobacco and liquor taxes. Thrift institutions, which are the nation's primary mortgage lenders and therefore must handle huge volumes of incoming payments each month, then adopted lockbox service through their correspondent commercial banks and gained the same benefits from it.

In the case of those corporations whose customers are located throughout the country, it may be advisable to establish several strategically located lockboxes so that incoming mail time is kept to a minimum. Such a corporation may ask its banks in San Francisco, Dallas, Chicago, Atlanta, and New York to provide identical lockbox service and subsequently to transfer funds to a central depository bank. This system of regional lockboxes gives the user the maximum benefit of availability.

Depository Transfer Checks

Many corporations and agencies of government receive incoming payments at dispersed locations each day and then require a means of inexpensively and rapidly moving the funds to a concentration account at a single bank. The **depository transfer check** serves this purpose. It is a preprinted, no-signature check that is prepared and deposited by the concentration bank and is drawn on the customer's local banks. It can be used *only* to move funds from one bank account to another and has the advantage of being far less expensive than a wire transfer.

When a depository transfer check system is being established, the user of the service supplies the concentration bank with a file containing all the necessary data (name of bank, transit number, routing symbol [if any], and account number) for each local account. Each reporting point then supplies the concentration bank with information, on a daily basis, showing the amount of its deposit to the local bank. The concentration bank then prepares checks drawn on each local account and makes a single deposit to the user's account. Complete reports are furnished each day showing the amounts drawn in from every local account. Telephone input and magnetic tape are among the common methods by which the amount of each local deposit is reported to the concentration bank.

Payment Services

Although the increasing adoption by wholesale customers of various forms of electronic funds transfer systems has reduced check volume, the nationwide use of checks is still approximately 100 million items daily. Disbursements for payroll, dividends, accounts payable, taxes, and freight payments account for much of the total volume, and the issuers face the chronic problem of matching all paid checks returned by the drawees against check registers and determining which items are outstanding at each statement period. In addition, unless the check issuers have agreed with their banks to adopt some method of truncation (referred to earlier in this text), they must also provide facilities to store the paid checks and gain access to them whenever necessary.

As part of the total product line in the cash management area, many banks provide answers to these problems through account reconciliation and microfilm archival service.

Account reconciliation uses the MICR data encoded on a customer's checks to provide a computer-generated listing that shows all paid checks in check number sequence. If required, the paid items can be sorted into check number order and returned with the listing. If the user provides the bank with magnetic tape or other input containing all the details of each issued check, the reconciliation prepared by the bank can also include a complete proof sheet, showing the check number and dollar amount of unpaid items and matching their total to the closing balance in the account. Through this service, the customer's time, effort, and expense in proving each bank statement can be reduced to a minimum.

Some time ago, banks in many parts of the world recognized that the traditional system of returning all paid checks to the issuer was unnecessary and expensive. Accordingly, they implemented a system that forms the basis for the **microfilm archival service** now offered by many American banks. It is a form of check truncation based on the assumption that a computerized listing of paid checks is, in effect, a statement by a drawee that each such item has been properly charged to the drawer's account. The accounting, legal, and tax professions have generally agreed to accept this evidence of issuance and payment. In microfilm archival service, paid checks are *not* returned to the customer. They are retained by the drawees after having been reduced to microfilm, and are subsequently destroyed. If the drawer ever requires additional proof of payment, the drawee supplies a photocopy, produced from the microfilm.

The use of these two services provides benefits to the bank as well as to its customers. The expensive and time-consuming tasks of posting, verifying, and mailing paid checks can be substantially reduced.

INFORMATION SERVICES

A financial officer in one of America's largest corporations has said that the term "cash management" is misleading because he never sees actual cash at all. Instead, he sees computer printouts, microfilm records, and terminals and screens in his offices. All incoming payments for his firm flow to lockbox banks, which generate magnetic tape that goes directly to the company's computers for daily updating of accounts receivable. Wherever possible, the company makes outgoing payments of funds through direct deposit to payees' bank accounts; in other cases, its checks are fully reconciled by the drawees and retained under microfilm archival service. The third application of this company's cash management program involves use of the most important single technique introduced by banks in recent years: the furnishing to customers, through terminals in their offices, of complete and timely information regarding daily book, collected, and available bank balances.

Just as the banks themselves have found it necessary to develop management information systems for their internal use, corporations, correspondent banks, and units of government have identified an increasing need for daily account data so that money transfer and investment decisions can be made quickly and available funds put to the best profitable use. With each increase in interest rates, corporate and institutional cash managers have greater opportunities to put idle funds to work and are under pressure from their superiors to keep demand deposit balances to a minimum. By investing excess funds, they are often able to generate substantial income for their organizations. One major corporation reports that its use of all the cash management services offered by its banks has enabled it to reduce its balances by $68 million. Another has increased its annual profits by $12 million through these methods. The key to the entire process is found in daily information.

In a fully integrated information system, the user, through terminals in its offices, receives daily reports of all the deposit and disbursement activity that has taken place on all its bank accounts each day. A corporation, correspondent bank, or government unit may designate a single bank to receive and consolidate reports from all depositories, or it may instruct each to report individually. In either case, it is made aware of the ledger balances, float, and available funds at each bank. The terminals through which this information is furnished can also be used to initiate wire transfers. Many banks have extended the range of this information service to include foreign as well as domestic bank accounts. Other banks have included stock market data and foreign exchange and money market rates in the daily reports they make available through customers' terminals.

Security is an important element in this cash management service. The customer must be provided with a unique identification code and number to gain access to the system, and further precautions may be built into the program so that no unauthorized party can issue wire transfer instructions to a bank.

Traditionally, most banks have looked for compensating balances to support their cash management services. However, in today's highly competitive and high interest rate environment, it is not realistic to expect knowledgeable and sophisticated cash managers to accept this method. Instead, they increasingly tend to pay their banks through direct fees for each service. By doing so, they free balances for other purposes and gain the benefit of a tax deduction for the direct expenses they incur. Similarly, wholesale customers today often send detailed proposals to several banks, outlining the range of cash management services they require and inviting the banks to respond with specific price quotations.

SAFE DEPOSIT SERVICES

The safe deposit facilities at banks today offer the same basic service that was provided many years ago by goldsmiths, who accepted precious metals and other valuables entrusted to them by their clients for safekeeping. The key word, then and now, is *protection*. Because banks, by their very nature, must have vault facilities for the protection of currency, securities, and collateral, it is logical that they should extend the use of those facilities by marketing the concept of protection to customers. However, safe deposit services are not offered solely because they are a traditional part of banking. They may, in addition, be considered as a new business tool to attract customers or as a defensive measure, designed to prevent existing depositors from seeking the services elsewhere and possibly moving account balances to other banks that do offer the service.

Upon proper identification, and with proper documentation in each instance, a bank may open a safe deposit box for an individual, an individual together with a **deputy** (agent) whom he or she appoints (and whose rights are comparable to those of an attorney-in-fact), for two or more individuals jointly, for a sole proprietor, for a partnership, for a corporation, or for a fiduciary. In the case of a corporation, the bank must obtain a separate corporate resolution authorizing the safe deposit relationship. Whenever a safe deposit box is rented, the bank must obtain whatever signature cards are appropriate. Typically, these cards include the terms of the contract between the customer and the bank. The bank then assumes responsibility for the adequate protection of the customer's property.

It is important to note the significant difference between the safe deposit and account relationships. The party renting a safe deposit box has every right to expect that the *identical* property placed in the box will be protected and can be retrieved when necessary. Frequently, this property is irreplaceable and unique. Jewelry, valuable documents, and family heirlooms, for example, must remain in the same condition as when the customer placed them in the box. On the other hand, a depositor who gives the bank $100 in coin and currency cannot expect to receive the identical coin and currency when a withdrawal is made.

Each bank that offers safe deposit services must be fully aware of the liability it is undertaking. It would be a tragic mistake for a bank to treat the safe deposit relationship casually and to neglect any action that provides protection for the customer.

In recent years, there have been many cases of burglaries in which highly professional thieves, using sophisticated electronic equipment, laser technology, and the most modern tools, have been able to penetrate the steel and concrete walls of bank vaults, bypass the alarm systems, and rifle not only the bank's own cash compartments but customers' boxes as well. If a customer claims that certain valuables, allegedly placed in a safe deposit box, have been removed without that customer's knowledge or authorization, the burden of proof is usually on the bank. It must prove that it did everything possible to provide protection. Any evidence of negligence on the bank's part in the control of its daily safe deposit operations, or any proof of defects in the construction of the vault itself, may serve as the single piece of evidence that convinces a judge or jury that the customer is entitled to damages.

Right of Access

The safe deposit contract and signature cards clearly stipulate which persons are permitted to have access to each box. Possession of a key *does not* establish this right of access. The best precaution a bank can take for its own protection against any future claims requires each individual desiring access to sign a slip of paper, which can be compared with the cards on file. Additional identification, such as a password or the use of a mother's maiden name, may be used to establish the right of access. If a bank is proved to have been negligent in verifying the identity of any individual who sought access to a box, its defense is immediately weakened. Carelessness in any single situation can be extremely detrimental. It is not sufficient for the bank to publish procedure manuals for safe deposit personnel; employees must implement those procedures with extreme care at all times.

In addition to exercising controls over the right of access, a bank may well employ many other safeguards and procedures in its daily safe deposit operations. The following are among the most common:

- Keys to unrented boxes should be under dual control at all times. By following this rule a bank can certify that no unauthorized party could have obtained a key, had a duplicate made from it, and used it after the box was rented.

- No member of the bank's staff should ever accept custody of a customer's key, for the same reason mentioned in the preceding paragraph.

- Safe deposit boxes should never be opened for a customer in the open area of the vault. Private rooms should be provided for the customers' use and should be searched after each occupancy. In this way the bank can attest to the fact that no observer was able to see the contents of a customer's box and thus to know if it was an especially attractive target for theft.

- For the same reason, no bank personnel, under normal circumstances, should have any knowledge of the contents of a box.

- When a customer terminates the safe deposit relationship and mails the keys to the bank, the box should be opened under dual control. If any contents are found in the box, it should be closed and locked. The bank should then require the customer to come to the safe deposit area to remove the contents.

- All safe deposit boxes require use of both a bank key and a customer's key to open them. The bank's key should never be referred to as a "master" key. Use of this term might give the impression that the bank has a single key that will open all boxes.

- In the event of a customer's death or legal incompetence, the bank must immediately observe all federal, state, and local laws.

Any question or doubt that arises in the daily operations of the safe deposit vault should be resolved in favor of *maximum* protection of the customer's property. The potential for claims and lawsuits is always high. The proper conduct of safe deposit operations may not generate substantial profits for a bank, but a single act of negligence—no matter how well-intentioned—can result in a court decision that creates a significant loss.

A question often arises as to the insurance that covers safe deposit operations. The contents of a customer's safe deposit box are not specifically insured, nor does federal deposit insurance apply to them. Rather, the customer is paying for the security that the bank's facilities are intended to provide, and a general liability policy, purchased by the bank, is usually in force.

OTHER SPECIALIZED SERVICES

The former board chairman of one of America's largest banks stated its marketing policy in these words: "We intend to supply every useful financial service anywhere in the free world where permitted to us by law and which we can perform at a profit." His attitude is shared by many major banks, which display a willingness to determine customer needs and wants and an ability to respond to them through new services. In many cases these services are far removed from the traditional narrow scope of banking.

It is not the purpose here to suggest that every bank should begin offering each of these services to every category of customer. Many banks accept the impossibility or impracticality of attempting to be all things to all people. Rather, the objective is to list these specialized services as further evidence of the dramatic changes in commercial banking. No longer do banks merely accept deposits, process payments, and extend credit, although those three functions still represent their major contributions to the economy. In today's highly competitive marketplace, banks often find that new services represent their only means of attracting new customers and retaining existing ones.

EFTS Services

Direct deposit systems are part of the overall EFTS approach to modern banking. They enable any paying agency to reduce the number of checks that would otherwise be issued, or to eliminate checks entirely. Examples include the magnetic tape that is furnished to financial institutions by the Social Security Administration for its regular payments to recipients or that is provided by branches of the armed forces and by corporations for payroll disbursing. These tapes can be processed through the network of automated clearinghouses (ACHs) so that the payee's account at any financial institution can be credited.

Point-of-sale terminals have now been installed in many stores, in conjunction with banks or other financial institutions. These facilities allow the purchaser of goods to pay for purchases through debits to an account and corresponding credits to the account of the seller. Automated teller machines allow customers to make deposits, withdrawals, and loan payments and to initiate transfers of funds between accounts. Pre-authorized payment systems eliminate the need for customers to issue checks for such standard monthly payments as insurance premiums and mortgage loans.

All such EFTS systems require specific security measures to protect users against any unauthorized transactions. Federal Reserve Regulation E addresses this point, as do state and local laws. Many banks now assign personal identification numbers (PINs) to their customers and program their automated facilities so that this number must be entered in conjunction with a bank card.

Payroll Services

Employers today must cope with a host of payroll problems that arise from complex federal, state, and local tax requirements, labor laws, and the need for both timely and completely confidential preparation of employees' pay. Many banks provide a highly customized payroll service, using the same equipment and technology employed in their own payroll processing. They can assume the entire burden of calculating each employee's gross pay, making all statutory and voluntary deductions, providing all current and year-to-date information, and computing the net amount. That amount can then be directly deposited to the employee's account with the bank, directed to another financial institution through the ACH network, or paid to the employee by check. The bank providing this payroll service enters into a contract that includes responsibility for rendering all necessary earnings and tax reports to units of government.

The customer benefits in this service include speed and accuracy in the preparation of each regular payroll, bonus, and overtime or incentive pay; complete confidentiality; guaranteed accuracy; and greatly reduced clerical work. The bank providing the service usually charges a direct fee based on the number of employees involved. Additional benefits to the bank may include the opening of new accounts for employees of the corporation, government unit, or correspondent bank using the service, and the temporary use of the taxes that are withheld from employees' pay.

Services to Correspondent Banks

To expand its correspondent network and build up its deposit base, a bank must be prepared to meet the specialized needs of other banks. Demand deposit accounting is one such service. Investment portfolio analysis is another, and it may be offered in conjunction with safekeeping facilities for the correspondent's securities. One bank may offer to prepare all the necessary Form 1099s for its correspondent, thereby providing the Internal Revenue Service with the required information on interest and dividend payments.

Thrift institutions are active users of the specialized services offered by their commercial bank correspondents. These include lockbox (for the daily collection of mortgage payments), payroll preparation, portfolio analysis, federal funds transactions, and account reconciliation (for the tellers' checks and money orders issued each day by the savings bank or savings and loan association).

SUMMARY

The banker of previous generations, who dealt with a limited market and believed that banking consisted only of attracting deposits, processing payments, and extending credit, would have great difficulty in appreciating the scope of commercial banking today. Innovation has become the key. There is an ongoing effort among banks to identify their markets, study the needs and wants of those markets, and develop and provide new or enhanced services that will benefit customers while generating profits.

A tremendous expansion of international banking has taken place since the end of World War II, and new service opportunities continue to open up as America's exports and imports increase. Earnings from all forms of international operations represent a major part of the income of many banks today.

Similarly, the area of cash management services has become an important contributor to the income of many commercial banks as customers have sought the benefits of new approaches to handling deposits and payments and supplying information. Through these services, float and clerical work can be reduced, availability of funds increased, and bank balances monitored and adjusted so that idle funds are put to profitable use.

Safe deposit services cannot be given any less attention than other areas of banking that require specific security procedures. Paramount in this area is the protection of customers' property, and every appropriate security measure must be taken to ensure that the bank is never negligent in its degree of care.

The increased capability of computers and the widespread acceptance of various applications of EFTS have also enabled commercial banks to broaden the range of their specialized services. It is only through service that they can meet the aggressive competition they encounter today from many other financial intermediaries.

QUESTIONS FOR DISCUSSION

1. How does a letter of credit, issued by a bank, protect the interests of both the importer and exporter of goods?

2. Define the following international banking terms:

    a. Irrevocable letter of credit
    b. Banker's acceptance
    c. Bill of lading
    d. Consular invoice

3. Why might a certificate of quality be required as part of a letter of credit transaction? Who would issue this certificate?

4. What benefits does trust receipt financing offer to an American importer?

5. List three international department services that would be helpful to an American exporter.

6. What purpose does a depository transfer check serve? Who creates the check?

7. For each of the following services, identify one benefit to the bank and one benefit to the user:

   a. Lockbox
   b. Payroll preparation
   c. Account reconciliation

8. Identify any five safeguards that a bank might use as protective measures in its safe deposit operations.

9. Assume that your bank is the correspondent for two thrift institutions in your community. Identify three specialized services that your bank might offer them.

10. The Smith Corporation, a customer of the First National Bank, has agreed to place its entire employee payroll on a direct deposit basis with that bank. What benefits can the Smith Corporation expect to gain from this service? How will the First National Bank benefit from providing the service?

Suggested Readings

Anderson, Stanley W. *The Banker and EFT.* Washington, D.C.: American Bankers Association, 1982.

American Bankers Association. *Bankers and Community Involvement.* Washington, D.C.: American Bankers Association, 1978.

American Bankers Association. *Letters of Credit.* (Programmed Instruction). Washington, D.C.: American Bankers Association, 1983.

American Bankers Association. *Safe Deposit Handbook.* Washington, D.C.: American Bankers Association, 1980.

American Bankers Association. *Safe Deposit Seminar.* Washington, D.C.: American Bankers Association, 1980.

California State Banking Department. *Money Orders and Travelers Checks. The Forgotten Payments Mechanism.* San Francisco: California State Banking Department, 1977.

Citibank. *Introduction to Commercial Letters of Credit.* New York: Citibank, 1976.

Oppenheim, Peter K. *International Banking.* 4th ed. Washington, D.C.: American Bankers Association, 1983.

Pezzullo, Mary Ann. *Marketing For Bankers.* Washington, D.C.: American Bankers Association, 1982.

Chapter 17

Banking Today and Tomorrow

LEARNING OBJECTIVES

After completing this chapter, you will have an understanding of

- the fundamental changes that have taken place in banking since World War II;

- the status of commercial banks in the financial marketplace today;

- the financial services offered today by major nonbank competitors;

- the advantages of banking-at-home systems;

- the key elements in a bank marketing effort; and

- the characteristics that successful banks of the future must possess.

When Americans use the word *revolution*, they usually are referring to the overthrow of a foreign government, or they may be using the word in one of its scientific senses (e.g., the revolutions per minute of an engine). Today, they would be equally correct if they used the same word in describing the world of banking. Not only has a revolution in banking taken place; it continues. No 20-year period in history has witnessed changes so numerous, so massive, and so permanent as did the span from 1961 to 1980. Yet there is no indication that the pace of change has slowed or that the financial turmoil of those 2 decades has ended. Rather, the start of the decade of the 1980s has been marked by additional drastic changes, and it seems safe to predict that evolutionary and revolutionary developments will create a financial marketplace of tomorrow that differs significantly from today's.

Consider the shock and amazement that the Rip Van Winkle of fiction would have felt had he been a banker who fell asleep in 1961 and awoke 20 years later. At the start of that period, a major bank in New York City introduced a new type of money market instrument, the large-denomination negotiable CD. As a result of that single innovation, the basic deposit structure of the banking industry began to change. The demand deposits on which bankers had traditionally relied began to shrink in proportion to the savings and time deposits that a new breed of customer found far more attractive. Instead of being an asset manager who could selectively lend and invest the interest-free deposits that steadily flowed into the system, the banker became a liability manager whose job it was to fund the institution by competitively attracting purchased money. Interest paid to depositors therefore has become the largest, the fastest growing, and the least controllable of all bank expense items. During 1981, America's 14,400 insured commercial banks paid out $139 billion in interest to depositors—a sum equal to 61 percent of their total operating expenses.

This fictional banker would never have heard of an organizational structure called the bank holding company (BHC), yet while he slept the BHC became the accepted format through which commercial banks were able to diversify their range of products and services. Leasing, mortgage servicing, customized services and products in the data processing field, investment counseling, and certain types of insurance coverage are profitably marketed today through BHCs, whose member banks hold three-quarters of the total assets of the entire commercial banking system. Almost without exception, America's major banks have formed bank holding companies, none of which existed before the early 1960s.

During the same 20-year period that began in 1961, bank cards were introduced in a large scale and helped to change both the lifestyles of millions of consumers and the retail lending practices of the issuing banks. Originally, these pieces of plastic were *credit* cards like those of the major oil companies or the travel-and-entertainment cards issued by such organizations as Diners Club and American Express. Credit cards can be used to obtain a tremendous variety of goods and services and are still widely issued by banks. However, in addition to the credit card, many banks now issue *debit* cards, so-called because their use creates a direct debit to the cardholder's account. For example, when an individual uses such a card in an automated teller machine to obtain a cash advance, or uses the card in a point-of-sale terminal at a store, an automatic charge is created and the debit is posted to the account, reducing the customer's balance.

The two decades through which banking's Rip Van Winkle slept also saw the start of the full-scale movement toward widespread applications of EFTS. Much to his surprise, he would find over 20,000 automated teller facilities now in place through which consumers conduct much of their banking business. He would notice the success of the Social Security Administration's direct deposit program, the increasing customer acceptance of EFTS as seen in pre-authorized monthly payment systems or the tape input now supplied to banks by insurance companies, and the movement toward check truncation.

Our mythical banker would also have to devote a great deal of attention simply to learning the new vocabulary that is part of banking today. Such terms as variable-rate mortgages, money market and All-Savers certificates, NOW accounts, country risk analysis, and explicit pricing would be unknown to him, and he would be on the same basis as a beginning student in trying to learn the full implications and effects of the Monetary Control and Community Reinvestment Acts. As he walked through his bank's offices, he would be bewildered by the extent to which desk-top terminals, microcomputers, and word processing equipment have changed the nature of daily clerical work. When he reached his desk each morning, today's banking would make it possible for him to find whole sets of reports supplied by modern management information systems. Virtually any type of data needed to help him in his daily work could be made available on short notice.

He would also find that his bank's role in its community had undergone a remarkable change during his slumber. Banks now accept the concept of social responsibility. They give to their communities instead of merely taking deposits from them, and they see themselves as corporate citizens whose own well-being is intimately tied to that of the city or town.

While our banker slept, the former personnel unit at his bank may have been replaced by a human resources department, through which new and enlightened methods of training and development are initiated and put into practice. Individuals are now hired and promoted without regard for race, sex, national origin, or other factors that could be used to discriminate. Supervisors have largely discarded the autocratic management style of their predecessors. They explain, motivate, and help, rather than merely ordering work to be done.

However, as our banker tried to comprehend and adjust to all the developments that had occurred during the 20 years, one change would stand out above all the others. It would reflect the steady deterioration of the banks' share of the financial marketplace and their loss of the exclusivity on financial services that they once possessed. Their efforts to compete with such nonbank intermediaries as Sears Roebuck, Merrill Lynch, and American Express are severely inhibited by laws and regulations that do not apply to these others. As a result, the decline in the percentage of the nation's financial assets held by commercial banks continues into the 1980s.

Commercial banking today envisions two possible sources of relief. Either legislators will begin to apply comparable regulations to the nonbanks, or they will relax some of the shackles that presently apply to banking. The former does not appear to be a realistic solution. Instead, banks must look to the latter; that is, they must seek deregulation of their own industry so that they can make the further changes that will enable them to survive.

The Garn-St Germain Act of 1982 provides an example of deregulation directly affecting commercial banks. Effective December 14, 1982, banks were authorized to offer a new type of account, specifically intended to enable them to compete with money market funds in the hope of attracting deposits back from those funds. The new accounts, commonly called money market accounts, require a minimum balance of $2,500 but permit the banks to pay unrestricted and competitive interest rates. At the same time, federal deposit insurance, up to the legal limit of $100,000, protects the depositor's funds. Certain restrictions apply to withdrawals from the accounts, but the combination of deposit insurance and high yields has made them extremely attractive. At the time the new accounts were introduced, money market funds had total assets of over \$230 billion; by year-end 1982 (less than 1 month later), the funds had decreased by approximately \$14 billion. The additional interest expense created for the banks as a result of these accounts will have to be carefully measured over the course of time; however, they have proved to be an effective competitive vehicle.

The traditional core business of banks—accepting deposits, processing payments, and extending credit—has shrunk in importance and will probably continue to do so as a result of intense competition from outside sources. Profit margins, i.e., the spreads between average interest rates that banks pay for funds and those they receive on loans and investments, have declined.

In 1963, the U.S. Supreme Court ruled that banking was "a unique line of commerce" and stated that commercial banks competed *only* with other commercial banks. The logic behind this opinion was difficult to understand in 1963 and is impossible to accept today. Commercial banks do *not* compete only with one another; they compete with a growing number of other financial intermediaries that enjoy advantages the banks are not legally allowed to possess.

Sears Roebuck operates 859 stores throughout the country and has 25 million active Sears cardholders, who have generated accounts receivable for the company of over \$7 billion. It owns a major insurance company (Allstate) and a savings and loan association in California. It has acquired large brokerage firms in both the stock market and real estate fields. Its plans call for the conversion of many of its existing stores into the true financial supermarkets of the future. Customers of these new Sears facilities will have ATMs at their disposal and will be able to handle a multitude of loan, deposit, and payment transactions without leaving the premises.

The American Express Company operates a travel and entertainment card system, a major insurance company, a large international bank, and one of the largest securities brokerage firms in the country. It owns a cable and satellite communications system, a research and consulting firm in the EFTS field, and a subsidiary that renders data processing services.

Merrill Lynch's cash management account gives the customer overnight investment of funds at money-market rates, borrowing privileges, a bank card, and a supply of checks. Merrill Lynch is also engaged in corporate lending, brokerage activities, insurance, and real estate.

The broad spectrum of financial services offered by these firms forces the banker of today to cope with a question his predecessor never had to face in 1961. In increasing numbers, customers—individuals, units of government, large and small businesses, and correspondent banks—are asking whether they need a commercial bank at all. Even the large corporations, formerly the prime customers of banks, now find it possible to borrow from each other in huge amounts through the commercial paper market, or to borrow from Merrill Lynch or another nonbank lender. If consumers find that their wants and needs can be met by credit unions (which offer higher interest rates on deposits and lower rates on loans) or thrift institutions (whose range of services has been broadened by their federal regulators), and if they can consistently obtain better yields through money market funds, they are likely to take advantage of these opportunities. Their actions will further reduce the market share held by banks.

To the extent that they are allowed to do so by regulatory authorities, commercial banks today must try to meet the competition through new or improved services of their own. In the consumer area, there is a specific example of this effort made possible through the new technology included under the term *automation.*

During 1981 almost 8,500 ATMs were delivered to financial institutions, bringing the total to over 20,000. Average transaction volume per ATM per month rose to 6,000, excluding simple balance inquiries.[1] ATMs have become the vehicle for handling many routine banking transactions that previously took place at tellers' windows. Their steady growth offers proof that a new breed of banker, through effective marketing to a new breed of customer, *can* produce results. It is noteworthy that the Texas National Bank has provided a further innovation in this area by combining ATMs with its night depository facilities for the convenience of customers.

Additional emphasis on automation has resulted in new systems that allow customers to do their banking at home. In many parts of the country, telephone banking has become part of the consumer's way of life. At year-end 1981, 167 commercial banks were offering some form of telephone bill payment service. They reported an average of over 16,000 transactions per month.[2]

Earlier in this text, information services for corporate, correspondent bank, and government customers were described as part of the overall cash management product line. These services can now be made available to individuals through home video systems, and one of the nation's largest commercial banks, in announcing the start of this service, pointedly remarked that the system was *not* in the future but rather in the immediate present.

A home computer, hooked up to the telephone and using the consumer's television set as a display screen, is necessary. The user is able to review and schedule bank-card payments, obtain balance information, and initiate mortgage payments or other periodic bills. In addition, the equipment can be used to pay directly from the user's account to participating utilities, merchants, and landlords.

BANK MARKETING TODAY

Throughout much of their history, commercial banks in America were the exclusive suppliers of many financial services but offered those services only to a restricted market. Their focus was on the corporate, correspondent bank, or government customer. The wants and needs of the customer were largely neglected. At the same time, the banks were operating in a seller's market; that is, they could afford the luxury of having customers come to them for services. As asset managers, the banks made selective decisions on loans and investments, using the steady stream of demand deposits that flowed in each year.

In the years since World War II, banks have learned to their dismay that vacuums do not exist for any length of time in the financial marketplace. If one type of institution does not act to fill the wants and needs of the market, another will quickly step in to do so. Thrift institutions, for example, improved their relative position tremendously in the postwar years simply by concentrating on meeting the needs of the consumers for mortgage loans. More recently, the money market funds have attracted huge quantities of money in a short period of time by identifying the need for high-yielding investment vehicles among people of relatively modest means and responding to that need.

The successes that banks have achieved, despite the intense competition that comes from unregulated financial intermediaries, result from a new recognition of the importance of the marketing function.

The term *marketing* should not be thought of as merely selling, or as a single activity performed by very few people in the bank. Rather, marketing today is understood to be an integrated set of activities in which the entire staff of the bank is involved. A total marketing plan in today's banking includes the following:

- Conducting research to identify the wants and needs of those types of customers that the bank wishes to attract and retain;

- Developing and managing the products and services that will meet those needs;

- Training staff members in the techniques of effective selling, and involving every staff member in some aspect of selling; and

- Generating increased business for the bank through actual selling to targeted markets.

To the banker who slept through the 1960s and 1970s, all of this represents a drastic change from the attitude that existed previously. In the past, the banker refused to think of himself as a salesman, and the techniques of mass marketing were ignored. In today's competitive marketplace, banks realize that it is essential to determine what the market segments want to buy, rather than simply determining what the banks want to sell. When that process has been completed, steps can be taken—as in the area of home banking or cash management information services—to meet the wants and needs of the target markets. The word target is important here, because it flows from the basic approach to the banking business that the board of directors and senior management have adopted. If the bank wishes to attempt to be all things to all people, its market is the universe; if, instead, it chooses to concentrate on a more limited approach, its marketing program will be adjusted accordingly.

Bank marketing today is not an activity that is carried out exclusively by a handful of officers or other staff members who have been made responsible for new business development. The most successful banks are those in which *all* personnel actually market the products and services to customers and prospects. Every clerk, teller, secretary, and safe deposit attendant can become a salesman for the bank simply by taking advantage of the inevitable interpersonal situations that arise in everyday life. Whenever a relative, friend, or neighbor mentions any type of financial need, a bank employee can immediately capitalize on the opportunity and suggest that his or her institution can meet that need. The sale of a bank service or product can easily result.

Cross-selling is an important part of the total marketing effort. The customer who already uses one service, assuming it meets his or her requirements for quality and timeliness, is automatically a target for others. Depositors who maintain personal checking accounts are prospects for safe deposit services, bank cards, travelers checks, and various types of loans. Profiles can be developed on corporate, correspondent bank, and governmental customers so that the marketing of specific services can be tailored to meet their situations and needs. Officers who have been assigned specific accounts should be fully aware of steps they can take to capitalize on the existing account relationship by selling additional services. Present customers always generate a very substantial part of the additional business that can be gained for a bank, and there is an additional benefit to the institution because those customers who use more than one service are less likely to change their affiliations and move their accounts to a competitor.

Bank marketing today recognizes the basic truth that other industries have known for many years: Customers do *not* buy products or services as such. Rather, they buy the *benefits* that they feel those products or services will provide. If the bank's marketing effort is to succeed, it must convince its customers that those benefits will, in fact, result if the customers "buy" those products or services.

BANKING FOR TOMORROW

It has been said that those who ignore the lessons of history are condemned to repeat its mistakes. By the same token, it is only through an analysis of all that is seen in the present that one can predict the future. The realities of today's financial marketplace must be faced. Ignoring them will not cause them to disappear in the future.

High on the list of these realities is the question in the minds of many bankers regarding their actual ability to survive. The U.S. financial system today includes over 40,000 depository institutions—commercial banks, savings banks, savings and loan associations, and credit unions.

A commercial bank with assets of $100 billion may at some point be competing for the same business with a credit union that has assets of $100,000. There simply is not enough room for all these institutions to continue to function in tomorrow's financial environment.

In conjunction with new telecommunication systems, computers have increased the speed and efficiency with which money can be moved from place to place throughout the world. As a result, many corporations have been able to develop their own in-house financial system. Because a few minutes at a computer terminal can give the financial officer up-to-date information on the organization's balances at every bank, and because money can be moved around the world at the speed of light, excess funds can immediately be placed wherever rates are highest, and demand deposits can be drastically reduced. Those banks that rely on the traditional excess balances left with them by their wholesale customers, and those that furnished only a small group of basic services to a very limited clientele, will find it difficult to survive.

Just as the banks in tomorrow's marketplace must deal with corporations that treat them differently and use them less extensively, so they must also deal with a new breed of consumer—more willing to accept change, more knowledgeable, better educated, and far more aware of the value of money to the institutions that compete for it. Some years ago, **disintermediation** was the term coined by thrift institutions to describe the outflow of funds from their accounts to other, higher yielding media. Today—and probably to an even greater extent tomorrow—the same word may be used to describe the movement of money *both* within banks and from them to other financial intermediaries. For example, it may refer to the fact that a customer withdraws his or her funds to place them in a money market fund; but it may also be used when a customer who has maintained excess funds in a checking account moves them to a savings account at the same bank, and from the savings account to a money market certificate, and from the latter to some other form of time deposit producing an even higher rate of return.

Banking for tomorrow must therefore be prepared to provide those financial services that will meet the new wants and needs of the consumer. The environment will continue to be highly competitive, and banks must recognize the intention of Sears Roebuck, among others, to move into this full range of services. Banking at home will be stressed as increased volume brings about cost reductions and the necessary computer systems become more readily accessible to customers. Indeed, one prediction has it that the market for two-way home banking systems, in which the consumer both receives balance information through a terminal and uses the same terminal to initiate transactions, will grow to 8 million households by 1990.

The Monetary Control Act of 1980 provides for a gradual elimination of all interest-rate ceilings (e.g., Regulation Q) in the banking industry, additional powers for mortgage lenders, and an increase in the regulatory scope of the Federal Reserve. Because the act's basic thrust is in the area of deregulation, it will increase the already competitive environment. Taken in conjunction with the other changes that have already been identified in the financial marketplace, the act is likely to

- Create a new system of "true cost" banking, in which customers will have to adjust to explicit pricing of services that formerly were provided without charge; pricing of loans will be adjusted accordingly.

- Hasten the introduction of variable-rate consumer and mortgage loans, so that lenders can adjust to money market changes.

- Weaken the traditional lines of separation between commercial banks and thrifts and allow for freer competition for consumer deposits, which are estimated at $1 trillion.

More than 12,000 commercial banks have deposits of $100 million or less. Many of them are located in states where thrift institutions have been the major competitors. That competition will be increased through the Monetary Control Act, which gave thrift institutions additional lending powers and authorized them to issue bank cards. The federal regulators of thrift institutions have already allowed interstate mergers in several cases and have authorized thrifts to install ATMs in all parts of the country.

INTERSTATE BANKING

Any discussion of tomorrow's banking must take into consideration the fundamental question of whether Congress will remove the existing barriers to full-scale interstate banking. The McFadden Act of 1927 guaranteed the rights of the individual states to control all branch banking within their borders and provided that state laws regulating branching were to apply to all banks, whether federal- or state-chartered. The Bank Holding Company Acts of 1956 and 1970, with the Douglas Amendment, provide that a bank holding company may not make acquisitions across state lines unless the legislatures of the two involved states have specifically extended reciprocal privileges. With the exception of Maine and New York, which passed this type of legislation leading to an interstate bank merger in late 1982, the net effect has been a total prohibition of branch banking across individual state borders.

The good intentions of the legislators who were responsible for these acts cannot be denied. Their goal was to limit the ability of the money-center giants to dominate the entire industry by opening branches in every part of the country. They feared a concentration of economic power in the hands of a relatively small number of banks. The country's banking tradition has always been one in which smaller individual banks were permitted to function as representatives of the free enterprise system. The objectives of those who drew up these acts may have been praiseworthy, but in the financial marketplace of tomorrow it is at best questionable whether the rationale can still be justified.

Until such time as the restrictions on full-scale interstate branching are relaxed, commercial banks can prepare for tomorrow by opening loan production and Edge Act offices in other states and, through the bank holding company, by making such acquisitions as the Fed may permit.

Commercial banks have steadily lost their relative position in the total financial marketplace. They no longer have their former exclusivity in supplying many financial services. Nevertheless, their importance to the nation's economy through their deposit, payment, and credit functions and the other services they provide cannot be overstated. The failure of a single bank has grave consequences in its community. History clearly shows how disastrous are the effects of a wave of bank failures, as in the years of the Great Depression. If the banks are to continue to maintain a key position among all financial institutions, and if it is in the national interest to have them do so, they must be given more freedom to compete with those suppliers of financial services whose operations are not subject to the same federal and state laws and regulations, who do not have to maintain reserves with the Fed, and who therefore possess significant competitive advantages.

THE ROAD TO SUCCESS

In attempting to predict what the banks of tomorrow will look like, how many of them will still be in existence, and what steps can be taken toward future growth and profitability even in the face of both competition and external constraints, several elements need to be examined. The essentials for success represent areas in which commercial banks have not displayed strength in the past. The key factors for success, rather than mere survival, are these:

1. Effective cost accounting and pricing;

2. Effective asset and liability management;

3. Effective marketing;

4. Effective short- and long-range planning; and

5. Innovation.

Cost Accounting and Pricing

The shift of the deposit base from demand to time and savings creates a need for comprehensive and effective systems of cost accounting. Added to this is the increased need for banks to institute adequate methods of pricing their services. The Monetary Control Act directed the Fed to adopt explicit pricing of its services to banks; these new costs must be recovered from those who use the services. The lack of emphasis on cost accounting and pricing in the past could be justified because of the existence of large, interest-free demand deposits, but that excuse no longer exists. Banks must know their costs, know how to explain their pricing systems to customers, and know how to recover their costs plus a profit margin in each case.

Asset and Liability Management

The changing deposit structure has forced bankers to become liability, rather than merely asset, managers. As part of this change in their life-style they must work to match the bank's assets against its liabilities and focus on the maturities in each case. The problems of thrift institutions in recent years, resulting from far higher costs for short-term money than the rates of return on their long-term loans, provide an object lesson for commercial banks.

The matter of compensation for both loans and nonloan products is critical, both in the areas of cost accounting and funds management. A continuation of the trend among customers to compensate banks with direct fees, rather than balances, can lead only to a further shrinkage in the demand deposit base. In the credit area, many customers now expect banks to use an "all-in-the-rate" system and to ignore completely the traditional requests for compensating balances.

Marketing

In tomorrow's highly competitive world, bankers must discard completely their former notion that selling was demeaning and unnecessary. If attrition does take place in the banking system, the survivors will undoubtedly be those who have done the best job of deciding which markets they wish to serve, learning the wants and needs of those markets, developing new services to meet those wants and needs, devising the strategies that will bring those services to the attention of the market, and training bank personnel in the techniques of selling. No bank can afford to sit back and wait for customers to approach it. Competitors have long understood the value of effective marketing; banks must now follow that lead.

Planning

Statistics indicate that in the past very few banks devoted much attention to planning. If the industry continues on that course, the risk is tremendous. Banks must try to shape their own destinies by deciding where they are at present, where they wish to be in the future, and what actions they need to take to attain that goal. The process involves analyzing the present position of the bank compared with those of other commercial banks and nonbank competitors and determining its customers' perceptions of the bank. This is followed by a setting of specific targets for the future and establishing specific strategies that will bring the desired growth and profits. Not every bank can do everything well or profitably. The planning process helps the institution to focus on its strengths in order to achieve the stated objectives.

Innovation

If, as predicted, there is a substantial reduction in the number of commercial banks, those that disappear from the scene are likely to be the victims of their own image in the minds of the public. Banks in general are thought of as being slow-moving and opposed to change. Those that consistently develop new or improved services are the exception to this rule and are immediately recognized as such by the marketplace. Within the framework of the regulations that affect it, a bank can serve a pioneer role by making transaction handling more convenient or more cost-effective to the user or by being the first in its community to supply a product that is wanted and needed. The bank that is perceived as progressive and responsive to customer wants and needs will gain a significant advantage in its attempts to meet the challenges of the future.

HUMAN RESOURCES MANAGEMENT

Tomorrow's banking will require the efforts of productive, motivated, dedicated personnel who have displayed an ability to adjust to change and to perform in a highly competitive environment. The five key factors previously listed as essential to the future success of banking are meaningless unless the right people are in the right positions. Banking must be thought of as providing careers, not merely jobs. The traditional bank emphasis on training and development will be increased even further to prepare staff members to face the tasks that lie ahead. Along with the increased skills that employees will need to handle increased responsibilities will come increased rewards and opportunities for personal growth. Just as the future of any bank may well depend on its ability to anticipate change and to manage change as it occurs, so the future of individuals in the banking industry depends on their ability to cope with the challenges their banks must face in the future. The former chairman of the Federal Deposit Insurance Corporation has summarized this:

The overriding challenge in the coming years will be finding out where you have the brains and putting them to work. More than ever before, banking will be dependent, totally dependent, on its people. Hardware and software are vital—but banking in the 80s (and beyond) will fly on the wings of its people.[3]

SUMMARY

In the years that have elapsed since the end of World War II, commercial banking has undergone a succession of revolutionary changes, including those that gave it a new deposit structure and a new type of organization in the holding company. More recently, banks have been faced with tremendous external change. Their nonbank competition has multiplied, both in numbers and in the quantity of financial services it can offer. Banks find themselves operating at a serious disadvantage in their efforts to meet this competition because of the laws and regulations that restrain their activities. America now has over 40,000 depository institutions, many of which may not be able to survive the pressures of further change. Those institutions that will constitute the banks of tomorrow will be characterized by an ability to meet challenges through a combination of key factors indicative of their ability to adjust to change.

QUESTIONS FOR DISCUSSION

1. Why is the large-denomination negotiable CD so important in our banking history?

2. Identify three major nonbank competitors in today's financial marketplace. What competitive advantages do they enjoy?

3. Identify three elements in an integrated system of bank marketing.

4. What opportunities might you, as an individual, have in your own bank's marketing effort?

5. Define the term disintermediation.

6. How does the McFadden Act restrict the branching activities of commercial banks?

7. "Borrowing short-term to lend long-term can be disastrous for a bank." Explain this statement.

NOTES

1. Linda Fenner Zimmer, "ATMs: Time to Fine-Tune and to Plan," *The Magazine of Bank Administration,* May 1982, p. 20.

2. Marjolijn van der Velde, "Home Banking: Where It Stands Today," *The Magazine of Bank Administration,* September 1982, p. 16.

3. Kenneth A. Randall, "As Banking Looks Ahead," *Bankers Monthly,* September 15, 1980, p. 22.

Suggested Readings

Baker, Jr., James V. *Asset/Liability Management.* Washington, D.C.: American Bankers Association, 1981.

Dessler, Gary. *Management Fundamentals.* Reston, Virginia: Reston Publishing Company, 1979.

Pezzullo, Mary Ann. *Marketing For Bankers.* Washington, D.C.: American Bankers Association, 1982.

Summers, Donald B. *Personnel Management in Banking.* New York: McGraw-Hill Book Company, 1981.

Sources of Current Information

American Banker (daily except Sat., Sun., Holidays)
525 West 42nd Street
New York, New York 10036

Bank Administration (monthly)
Bank Administration Institute
60 Gould Center
Rolling Meadows, Illinois 60008

Bank Marketing (monthly)
Bank Marketing Association
309 West Washington Street
Chicago, Illinois 60606

Bankers Magazine (bi-monthly)
Warren, Gorham and Lamont
210 South Street
Boston, Massachusetts 02111

Bankers News Weekly (weekly)
American Bankers Association
1120 Connecticut Avenue, N.W.
Washington, D.C. 20036

Banking (monthly)
(Journal of the American Bankers Association)
Simmons-Boardman Publishing Corporation
350 Broadway
New York, New York 10013

Federal Reserve Bulletin (monthly)
Division of Administrative Services
Board of Governors of the Federal Reserve System
Washington, D.C. 20551

Issues in Bank Regulation (quarterly)
Bank Administration Institute
60 Gould Center
Rolling Meadows, Illinois 60008

See also regional Federal Reserve publications.

These items represent only a few of the many resources available for banking information and study. For further information, contact the ABA Library at (202) 467-4180, or write to:

> Library Assistance
> American Bankers Association
> 1120 Connecticut Avenue, N.W.
> Washington, D.C. 20036

Glossary

ABA Transit number. A unique identifying number assigned to each bank by the American Bankers Association National Numerical System. The transit number has two parts, separated by a hyphen. The first part shows the city, state, or territory in which the bank is located; the second part identifies the bank itself. The transit number appears in the upper right corner of checks as the numerator (upper portion) of a fraction.

Acceptance. A time draft (bill of exchange), on the face of which the drawee has written the word *accepted*, the date it is payable, and his or her signature. An acceptance is an obligation that the drawee has agreed to pay at maturity. After having accepted the draft, the drawee is known as the acceptor. See also **Banker's acceptance**, **Trade acceptance**, and **Certified check**.

Access. The right of entry to a safe deposit box so that authorized parties can examine, add to, or reduce the contents.

Account analysis. The process of determining the profit or loss to a bank in handling an account for a given period. It shows the activity involved, the cost of that activity as determined by multiplying unit costs by transaction volume, and the estimated earnings on average investable balances maintained during the period after all expenses have been listed.

Account reconciliation. The process for determining the differences between two items of an account to bring them into agreement, e.g., reconciling a bank statement and a checkbook.

Accounts receivable. Money owed to a business enterprise by customers for merchandise or services sold to them on open account, without a formal note or other evidence of debt.

Accrual accounting. The method of accounting that records all income when it is earned and all expenses when they are incurred.

Adjustable rate loan. See **Variable rate loan**.

Administrator. A party appointed by a court to settle an estate when (1) the decedent has left no valid will, (2) no executor is named in the will, or (3) the named executor cannot or will not serve. The legend *c.t.a.* with the word *administrator* means that the terms of the will dictate the settling of the estate.

Advice. A written acknowledgment by a bank of a transaction affecting an account, e.g., debit or credit advices.

Advised line of credit. A line of credit that has been confirmed in writing to the customer by the bank. See **Line of credit**.

Advising bank. A bank that has received notification from another financial institution that a Letter of Credit has been opened by an importer or customer. The advising bank will then contact the exporter reaffirming the conditions and terms of the Letter of Credit.

Agency. The relationship between agent and principal. The agent acts on behalf of the principal while the latter retains legal title to property or other assets.

Altered check. A check on which a material change, such as in the dollar amount, has been made. Banks are expected to detect alterations and are responsible for paying checks as originally drawn.

American Bankers Association (ABA). An organization of banks, founded in 1875, to keep members aware of developments affecting the industry, to develop educated and competent bank personnel, and to seek improvements in bank management and service.

American Institute of Banking (AIB). A section of the American Bankers Association founded in 1900 for the purpose of providing banking-oriented education for bank employees. AIB's activities are carried on through chapters and study groups throughout the country. In addition to its regular classes, the Institute conducts correspondence courses. Membership and enrollment are open to employees and officers of ABA member institutions.

Amortization. The periodic reduction of an outstanding loan amount through regular payments.

Annual percentage rate (APR). The cost of credit on a yearly basis. Expressed as a percentage, the APR results from an equation that considers three specifically defined factors: the amount financed, the finance charge, and the term of the loan. The APR is usually expressed in terms of the effective annual simple interest rate.

Asset. Anything owned by an individual or business that has commercial or exchange value. Assets may consist of specific property or of claims against others, in contrast to obligations due to others (liabilities).

Attorney-in-fact. A party who has been authorized by a bank's depositor to issue instructions to that bank regarding an account. The form by which the depositor conveys this authority is called a **power of attorney**. The rights of an attorney-in-fact last until revoked or until the depositor dies.

Auditor. In banking, an individual, usually appointed by the bank's directors and reporting directly to them, who is responsible for examining any and all phases of the bank's operations.

Authorized signature. The signature of the individual(s) who has the legal right to issue instructions.

Automated clearinghouse. A computerized facility that performs the clearing of paperless entries between member depository institutions.

Automated teller machines (ATMs). Electronic facilities, located inside or apart from a financial services institution, for handling many transactions automatically.

Automatic transfer service (ATS). A service by which a bank moves funds from one type of account to another for its customer on a preauthorized basis.

Availability schedule. A list showing the number of days that must elapse before deposited checks can be considered converted into usable funds.

Average daily float. See **Float**.

Balance. The amount of funds in a customer's account.

Balance sheet. A detailed listing of assets, liabilities, and equity capital accounts (net worth), showing the financial condition of a bank or company as of a given date. A balance sheet illustrates the basic accounting equation: assets = liabilities + net worth. In banking, the balance sheet is usually referred to as the **statement of condition**.

Balloon payment. The last payment on a loan that is substantially larger than the previous payments.

Bank check. A check, also known as a cashier's, treasurer's, or official check, drawn by a bank on itself. Since the drawer and drawee are one and the same, acceptance is considered automatic and such instruments have been legally held to be promises to pay.

Bank draft. A check drawn by a bank on its funds deposited with another bank.

Bank examination. Detailed scrutiny of a bank's assets, liabilities, income, and expenses by authorized examiners representing a federal or state agency. The examination is intended to ensure that the bank is obeying all laws and regulations, is properly stating its financial condition, and is being soundly operated.

Bank holding company. A corporation that owns or controls one or more banks through ownership of stock. All bank holding companies come under the jurisdiction of the Federal Reserve.

Bank statement. A report, rendered by a bank to its customer, showing the account balance at the start of a period, the transactions affecting the account, and the closing balance. Paid checks are usually returned to the customer with the statement, along with debit and credit advices.

Banker's acceptance. A time draft drawn on a bank and accepted by that bank. See also **Acceptance**.

Bankers blanket bond. A broad-coverage insurance policy that provides protection against such hazards as embezzlement, burglary, robbery, fraud, and forgery.

Barter. Direct physical exchanging of merchandise.

Batch. A group of deposits, checks, or other work that has been assembled for proof and processing purposes.

Bearer. The party who is in possession of a check, security, or title document. A check made payable to "Cash" is a bearer instrument.

Beneficiary. The party who is to receive the proceeds of a transaction, such as a letter of credit, insurance policy, or trust.

Bilateral contract. An agreement or contract made between two persons or two groups.

Bill. Money; paper currency.

Bill of exchange. See **Draft**.

Bill of lading. A document issued by a transporter of goods (carrier) for the merchandise being shipped. It may be issued in negotiable or nonnegotiable form and is a contract to ship the merchandise, a receipt for it, and a document of title.

Blank endorsement. The signature of a person or business on an instrument (check, note) making it payable to the holder in due course and negotiable without restrictions.

Board of Governors. The seven-member group, appointed by the President and confirmed by the Senate for 14-year terms, that directs the operations of the Federal Reserve System.

Bond. An instrument that evidences long-term debt. The issuer (a corporation, unit of government, or other legal entity) promises to repay a certain sum of money at a specified date. Bonds may be registered (i.e., they identify the lender) or bearer (i.e., they do not identify the lender).

Bond of indemnity. A written instrument issued to protect another party against possible loss.

Book balance. See **Ledger balance**.

Bookkeeping department. The unit in a bank that maintains and updates all records of depositors' accounts. It is also called the demand deposit accounting (DDA) unit.

Branch bank. A bank that maintains a head office and one or more branch locations.

Bulk cash. Rolled or bagged coin and/or banded currency.

Cable transfer. The transfer of funds to or from a foreign country through cable instructions.

Call report. A sworn statement of a bank's financial condition as of a certain date, submitted in response to a demand made by supervisory agencies or authorities.

Capital. An accounting term describing the excess of assets over liabilities. A bank's capital accounts include money raised through the sale of stock, retained profits, and borrowings in the form of notes or debentures.

Capital ratio. A measurement of profitability determined by dividing stockholders' equity by total assets.

Cash (a check). To give money in exchange for a check drawn on another financial institution.

Cash accounting. The accounting system which posts debits and credits *only* when money is actually received or paid.

Cash items. Any items (commonly, checks and other instruments payable on demand) that a bank is willing to accept for immediate but provisional credit to customers' accounts.

Cash letter. An interbank transmittal letter, resembling a deposit slip, used to accompany cash items that are sent from one bank to another.

Cash management. Payment and collection services for corporate customers to speed collection of receivables, control payments, and efficiently manage cash.

Cash surrender value. The amount that an insurance company will pay to the insured upon surrender of a policy.

Cashier's check. See **Bank check**.

Certificate of deposit. A formal receipt for a specified amount of money left with a bank. It is commonly called a CD. Such deposits may bear interest, in which case they are payable at a definite date in the future or after a specified minimum notice of intention to withdraw; or they may be non-interest-bearing, in which case they may be payable on demand or at a future date. CDs may be issued in negotiable or nonnegotiable form. They are payable only upon surrender with proper endorsement, and are carried on the bank's general ledger under the heading "Certificates of Deposit" rather than on individual ledgers under the names of the persons to whom originally issued.

Certificate of origin. A document issued to certify the country of origin of goods or merchandise.

Certificate of quality. A document issued by an appraiser attesting that goods being shipped conform to the buyer's orders.

Certified check. A depositor's check across the face of which an authorized party in the drawee bank has stamped the word *certified* and has added a signature. Through certification of a check, the drawee guarantees that sufficient funds have been set aside from the depositor's account to pay the item. Legally, certification is similar to acceptance of a draft, and therefore the instrument becomes the bank's promise to pay.

Charter. A document issued by a state or federal supervisory agency authorizing a bank to conduct its business. The terms and conditions under which the bank can operate are enumerated in the charter.

Chattel. Any article of personal property.

Chattel mortgage. A lien giving another party an interest in certain property.

Check. A demand draft drawn on a bank.

Check digit. A suffix numeral used by bank computers, using a programmed formula, to test the validity of an account number or bank number.

Check routing symbol. The denominator (lower portion) of a fraction appearing in the upper right corner of checks drawn on all Federal Reserve member banks. The ABA Transit Number is the upper portion of this fraction. The check routing symbol identifies the Federal Reserve district in which the drawee is located, the Federal Reserve facility through which it can be collected, and the immediate or deferred availability assigned to the check under the Fed schedule.

Clearing. The process or method by which checks and/or other point of sale transactions are moved, either physically or electronically, from the point of origin to the bank or other financial institution that maintains the customer's account record.

Clearing item. A check or item in the process of collection from another financial institution. See **Clearing**.

Clearinghouse association. A group of banks that voluntarily establish a clearinghouse (meeting place) for the exchange and settlement of checks.

Coin. Metallic money. In contrast, paper money is referred to as currency.

Collateral. Property pledged by a borrower to secure a loan. If the borrower defaults, the lender has the right to sell the collateral to liquidate the loan.

Collateral note. A promissory note that pledges certain property as security for a debt.

Collected balance. Cash plus the checks deposited in the bank that have been presented to the drawee bank for payment and for which payment has actually been received.

Collection item. The opposite of a cash item, also called a noncash item. Collection items receive deferred credit to accounts, often require special handling, are usually subject to special fees, and do not create float.

Commercial bank. A full-service institution that offers deposit, payment, and credit services to all types of customers, in addition to other financial services.

Commercial invoice. A document listing goods sold and/or shipped and indicating the price and terms of the sale.

Commercial letter of credit. An instrument issued by a bank, substituting the credit of that bank for the credit of a buyer of goods. It authorizes the seller of the merchandise to draw drafts on the bank and guarantees payment of those drafts if all the stated terms have been met.

Commercial loan. Credit extended by a bank to a business firm, most frequently on a short-term and unsecured basis.

Commercial paper. Short-term, unsecured notes issued by major corporations of unquestioned credit standing as a borrowing medium.

Common stock. Evidence of ownership of a corporation. Common stockholders have rights inferior to those who hold the corporation's bonds, preferred stock, and other debts; however, common stock may carry voting rights superior to those of other issues.

Compensating balance. The balance that a borrower must keep on deposit in order to ensure a credit line, to gain unlimited checking privileges, and to ensure favorable treatment by a bank in times of high interest rates (as part of a loan agreement).

Comptroller of the Currency. An official of the U.S. government, appointed by the President and confirmed by the Senate, who is responsible for the chartering, examining, supervising, and liquidating of all national banks.

Conservator: A court-appointed official responsible for the care and protection of the interests of an estate.

Conservatorship. See **Guardianship**.

Construction loan. A short-term loan to finance the cost of construction. The lender makes payment to the builder/owner at periodic intervals as the work progresses. The loan is repaid upon completion of the construction project, usually by proceeds from a mortgage loan.

Consular invoice. A form of certification, by a consul or other government official, covering a shipment of goods. It is used to ensure that the shipment does not violate any laws or trade restrictions and also provides the government with statistical information on imports.

Consumer credit. The general banking term for loans extended to individuals or small businesses, usually on an unsecured basis and providing for monthly repayment. Also referred to as personal loans, personal finance, or installment credit.

Contract. An agreement between two or more persons, consisting of a promise or mutual promises that the law will enforce.

Contributory trust. An employee trust fund, either pension or profit-sharing, into which both the employer and employees make payments.

Corporate indenture. See **Indenture**.

Corporate resolution. A document presented to a bank by a corporation that defines the authority given to each of its officers, specifies who may sign checks, and who may conduct the business of the corporation. The powers delineated in the document are granted by the corporation's board of directors.

Corporation. A legal entity totally separate from people who own, manage, and work for it, with all rights and responsibilities of an individual person.

Correspondent bank. A bank that maintains an account relationship and/or engages in an exchange of services with another bank.

Cost accounting. An accounting system that relates all direct and indirect costs and expenses to the specific function performed.

Counterfeit money. Spurious (bogus) coins and currency that have been made to appear genuine. The act of creating counterfeit money is a felony, and those responsible for it are subject to long prison terms and heavy fines. The U.S. Secret Service, a bureau of the Treasury Department, is responsible for tracking counterfeiters.

Country collections. A term describing all items that are being sent to drawees outside the geographic area in which the sending bank is located.

Coupon. One of a series of promissory notes of consecutive maturities, attached to a bond or other debt certificate and intended to be detached and presented on their respective due dates for payment of interest.

Credit. An advance of cash, merchandise, or other commodity in exchange for a promise or other agreement to pay at a future date, with interest if so agreed.

Credit balance. The net amount of funds in an account indicating an excess of total credits over total debits.

Credit department. The unit within a bank in which all information regarding borrowers is obtained, analyzed, and kept on file. This department's work also includes answering inquiries from outside sources. A bank's credit files contain the history of its account relationships and include all memoranda, letters, financial statements, and other material that must be retained.

Credit risk. The possibility that a debtor may not be able to repay. See also **Market risk**.

Credit union. A voluntary cooperative association of individuals having a common bond (e.g., place of employment), organized and chartered to accept deposits and extend loans.

Creditor. Any party to whom money is owed by another.

Cross-selling. Employee efforts to sell financial services other than the service he/she is performing.

Currency. Paper money, as opposed to coin.

Custody. A banking service that provides safekeeping for a customer's property under written agreement and also calls for the bank to collect and pay out income and to buy, sell, receive, and deliver securities when ordered to do so by the principal.

Cycle statement system. A system of dividing bank depositors' accounts into groups whose statements are then mailed at staggered intervals (cycles) during the month, thereby distributing the work-load more evenly.

Daily transaction tape. In fully automated demand deposit accounting, the magnetic tape or disc record of each day's debits and credits to all accounts, usually in account number sequence. The daily transaction tape is also referred to as the entry run.

Debenture. An unsecured note of a corporation or bank.

Debit. A charge against the customer's deposit or bank card account. A debit entry usually increases the balance of an asset or expense account and decreases the balance of a liability or equity account.

Debit balance. The lack of funds in an account indicating an excess of total debits over total credits.

Decedent. A person who has died. The term is used in connection with wills, estates, and inheritances.

Deed. A written document transferring title to real property.

Deferred account. An account set up for check collection purposes (usually by the Federal Reserve).

Delivery. The transfer of the possession of an item from one person to another.

Demand deposit accounting. A term that refers to the processing, tracking, and accounting for the demand deposits of a bank.

Demand deposits. Funds that may be withdrawn at any time, without prior notice to the bank. Checking accounts are the most common form of demand deposits.

Demand draft. A written order to pay at sight, upon presentation. A check is a demand draft drawn on a bank.

Demand loan. A loan with no fixed maturity date, payable when the bank calls for it or when the borrower chooses to repay it.

Deposit. Any placement of cash, checks, or other drafts with a bank for credit to an account. All deposits are liabilities of a bank, since they must be repaid in some form at some future date.

Deposit function. The banking process by which funds are accepted for credit to a demand or time account. In the case of checks, the deposit function includes conversion of the items into usable, available funds.

Deposit slip. A listing of items given to a bank for credit to an account. A copy of the deposit slip may serve as a receipt for the customer.

Depository Institutions Deregulation Committee (DIDC). A group of officials, supervising commercial banks and thrift institutions, created under the terms of the Monetary Control Act of 1980.

Depository transfer check. A preprinted, no-signature instrument, used only to move funds from one bank account to another.

Deputy. An individual authorized by the holder of a safe deposit box to have access to that box. The deputy has rights similar to those of an attorney-in-fact.

Direct deposit. The process by which a payor delivers data by electronic means directly to the payee's bank for credit to his/her account. Examples include the Federal Government's direct deposit program for social security checks and employee payroll checks.

Direct presentment. A direct demand for acceptance or payment made by the holder of a negotiable instrument upon the maker of a note or the drawer of a check or draft.

Direct verification. The auditing procedure by which a bank confirms account balance, loan, or other information through direct contact with its debtors or creditors.

Directors. The individuals who comprise the board of directors and therefore constitute the active governing body of a corporation. Directors are elected by stockholders.

Discount. Interest withheld when a note, draft, or bill is purchased, or collected in advance at the time a loan is made.

Discount rate. The rate of interest charged by the Federal Reserve on loans it makes to its member banks or to other financial institutions.

Discount register. A bank's book of original entry, in which a daily record is kept of all loan department transactions. Loans made or paid, interest collected, and payments received would be entered in this register.

Dishonor. A drawee's refusal to accept or pay a check, draft, or other instrument presented, or refusal by the maker of a note to pay it when it is presented.

Disintermediation. The flow of funds from interest-bearing time accounts into short-term investments (stocks, bonds) for higher interest rates.

Documentary draft. A written order to pay, accompanied by securities or other papers to be delivered against payment or acceptance.

Dormant account. A customer relationship that has had no activity for a period of time.

Double-entry bookkeeping. An accounting system based on the premise that for every debit there must be equal, corresponding credits; i.e., all transactions must be posted twice.

Draft. A signed, written order by which one party (the drawer) instructs another (the drawee) to make payment to a third (the payee). In international banking, a draft is often called a bill of exchange.

Drawee. The party who is directed by the drawer to make a payment. In the case of checks, the drawee is a bank.

Drawer. The party who issues a set of written instructions to a drawee, calling for a payment of funds.

Drive-in window. A service offered to the public by banks where a teller window faces the outside of a bank building allowing customers to transact business without leaving their cars.

Dual banking system. All commercial banks in the United States must be chartered, either by the state in which they are domiciled or by the federal government through the office of the Comptroller of the Currency. The side-by-side existence of both state-chartered and national banks creates a *dual* system.

Dual control. A bank procedure requiring that two members of the staff be involved in a transaction.

Dual posting. The bookkeeping system in which all transactions affecting accounts are recorded twice, once each by two different individuals.

Edge Act. Federal legislation, passed in 1919, allowing banks to establish offices outside their own states purely for the purpose of assisting in foreign trade transactions.

EFTS. The common acronym for electronic fund transfer systems, i.e., the use of automated technology to post to accounts. EFTS applications eliminate or reduce the use of checks or other paper.

Employee trusts. Pension and profit-sharing trust funds established by employers for the benefit of employees.

Endorsement. Legal transfer of one's rights to an instrument.

Entry run. See **Daily transaction tape**.

Equity. Ownership interests. Corporations obtain equity capital through the sale of certificates of ownership, such as common and preferred stock; these are known as equity securities.

Escheat. The legal principle by which a state government is entitled to receive funds that have remained in dormant accounts for a stated period of time.

Escrow. The holding of funds, documents, securities, or other property by an impartial, trusted third party for the other two participants in a business transaction. When the transaction is completed, the escrow agent releases the entrusted property.

Escrow agent. A third party in a transaction who acts as the agent for both the buyer and the seller and who carries out the instructions of both and assumes the responsibilities of handling all the paperwork and disbursement of funds.

Estate. The sum total, as determined by a complete inventory, of all the assets of a decedent.

Exchange charge. A fee deducted from the face amount of a check by the nonpar bank on which it is drawn; also known as a settlement charge. All exchange charges must be debited to the depositor from whom the checks were received.

Executor. A party named in a decedent's valid will and made responsible for settling the estate. Executors must be qualified by a court before they can act.

FDIC assessment. The annual premium, equal to one-twelfth of 1 percent of average deposits, that FDIC members pay for their insurance coverage.

Federal Deposit Insurance Corporation (FDIC). The agency of the federal government established in 1933 to provide insurance protection, up to a stated limit, on depositors' accounts. All national banks and all Fed member banks must belong to FDIC; mutual savings banks may join if they wish.

Federal funds transactions. Debits or credits through the accounts of member institutions at the Federal Reserve. Transfers between banks may be made in Fed funds, or excess reserves may be borrowed or loaned.

Federal Reserve banks. The 12 institutions, one in each Federal Reserve district, that deal primarily with member banks and the government. In addition to their main offices in each district, Federal Reserve banks maintain branches and Regional Check Processing Centers as necessary.

Federal Reserve notes. The paper money issued by one of the Federal Reserve banks and officially designated by the federal government as legal tender, to be accepted in payment of all debts. Each note is an interest-free promise to pay on demand issued by the Federal Reserve Bank.

Federal Reserve System. The organization created by the 1913 Federal Reserve Act. The system includes the 12 Federal Reserve banks and their branches, plus the member banks, which are its legal owners. The Board of Governors, headquartered in Washington, exercises overall control over the nationwide operations of the Federal Reserve System ("the Fed").

Federal Savings and Loan Insurance Corporation (FSLIC). The counterpart agency of FDIC, created by the federal government to provide deposit insurance for customers of thrift institutions.

Fiduciary. An individual, bank, or other party to whom specific property is turned over under the terms of a contractual agreement.

Financial instrument. Any written document that has monetary value or that evidences a monetary transaction.

Fiscal policy. The activities of Congress and the federal government in the areas of taxation and the budget.

Float. The dollar total of deposited cash items that are in the process of collection from drawee banks; also known as uncollected funds. In general, float has no value to the bank of deposit or to the depositor; hence, the amount of a bank's daily float directly affects its earnings potential. A customer's average daily float is often calculated for purposes of account analysis.

Floor plan financing. Loans made to finance dealers' inventory purchases, such as automobile dealers.

Forged check. A demand draft, drawn on a bank, on which the maker's signature is not genuine.

Forgery. The legal term for counterfeiting a check or other document with the intention to defraud.

Free banking laws. The statutes passed by various states during the nineteenth century making it possible for banks to open and operate with a minimum of chartering requirements or other governmental controls.

Garn-St Germain Act. The federal legislation passed in 1982 directing the DIDC to authorize the opening of new types of interest-free accounts and extending the powers of federal regulatory authorities to assist banks and thrift institutions that encounter financial difficulties.

General ledger. The consolidated, summary books of account for an entire bank. The general ledger unit records all changes in the bank's financial condition and provides the material for all call reports and published statements of condition. All subsidiary ledger figures, such as branch and departmental totals, are brought together in the general ledger.

Genuine signature. The actual, valid signature of the maker of a check.

Glass-Steagall Act. The banking legislation passed in 1933; also known as the 1933 Banking Act.

Global risk analysis. An examination of the elements and sources of risk involved in international trade and lending.

Guardian. A bank, individual, or other party named by a court to manage the person and/or property of a minor or incompetent.

Guardianship. The title given to a court directive that establishes a bank, individual, or other legal entity to manage a person and/or property of a minor or incompetent.

Guidance line of credit. A line of credit that is established only for the bank's internal use.

Hard money. Metallic, as distinguished from paper, money.

Hold. The restriction on payment of part or all of the balance in an account.

Holder in due course. As defined in the Uniform Commercial Code, a party who accepts an instrument in good faith, for value, and without notice that it has been dishonored or is overdue, or that there is any claim against it.

House check. Synonymous with ON-US check. A check deposited or otherwise negotiated at the bank on which it is drawn.

Income. A gain arising from capital or labor either accrued or earned and usually measured in money or its equivalent.

Income statement. A record, also known as a profit and loss statement, of the income and expenses of a bank or business, covering a stated period of time.

Indenture. The formal agreement executed by an issuer of bonds.

Individual Retirement Accounts (IRAs). Trust funds established by an individual for retirement purposes, as authorized by Congress. Contributions to IRAs are deductible for tax purposes.

Informal account. A bank account opened without detailed, legal documentation.

Informal trust. A trust fund established with a bank without court appointment or other legal documentation; also called Totten trust.

Installment loan. Direct loans to individuals that are repaid in fixed, periodic payments. Installment loans are often secured for debt consolidation, payment of taxes, hospital expenses, or educational purposes.

Institutional trust. A trust fund consisting of assets of a university or other institution turned over to a bank to be invested and managed.

Insufficient funds. A banking term indicating that the maker's balance does not contain sufficient funds to cover a check or checks; commonly abbreviated NSF, "not sufficient funds."

Insurance certificate. A document usually issued by an insurance firm that provides a degree of security and protection for merchandise during transit.

Insured bank. A bank that is a member of FDIC.

Interbank loan. The extension of credit by one bank to another.

Interest. Money paid for the use of money.

Intestate. The legal term describing a decedent who has not left a valid will.

Investment. The exchange of money, *either* for a promise to pay at a later date (e.g., bonds) *or* for an ownership share in a business venture (e.g., stocks).

Investment portfolio. The sum total of the various types of securities owned by a bank, a business, an individual, an institution, or an entity of government.

Invoice. A commercial bill for goods or services rendered.

Irrevocable. The term used for a letter of credit that cannot be canceled or modified, except by full mutual agreement between the parties.

Issuing bank. A bank that issues a letter of credit based on the application and needs of the importer.

Joint account. A bank relationship in the names of two or more people. Joint accounts may carry rights of survivorship or may be established on a tenants-in-common basis without such rights.

Joint tenancy. Two or more people who hold equal ownership of property. It conveys a "right of survivorship" among the tenants or owners. A tenant may convey his or her separate interest during life, but upon death his or her interest will pass to the surviving joint tenant(s) rather than to heirs or through a will of the deceased tenant.

Journal. An accounting record of original entry in which transactions are listed and described in chronological order.

Keogh account. A bank account established under the terms of the Keogh Act (H.R. 10) for self-employed individuals for retirement purposes. Contributions to Keogh plans are deductible for tax purposes.

Kiting. Attempting to draw against non-existent funds for fraudulent purposes. A depositor writes a check in an amount to overdraw the account in one bank and makes up the deficiency by depositing into that same account a check drawn on another bank in which there is also insufficient funds.

Ledger. An accounting record of final entry in which transactions are posted according to the accounts that are affected.

Ledger balance. The record of the balance in a customer's account per the bank records. The ledger balance may not reflect all deposits if the bank has not yet received actual payment for them. Also referred to as book balance.

Legal reserves. The portion of banks' demand and time deposits that must be kept in the form of cash or acceptable equivalents for depositors' protection. Federal Reserve member banks maintain these reserves with the Fed in their district; others may either keep reserves with the Fed itself or with a correspondent that is a Fed member.

Legal tender. Currency, backed by a government, that is acceptable in payment of all public and private debts.

Letter of credit. A bank instrument that substitutes the credit of that bank for the credit of another party, such as the buyer of merchandise.

Liability. Anything owed by a bank, individual, or business. A bank's largest liability is the sum total of its demand and time deposits.

Liability ledger. The record maintained by a bank's loan department showing the indebtedness of each borrower.

Lien. 1) Qualified right of property that a creditor has in or over specific property of a debtor as security for the debt or for the performance of an obligation. 2) A legal claim or attachment, filed on record, against property as security for payment of an obligation. See **Chattel mortgage**.

Line of credit. The predetermined maximum amount that a bank will lend to any borrower. Confirmed lines of credit are made known to the customer; guidance lines of credit are for the bank's internal use only.

Liquidity. The quality that makes an asset quickly and easily convertible into cash; *also,* the ability of a bank, individual, or business to meet current debts.

Liquidity needs. The amount that a bank calculates is necessary to cover estimated withdrawals or payments of funds and to meet the legitimate credit demands of customers.

Living trust. A trust fund that becomes effective during the lifetime of the trustor (settlor).

Loan. A business contract between a borrower and lender covering an extension of credit.

Loan participation. The sharing of a loan to a single borrower by two or more banks.

Lobby depository. A vault located within the lobby of a bank that permits customers to deposit funds without the assistance of a teller.

Local items. Checks drawn on other banks within the same city.

Lockbox. A banking service that assumes responsibility for receiving, examining, and processing incoming checks for a customer.

Magnetic ink character recognition (MICR). The American Bankers Association program that provides for encoding of checks and documents with standard characters in magnetic ink so that they can be electronically "read" and processed.

Mail deposit. A deposit received through the mail as opposed to an over the counter transaction.

Maker. The party who executes an instrument, such as a check, draft, or note; also frequently referred to as the drawer.

Managing agent. The service by which a bank or other party assumes an active role in the management of another's property.

Margin. The excess of the value of collateral over the amount loaned against it. Also, the difference between the purchase price of a security and the amount actually paid at the time of purchase.

Market risk. The possibility of decline in the current value of a security; the loss that the holder of an investment may have to assume at the time of sale.

Master file. The updated record, also known as master tape or disk, of the closing balance in each account at a bank. It is produced by merging the previous day's master tape with the current day's transaction tape (entry run).

Maturity. The date on which a note, draft, bond, or acceptance becomes due.

Maturity tickler. The reminder file maintained by a bank according to due dates to ensure that notes will be presented as they fall due.

Medium of exchange. Any commodity, including money, that is widely accepted in payment for goods or services on the basis of its recognized value.

Member bank. An institution that belongs to the Federal Reserve System.

Merge. 1) The combination of two or more formerly independent firms under a single ownership. 2) To combine into one sequenced file form two or more similarly sequenced files without changing the order of the items.

Microfilm. The photographic process that reduces checks and other documents for record-keeping and storage purposes.

Missort. A check or other instrument routed in error.

Monetary Control Act. The 1980 legislation that created the Depository Institutions Deregulation Committee, provided for the gradual phase-out of interest-rate ceilings, made all financial institutions subject to reserve requirements, and gave expanded powers to thrift institutions.

Monetary policy. The general term for the actions taken by the Federal Reserve to control the flow of money and credit.

Money. Legal tender; coin and currency declared by a government to be the accepted medium of exchange.

Money market certificate. A nonnegotiable instrument, issued by a bank or thrift institution, carrying a 26-week maturity. The minimum amount is $2,500 and the rate of interest is tied to the current rate on U.S. Treasury bills.

Money market deposit account. An account authorized by the Depository Institutions Deregulation Committee (DIDC) that provides banks and savings and loans with a competitive instrument with which to compete with money market funds.

Money market fund. A mutual fund that pools investors' contributions and invests them in various money market instruments.

Money supply. The total amount of funds available for spending in the nation at any point in time.

Mortgage loan. Real estate credit, usually extended on a long-term basis with the property as security.

Municipal. A bond issued by any government, or agency or authority of government, other than the federal government.

Mutual savings bank. A thrift institution that has no stockholders and is owned by its depositors.

National bank. A commercial bank operating under a federal charter and supervised by the Comptroller of the Currency. The word *national* must appear in some form in the bank's corporate title.

National bank note. A type of currency issued by the United States now being retired from circulation. National bank notes were backed by U.S. Government bonds.

National numerical system. See **ABA transit number**.

Negative verification. The auditing system by which a letter regarding balances, loans, or other data is sent to a customer; a reply is called for *only* if there is a discrepancy between the balance or other facts reported by the bank and the customer's own records.

Negotiable instrument. An unconditional written order or promise to pay a sum of money that is easily transferable from one party to another. Various laws set forth the qualifications of negotiable instruments and the rights and liabilities of their holders.

Net worth. Shareholders' equity in a bank or business; the excess of assets over liabilities.

Night depository. A small vault located on the inside of a bank but accessible to customers outside the bank for depository purposes. It is a convenient service offered to merchants wishing to deposit receipts after regular banking hours.

Noncash item. Any instrument that a bank declines to accept on a cash basis; a collection item. Credit is not posted to the customer's account until final settlement takes place.

Nonearning asset. The valued assets of a bank that do not produce revenue, income, or earnings potential for the institution, such as furniture, fixtures, equipment, and other materials used to transact bank business.

Nonpar bank. An institution that is not a Fed member and deducts an exchange charge from the face amount of checks drawn on it.

Non-performing loan. A bank loan that produces no income and becomes a nonearning asset. Loans of this category usually are related to or precede foreclosure or charge-off action.

Note. A written promise to pay.

NOW account. A special account, authorized by act of Congress, that allows the customer to earn interest while at the same time having check-writing privileges.

NSF. See **Insufficient funds**.

Officer. Any principal executive of a corporation or business to whom authority has been delegated, usually by the board of directors and/or senior management.

Official check. See **Bank check**.

On-us check. A check cashed or deposited at the same bank on which it is drawn. Also called a "house" check.

Open market operations. Sale and purchase of government securities on the open market by a central bank in order to influence the size of the money supply. In the United States, the Federal Reserve System uses open market operations as a major tool for implementing monetary policy.

Opening bank. See **Issuing bank**.

Order. Identification of the one to whom payment of funds should be made as in "Pay to the Order of."

Overdraft. A negative (minus) balance in an account, resulting from the paying of checks for an amount greater than the depositor's balance.

Par value. The nominal worth of a bond, note, or other instrument.

Participation. See **Loan participation**.

Partnership. A business venture operated by two or more individuals.

Partnership agreement. A contract or covenant between the partners of a business wherein the rights, duties, and responsibilities of each are clearly delineated and defined.

Passbook. A record, supplied by a bank, showing customer transactions on an account.

Pay. 1) To pay a check in cash. 2) To debit a check against a customer's account when same is presented for payment through clearing channels.

Payee. The beneficiary of an instrument; the party to whom payment is to be made.

Paying agent. The service by which a bank disburses dividends on a corporation's stock or the interest and principal on bonds or notes.

Paying teller. A bank representative responsible for the paying and cashing of checks presented.

Pension. A fixed sum paid to an individual or his/her family on a regular basis, usually by an employer following the individual's retirement from service.

Platform. A term generally used to describe that portion of a bank's lobby where officers, new accounts, and customer service personnel are located.

Positive verification. The auditing system under which every customer contacted during an audit must reply to the bank's letter of inquiry regarding balances, loans, etc.

Postdated check. An item bearing a future date. It is not valid until that date is reached.

Power of attorney. The legal document by which one party is authorized to act on behalf of another. See **Attorney-in-fact**.

Preauthorized payments. A convenience service offered to customers that enables a debtor to request that funds be transferred from his/her deposit account to a creditor's account on a regularly fixed basis.

Preferred stock. Securities that give the holder a right to share in a bank's or corporation's profits before common stockholders. If the institution is liquidated, preferred stockholders have a prior claim on its assets over common stock-holders and certain other creditors.

Presenting bank. A bank that forwards an item to another for payment.

Prime rate. The interest rate charged by a bank to its best, most creditworthy customers.

Principal. (1) The sum of money stated in a contract, an account or a financial instrument as distinguished from the sum of money actually to be paid, e.g., the amount of a loan or debt exclusive of interest. (2) A person who is primarily liable on an obligation. (3) A person appoints another person to act for him or her as agent. (4) The property of an estate other than the income from the property. (5) The individual with primary ownership or management control of a business.

Probate. The judicial determination concerning the validity of a will and all questions that may pertain to that will.

Profit-and-loss statement. See **Income statement**.

Profit-sharing trust. A fund in which an employer sets aside a portion of annual profits for the benefit of the employees.

Promissory note. A written promise committing the maker to pay a sum certain in money to the payee, with or without interest, on demand or at a fixed or deter-minable future date.

Proof. Any process that tests the accuracy of a function or operation; also known as balancing.

Proof department. The central unit in a bank that sorts and distributes checks and other work and arrives at control figures for all transactions.

Proof machine. Equipment that simultaneously sorts items, records the dollar amount of each item, provides totals for each sorted group, and balances the total to the original input amount.

Proprietor. A person who has an exclusive right or interest in a business or in property.

Proprietorship. A business venture operated by a single owner.

Protest. A legal document, usually notarized, that provides evidence that an instrument was presented and dishonored.

Prove. The process of verifying the accuracy of calculations performed by an individual or department.

Public funds. Accounts established for any government, agency of government, or political subdivision.

Purpose statement. A signed affidavit from a borrower whose loan is secured by certain types of stock market collateral. Under Regulation U of the Federal Reserve, the borrower must state the use(s) to which the proceeds of the loan will be put.

Qualified endorsement. An endorsement on a check or other instrument containing the words *without recourse* or similar language intended to limit the endorser's liability.

Quick deposit box. See **Lobby depository**.

Raised check. An item on which the dollar amount has been fraudulently increased.

Receiving teller. A bank representative who accepts and verifies deposits and issues receipts for them but has no paying or cashing duties.

Redlining. Systematic exclusion of certain geographic areas—usually high-risk, low-income neighborhoods—from mortgage investment.

Regional Check Processing Centers (RCPCs). Special facilities established by the Fed in its 12 districts to expedite the handling, presenting, and collecting of transit checks.

Registrar. A bank or trust company appointed by a corporation to ensure that the number of shares of outstanding stock does not exceed the authorized number. A registrar is agent for both the corporation and the latter's stockholders, since it protects the interests of both.

Repurchase agreements (Repos). Contracts between a seller and buyer, usually involving federal government obligations. The seller agrees to buy back the securities at an agreed-upon price after a stated period of time. Repos are often executed on an overnight basis.

Reserves. Portions of a bank's funds set aside to meet legal requirements or for known or potential expenses or losses.

Resolution. An official document, executed under seal by a corporation, certifying that specified officers can open a bank account for the corporation and conduct business with the bank on its behalf.

Restrictive endorsement. An endorsement that limits the future actions of the next holder; the most common example includes the words "For Deposit Only."

Return items. Checks, drafts, or notes that have been dishonored by the drawee or maker and are sent back to the presenting party.

Return on assets (ROA). A financial measurement that indicates how efficiently the bank's assets are being employed. It is usually determined by dividing Net Profits by Assets, although there are more sophisticated formulas available for pinpointing accuracy.

Return on equity (ROE). A financial measurement that indicates how efficiently the bank's equity capital is invested. It is usually determined by dividing Net Profit by Net Worth (Equity), although varying formulas are available for more sophisticated measurements.

Revocable. A term usually associated with letters of credit. It allows a document to be cancelled or amended by either party without the approval of the other.

Revolving credit. A line of credit arrangement that permits the customer to withdraw funds or charge purchases up to a specified dollar limit. Also referred to as open-end credit.

Right of survivorship. The right of one individual to take full possession of a specific asset upon the death of the co-owner.

Routing symbol. See **Check routing symbol**.

Safekeeping. The banking service by which the bank issues a receipt for, maintains records of, and provides vault facilities for a customer's property.

Safety. The ideal perception by customers that the bank is in a position to honor all anticipated demands for withdrawal of funds, and the measures the bank takes to protect the funds entrusted to it.

Savings account. An interest-bearing relationship, used by the customer to accumulate funds. Savings accounts have no fixed maturity date.

Savings and loan association. A federally or state-chartered thrift institution that accepts various forms of deposits and uses them primarily for mortgage loans.

Savings bank. A thrift institution specializing in savings accounts but also offering other forms of deposit relationships. See also **Mutual savings bank**.

Savings certificate. A written instrument evidencing the depositing of a stated sum of money. The rate of interest and maturity date are usually specified. The certificate must be surrendered to the bank to obtain funds.

Security officer. A bank representative who has been given responsibility for various phases of internal controls, often including the detecting of fraud and the maintaining of alarm systems and other protective devices.

Service charge. A fee levied by a bank for services rendered to a depositor or other customer.

Settlor. A person who creates a trust (such as a living trust) to become operative during his/her lifetime. Also called "donor," "grantor," and "trustor."

Share draft. A check-like instrument issued by the customer of a credit union, drawn against the deposit balance at that institution, and used as a payment medium.

Sight draft. A written order to pay upon delivery or presentation.

Sight letter of credit. An instrument issued by a bank to an individual or corporation by which the bank substitutes its own credit for that of the individual or corporation. A sight letter of credit permits payment of the funds upon immediate presentation of the documents evidencing a shipment of goods.

Signature. A sign or mark made by the drawer or maker of a negotiable instrument. A signature may include marks, thumbprints, and be printed, typed, or stamped.

Sorter-reader. Electronic equipment having the ability to "read," sort, and process MICR-encoded checks and other documents.

Special endorsement. An endorsement that names the party to whom an instrument is being transferred.

Specie. "Hard" currency; gold and/or silver.

Split deposit. A transaction in which a customer wishes to have part of a check credited to an account and the remainder paid out in cash.

Spot audit. A procedure by which certain bank accounts, procedures, or areas are selected at random for testing.

Spread. 1) The difference between the return on assets and the cost of liabilities. 2) The difference between the buying rate and selling rate of a foreign currency or marketable security (stock, bond).

Stale-dated check. An instrument bearing a date 6 months or more prior to its presentation.

State bank. A commercial institution chartered by the state in which it is headquartered.

Statement of condition. See **Balance sheet**.

Stop payment. A depositor's instructions to the drawee, directing it to dishonor a specific item.

Subsidiary ledger. A breakdown of the General Ledger into individual records of various banking activities, such as mortgage loan accounts, savings accounts, loans in process, and numerous other account designations.

Super NOW account. An account authorized by the Depository Institutions Deregulation Committee that is similar to the money market deposit account but differs in that it 1) subjects the funds to reserve requirements, 2) is not available to corporations, and 3) has no limit to monthly transaction volume.

Surplus. A bank's funds derived from retained earnings over a period of time and from stockholders' contributions.

Survivorship. The right, subject to legal considerations, of a surviving party to the property of a decedent.

Sweep account. A relationship in which all the funds in a depositor's account, over and above a specified figure, are automatically transferred into an investment pool.

Tenants in common. The holding of property by two or more persons in such a manner that each has an undivided interest that (at the death of one) passes as such to the heirs or devisees and not to the survivor or survivors.

Terminal. An electronic device, often connected to a computer, that can supply information and accept instructions to initiate transactions.

Testamentary trust. A trust fund created under the terms of a will.

Testate. Having made and left a valid will; as opposed to intestate.

Testator. A decedent who has created a valid will.

Time deposit. An account on which time limitations on withdrawal are enforced to receive a given return.

Time draft. A written order directing that payment be made at a fixed or determinable future date.

Time letter of credit. An instrument issued by a bank to an individual or corporation by which the bank substitutes its own credit for that of the individual or corporation. A time letter of credit specifies a date when payment must be made.

Time loan. An amount of credit extended with a specific repayment date.

Title. Legal evidence of ownership of property.

Totten trust. See **Informal trust**.

Trade acceptance. A time draft drawn on the buyer of goods by the seller and accepted by the buyer before maturity.

Trade name. A fictitious name, often called trade style, used for business purposes. The laws of many states require that trade names be legally registered.

Transaction account: A term used to describe all relationships with financial institutions that permit transfers of funds to third parties.

Transit check. Any item that a bank chooses to classify as not payable locally. Transit work usually consists of checks drawn on out-of-town banks.

Transit number. See **ABA transit number**.

Travelers checks. Negotiable instruments sold by a bank or other issuer in various denominations for the convenience of individuals. They are readily convertible into cash upon identification, which normally consists of a signature affixed in the presence of the cashing party.

Traveler's letter of credit. An instrument issued by a bank for the convenience of an individual who is going abroad. It must be negotiated at a foreign branch of the issuing bank or at an office of a foreign correspondent bank. It allows the traveler to draw drafts against it to obtain local currency.

Treasurer's check. See **Bank check**.

Truncation. A banking system that reduces the need to send or otherwise physically handle checks for customers' accounts. Checks are stored at the point of entry.

Trust. An arrangement or contract established by agreement or declaration, by a will, or by order of a court, under which one party (the trustee) holds legal title to property belonging to another party with a specific benefit in mind.

Trust company. A financial institution chartered to offer trust services. Depending on the terms of its charter, it may also be authorized to offer banking services.

Trust receipt. A written agreement creating a special type of secured loan, and often extended to a buyer or other importer of goods. The borrower is allowed to take possession of merchandise to which the bank holds legal title.

Trustee. The party holding legal title to property under the terms of a trust.

Trustor. The party whose property has been turned over to a trustee; also known as a settlor.

Truth-in-lending laws. Federal and/or state laws requiring that a lender provide the borrower with full information regarding the terms and conditions of a loan.

Uncollected funds. See **Float**.

Uniform Commercial Code. The body of laws, adopted in whole or part by all states, pertaining to various types of financial transactions.

Uniform Fiduciaries Act. A government statute that contains provisions that apply directly to fiduciary or trust accounts. The act provides guidelines for banks on the type and extent of documentation that is required on fiduciary accounts and policing policies related to the security of such accounts.

Uniform Gifts to Minors Act. Legislation that provides tax relief for individuals who make irrevocable gifts of money or other property to underage beneficiaries.

Unit bank. An institution that maintains no branch offices.

Unit teller. A bank representative who handles both paying and receiving functions.

Unsecured loan. Credit extended without collateral.

Updating. Modifying a master file with current information.

Usury. Excessive or punitive interest charges.

Variable rate loan. A type of loan that allows for periodic adjustment of the interest rate in keeping with a fluctuating market. Also referred to as an adjustable rate loan.

Verification. The auditing process in banking by which bank records are confirmed through direct contact with customers.

Ward. A person who by reason of minority, mental incompetence, or other incapacity is under the protection of the court either directly or through a guardian, committee, curator, or conservator.

Warehouse receipt. A document evidencing the storage of specified property in a bonded facility. The receipt may be issued in negotiable or nonnegotiable form and serves as a title document.

Wildcat banking. The system that established bank offices at remote locations for the redemption of notes.

Will. A formal, written, witnessed instrument by which a person gives instructions for the disposition of his or her estate.

Wire fate. Special instructions accompanying the presenting of an instrument asking that the sending bank be notified by wire whether or not the instrument is honored.

Wire transfer. A transaction by which funds are moved electronically from one bank to another, upon a customer's instructions, through bookkeeping entries at the two banks.

Without rights of survivorship. An account in which the joint tenancy ends upon the death of one of the parties.

Working capital. The excess of a business venture's current assets over its current liabilities; the liquid funds available to a business for its daily needs.

Writ of attachment. A legal document, frequently served on a bank, making the assets of a debtor subject to the terms of a court order.

Zero proof. A banking procedure by which a control figure is first entered into a machine or system. All postings are successively subtracted from that figure to arrive at a zero balance, thus indicating that all entries have been correctly posted.

Index

About the Author

Eric N. Compton, the author of three textbooks on banking, is a vice president in the International Institutional Banking Department at Chase Manhattan. He is responsible for all Credit Analysis Seminars offered by Chase to correspondent banks throughout the world. He serves as an instructor in those programs.

Mr. Compton's banking career, which includes experience in the Installment Loan, Marketing Training, and Management Development areas, began in New York City in 1950. He has also served as a relationship manager in the branch system and as a team leader in the Cash Management Sales and Government Banking divisions.

Since 1961, he has served the American Institute of Banking in New York as a faculty member, and is a past president and former trustee of that chapter.

Principles of Banking

Date: _____

This questionnaire is designed to get reader opinions on the adequacy and relevance of the text. Your comments, both positive and negative, will influence the design and content of future AIB textbooks. Thank you for your assistance.

I. Background Information

A. In this course I was a(n): ☐ instructor   ☐ student

B. Highest educational attainment:
☐ High School   ☐ Some College   ☐ BA/BS Degree   ☐ Advanced Degree

C. I am a(n): ☐ Officer   ☐ Non-Officer   ☐ Non-Bank Employee

D. Asset Size of Bank:
☐ $0-100m   ☐ $101-500m   ☐ $501-1b   ☐ Over $1b

E. My major job responsibility is _____

F. I am pursuing an AIB diploma: ☐ Yes   ☐ No

II. The Materials

Please rate the text according to the criteria below. Check the box that most closely corresponds with your opinions.

Thoroughness:	☐ covers too little of subject	☐ Covers sufficient content	☐ Covers too much unrelated content
Difficulty Level:	☐ Too basic	☐ Appropriate for level of course	☐ Too difficult
Interest Level:	☐ Dull and uninteresting	☐ Acceptable	☐ Very interesting
Organization:	☐ Sequenced logically	☐ Not in logical sequence	
Timeliness:	☐ Most content was current	☐ Most content was outdated	
Practicality:	☐ Too theoretical	☐ Has sufficient practical application	

Please rate the *overall effectiveness* of the text by circling the number which represents your opinion.

Very effective as a learning aid   Ineffective as a learning aid

5   4   3   2   1

III. Comments

A. Can you make any suggestions for improving the book?

_____

_____

_____

B. Would you recommend this book to someone who needs to know this information?

☐ Yes   ☐ No

STAPLE HERE

FOLD IN HALF AND STAPLE

FOLD HERE

No Postage
Necessary
If Mailed
In The
United States

BUSINESS REPLY MAIL

First Class   Permit No. 10579   Washington, D.C.

Postage Will Be Paid by

Education & Field Relations
Education Policy & Development Group
American Bankers Association
1120 Connecticut Avenue
Washington, D.C. 20036